THE BATTLE OF TH
LITTLE BIG HORN

THE BATTLE OF THE LITTLE BIG HORN

A New Appraisal

WENDY ANN WALLACE

Pen & Sword
MILITARY
AN IMPRINT OF PEN & SWORD BOOKS LTD.
YORKSHIRE – PHILADELPHIA

First published in Great Britain in 2023 by
PEN AND SWORD MILITARY
An imprint of
Pen & Sword Books Limited
Yorkshire – Philadelphia

ISBN 978 1 39904 671 8

A CIP catalogue record for this book is available from the British Library.

Typeset in Times New Roman 10.5/13 by
SJmagic DESIGN SERVICES, India.
Printed and bound in the UK by CPI Group (UK) Ltd.

Pen & Sword Books Limited incorporates the imprints of Atlas, Archaeology, Aviation, Discovery, Family History, Fiction, History, Maritime, Military, Military Classics, Politics, Select, Transport, True Crime, Air World, Frontline Publishing, Leo Cooper, Remember When, Seaforth Publishing, The Praetorian Press, Wharncliffe Local History, Wharncliffe Transport, Wharncliffe True Crime and White Owl.

For a complete list of Pen & Sword titles please contact
PEN & SWORD BOOKS LIMITED
47 Church Street, Barnsley, South Yorkshire S70 2AS, United Kingdom
E-mail: enquiries@pen-and-sword.co.uk
Website: www.pen-and-sword.co.uk

or

PEN AND SWORD BOOKS
1950 Lawrence Rd, Havertown, PA 19083, USA
E-mail: uspen-and-sword@casematepublishers.com
Website: www.penandswordbooks.com

MIX
Paper | Supporting responsible forestry
FSC® C013604

Contents

Author's Note

Conspirators and murderers generally do not leave a paper – trail for historians like myself to follow. Thus, it took me over thirty years to reach the conclusion recorded in this book and its sequel. The results are based on numerous letters written during the time these events occurred, (one such letter was chased across three States!) and at later times when corresponding with me, giving me quotes from their ancestor's diaries and other papers. Such a history has never been recorder before and piecing everything together gave a very different perspective on the whole affair. Obviously, some of the language used represents the times of the events and does not reflect the attitudes of the author or the publishers, in modern times.

Introduction

No other battle in American history has gripped the imagination like the Battle of the Little Big Horn. The sheer enigma of George Armstrong Custer draws you like a magnet to unravel the mysteries that shroud this conflict. Equally, there have been more books written about the fight than you can imagine. So I see you shrug your shoulders and hear you ask "why write another book on such a hackneyed subject?" The answer is simple. For the last forty or more years I have conducted a deep research into the event and this new research has led me to believe that although many books have been published on the subject, the authors have not looked beyond the accepted versions and demand more. This book does and the answers will astound you, but I should start at the beginning of my journey, a journey that has taken so many years of research, preparation and writing.

I have always loved the Wild West and read as many books as I could to understand the subject. My mother loved the western TV shows and read piles of western fiction; my father was deeply interested in all kinds of history, so I was doomed from the start, there was literally no hope for me. In 1970 a book made its debut which made me seriously think about the history I was reading. My father bought it on his way home from work and it was titled *'War Cries on Horseback'*. It was written by Stephen Longstreet who, at the time, was neither an authority on the Indian wars nor an established author, but it looked at the conflict from a different perspective. Nevertheless, I read the book and enjoyed it very much, allowing his words to permeate my senses and question the accepted history of this era.

Custer was not a glory hunter and he was most certainly not a fool, although he was a very complex man. Since his untimely death in 1876, controversy has raged concerning the reasons for his demise, with the big question, why? Why did he die? Could it be that the native Americans were the instruments of death rather than the cause? If that is so, what were the causes and who continued to orchestrate the eventual outcome?

Using original documents and contemporary sources from both sides, records of the events that led up to that terrible battle and official reports, the outcome and future prospects can be carefully pieced together. It is these sources that reveal that a conspiracy to eliminate Custer did, in fact, exist. The documents are incomplete and confusing, often conflicting with each other and generally misleading. Contemporary accounts occasionally add to the confusion, but careful examination of them can be quite revealing. No, I am not a so called 'conspiracy nut'. That is an awful expression that labels anyone who strays from the accepted versions of historical events and I believe it is extremely insulting. However, I am a historian and I can live with the insults until the truth is finally revealed.

The accepted official version of the battle was assembled in haste soon after the event. It was written primarily to glorify the dead and vilify the victors, after all Custer was a national hero of the Civil War. But it was this early version that has remained as the foundation for all other written works as the truth of what happened. I believe that it is not the truth and to honour the dead the truth must be told. So now we can say that everything you thought you knew about the events concerning the battle and Custer's death is probably wrong and start again from scratch.

Stephen Longstreet states in his book that *'the only survivor of the Seventh Cavalry at the Little Big Horn was a horse'*. This is not strictly true. Reno and Benteen survived the hostile assaults, along with the majority of the men in their battalions and several horses were found, severely wounded but still standing on the battlefield. Their injuries were too severe to treat and so they were destroyed. One horse stood out from all the others and that was 'Comanche', Captain Keogh's faithful charger. He was instantly recognised and although he had some very nasty wounds, it was decided to save him and make him a symbol of the heroism the fight portrayed. Many historians have fallen foul of the facts concerning 'Comanche', as did Longstreet.

There were other survivors too, the hostiles themselves. For many years these participants would not speak of the fight for fear of retribution and when they did, they were largely ignored as their version contradicted the already established account. Proof of their accounts, their pictographs, lay locked away gathering dust for years. A terrible transgression that, again, suppressed the truth.

The political side is more difficult to define, for it was here that the conspiracy had its roots. It is a known fact that most conspiracy theories concentrate on the darker side of human nature and the ability or use of power of people in high positions to enact their cruel intentions. What we have here is no different from that. It is always dangerous to allow a few politically positioned people in power to orchestrate their own private executions in order to contain any threats they may perceive to be rising against them. George Custer was a political threat to the incumbent President, Ulysses S. Grant, and his faithful servants, Generals Sherman and Sheridan. All three have their reasons for personally disliking Custer and the very thought of him becoming their next President was an anathema to their very existence. However, they were not the only ones who could not bear the thought of Custer being their next President. Rutherford B. Hayes also had aspirations of entering the White House and with the help of his Civil War compatriot, General George Crook, he would become the 19th President of the United States with no George Custer to oppose him. The populace and the media may have wanted Custer as their President but those in positions of power did not.

The act of conspiracy has played a major part in the politics of the United States, before and since its formation as an independent nation and conspirators (on the whole) are very cunning and adept at concealing their dastardly deeds. None more so than here. However, no conspiracy can remain concealed forever and the truth will work its way to the surface eventually.

The passage of time has not lessened the need to set the records straight. Lies about momentous events infiltrate the system and corrupt all of us that choose to believe them. It has not been easy to sift through all the documents, but the relentless search has paid off. The truth can now be exposed and the establishment of the historical inaccuracies can be corrected. The hostiles were forced into taking the action they did by greedy politicians and they, unwittingly, became the instrument of death. Custer was deliberately put in an untenable position from which only death was the possible release, by those same powerful people who not only hated him but were afraid of him. Perhaps they even envied him, all things are possible. I have done my part by bringing you the truth. I hope you enjoy my efforts.

W.A. Wallace
January 2020

PART ONE

'The hour was sad I left the maid,
A lingering farewell taking;
Her sighs and tears my steps delayed,
I thought her heart was breaking.

In hurried words her name I blessed,
I breathed the vows that bind me;
And to my heart in anguish pressed,
The girl I left behind me.'

Samuel Glover

Chapter 1

Land of the Greasy Grass

Stretched across the Montana-Wyoming border lie the soaring heights of the Big Horn Mountains. Forming part of the eastern slopes of the vast Rocky Mountains, the impressive Big Horn range attains a height of some 3500 metres in the heart of the Big Horn National Forrest. It is from these precipitous hills and deep narrow ravines that the Little Big Horn emerges to begin its tortuous course north and its eventual confluence with the Big Horn River, only 20 Kilometres south of the Yellowstone.

Some 130 Kilometres in length, the Little Big Horn is a fast flowing river that ranges from 21 to 36 metres in width. Its pebbled bottom gives way to soft but abrupt banks that makes crossing of it treacherous at the best of times. Depending on the width, the water is some 61 centimetres to 1.5 metres in depth, becoming shallower at the natural fords.

Leaving the Big Horn Mountains in the south, the Little Big Horn first passes the rocky peaks of the Wolf Mountains to the south-east and then the more gentler slopes of the Rosebud Mountains to the north-east. As it twists and turns on its way through these deep canyons, steep rocky cliffs slowly give way to the soft undulating prairie lands, where the grass is green and scattered groves shelter clusters of cottonwood and box-elder trees. Here, the valley of the Little Big Horn is broad, open and copiously fertile.

These gently rolling hills are periodically broken by gullies and small ravines; scars eroded into the landscape by the unforgiving elements of wind and water, that have ravaged these lands from the beginning of time. These gullies traverse the hillsides at random, some providing protection to the many little tributaries that meander into the Little Big Horn, leaving others to form wide, dry gulches that harbour only the dry sands of the empty rivulets. In an article written in 1877, concerning his participation in the 1876 summer campaign, Colonel John Gibbon wrote of the area:

> 'The Little Big Horn is a stream with some singular features. It winds through its valley in a very crooked bed, bordered in many places with high precipitous banks, and is generally through this

> part of its course very sluggish and wherever this is the case the water is deep enough to swim a horse. At various intervals between these sluggish parts the water becomes shallow enough to admit of fording, and goes rippling along to form the next deep spot below.
>
> About a mile (1.6 Kilometres) below the bluffs occupied by Colonel Reno's command the river makes a considerable bend to the north-ward, and sweeping round towards the south again, cuts its course well into the bluff on the north bank, and leaves the valley on the south bank. In this curve the Indian camp was located.......
>
> Close by [us] are two such fords as I have described, and crossing one of these we move up the right bank of the stream which here runs nearly due south. On our right is the wooded bank of the river, the intervening space between the cottonwood trees being filled up with brush wood. On our left the valley opens out into grass-covered prairie, fringed on its southern side and again on its western side, where the stream curves to the north again, with timber and brush wood.
>
> Riding up the stream we come to the point where, after cutting the bluffs skirting it on the north, it turns sharply to the south. Here the ground commences to rise before us in gently sloping hills separated by little valleys.......
>
> Just before this valley joins the valley of the river, the bottom has been cut into a gulch some 8 or 10 feet (2.4 to 3 metres) deep, and this is filled with brush wood nourished by the moisture of the rain-water, which doubtless cut out the gulch.'

Such is the area of the Little Big Horn valley. It has changed very little since those fateful days in June 1876, with only the addition of a few highways to connect the townships that sprang up at a later date. In those wild, uncertain days the untamed prairie stretched as far as the eye could see and beyond. Free open land that was rich in vegetation and just as abundant in game. It was here that the hunter could find numerous pockets of antelope, elk and deer to satisfy his hunger and vast herds of buffalo to not only feed him, but clothe him as well.

The Indians called this area 'the land of the greasy grass' and it is easy to understand why. For the nomadic tribes it provided everything they would need. However, nature had been exceptionally cruel during the winter of 1875/1876 and uncontrollable circumstances had the region in the grip of freezing weather and almost bereft of any game.

THE BATTLE OF THE LITTLE BIG HORN

Spring had come late to Montana in 1876. The snow in the mountains had not melted until May, causing the Little Big Horn to run deeper and widen its banks. Although the soils of the surrounding plateau were now reasonably dry, the steep clay banks of the river were still saturated with unseasonal moisture making them soft and treacherous.

Where the Indians had camped to the west of the river, it was some 36 metres in width and deep enough to swim a horse. However, situated north and south of the encampment were some natural fords, where the banks sloped gently to the water's edge and the pebbles embedded in the sandy bottom afforded a little protection against horses hooves that would otherwise slip beneath the fast flowing water. Here, some 50 Kilometres from its emergence out of the Big Horn Mountains, the undulating prairie sloped up several metres to become a level grassy bench that provided an ideal campsite. Towards the west, these gentle slopes gradually became rocky peaks as the ash-grey mountains rose to dominate the horizon.

The Sioux Nation knew this region well. Indeed, they had been drifting to and from this land of plenty for many generations. As the vast buffalo herds moved further north so the nomadic natives followed them, for to these people the buffalo formed the very basis of their existence. The Lakota tribes were predominantly meat eaters; tall in their stride and proudly strong in their build. They were the lords of the sprawling hills and masters of the yawning plains. Their domain ranged from the Big Horn Mountains on the edge of the Rockies to the Black Hills in Dakota Territory. Here, the Indians roamed free as the buffalo and their warriors could practice their skills in challenging the bears that also shared their country.

Following the bitter Red Cloud War (1866 to 1868), a peace commission was convened at Fort Laramie in 1868 to determine the ownership (amongst other things) of these enormous hunting grounds. The great Ogalalla Chief, Red Cloud, was adamant in maintaining the rights to this area as he grimly stated his terms to the government representatives assembled at the fort:

> "Clear the Bozeman Trail that leads to the goldfields of Idaho and Montana, and abandon the army forts along the route."

After some lengthy deliberation, the commission agreed to accept Red Cloud's terms and they drafted a peace treaty for all to sign, with the following inclusion:

> '…….the country north of the North Platte and east to the summits of the Big Horn Mountains shall be held and considered to be 'un-ceded' Indian Territory.

> …….No white person or persons shall be permitted to settle upon or occupy any portion of the same; nor without consent of the Indians first had and obtained, to pass through the same."

Red Cloud finally signed the treaty on 6th November 1868, after the army had completely withdrawn from the area and all the forts had been razed to the ground. However, the contents of this treaty were extremely ambiguous, ultimately proving to be highly controversial. Whether or not this 'un-ceded' Indian Territory actually stretched as far as the Yellowstone and included the bountiful game regions of the Powder and Tongue valleys, was hotly debateable. The Sioux, who could not conceive the idea that land had boundaries, insisted that it did and constantly crossed the borders east of the Big Horn Mountains that the treaty allowed them. (It should be noted here that the Indians could not read the actual words written in the treaty themselves and, as such, had to rely on the interpreters who were usually present at such meetings to translate for them. These so-called interpreters were not always themselves truthful or trustworthy. Indeed, for the most part they were rogues who would just as soon kill the Indians as look at them.)

Therefore, firmly believing this land was theirs, the wandering Indians frequently traversed the boundaries and roamed the grasslands in search of game or to make war on their traditional enemies, the Crows. It is a known fact that by 1875, when most of the Indian tribes had been forced onto reservations, the military commanders in the west were fully aware of the yearly exodus of numerous Indians from the agencies to spend the winters in their hunting grounds, only to witness their return in the Spring.

Thus, this beautiful region of green, wind swept hills and high mountain peaks, made fertile by the clear flowing waters of the many rivers and their tributaries, was a smouldering-powderkeg in the 1870's, with the two opposing cultures ready to put a match to the ever-decreasing fuse.

Chapter 2

The Way of the Red Man

Between the dense woodlands of the east and the mountainous ranges of the west lies the grassy expanse of the Great Plains. From the Canadian border the Great Plains reach as far south as the desert lands of Texas and New Mexico. In 1876 it was a wild and inhospitable region, displaying a beauty that only Mother Nature could create.

This was the homeland and hunting grounds of some of the most colourful and wildly romantic characters of western history; the Plains Indians. Names such as Red Cloud, Spotted Tail, Dull Knife, Gall, Roman Nose and, of course, the fabulous Crazy Horse and Sitting Bull, still make the blood tingle with unrivalled excitement. Great battles such as Sand Creek (1864), the Fetterman Fight (1866), the Washita (1868), the Rosebud (1876), The Little Big Horn (1876) and Wounded Knee (1890), have carved history deep into these lands with the blood of the brave men who died fighting for their beliefs, both red and white. However, there was much more to the Plains Indians than their famous warriors or immortal battles. Much more. They had complex cultures and beliefs that went much deeper than the white settler's ploughshare.

Many of the numerous tribes had been gradually pushed west onto the Plains, as the white colonists had surged across the Appalachian Mountains in their hungry quest for land. Those who already roamed the vast Plains were instantly displaced and pushed even further west or north as the immense tidal wave gathered momentum. For the settlers it was just pure greed and a selfish belief, 'Manifest Destiny'. For the Indians it was a case of move out of the way or be annihilated. The Indians gave way. However, there is evidence that shows a distinct similarity between the languages of some of the Plains Indians with those of the Woodland nations (the Cheyenne, for example) thus proving they all once shared the same region.

By 1876, complicated structures within the native population had separated the numerous tribes to form their own identities: The Arapaho, Arikara, Assiniboin, Atsina (or Gros Ventre, also known as the Hidatsa), Comanche, Cree, Crow, Gosiute, Iowa, Kansa, Kiowa, Mandan, Missouri, Northern Cheyenne, Omaha, Osage, Pawnee, Piegan, Ponca, Shoshone, Southern

Cheyenne, Ute and, of course, the great Sioux Nation. Many of these names have now faded into obscurity living on only in the annals of history.

The Sioux were the largest of the Indian nations that inhabited the Plains and were divided into three divisions, each of which were further divided into numerous tribes, thus: the Dakota or Santee division, with the Mivdekanton, Sisseton, Wahpekute and Wahpeton Sioux; the Lakota or Teton division, encompassing the Blackfoot, Brulé, Hunkpapa, Minniconjou, Ogallala, Sans Arc and Two Kettle tribes; and, lastly the Nakota or Wiciyela division comprising of the Yankton and Yanktonai Sioux.

It is interesting to note that although these Plains dwellers numbered approximately 35 tribes in total, the overall number of this population (at this time) barely rose above 100,000, a surprisingly small number considering the huge area they occupied.

There was good reason for these indigenous people to be nomadic. It didn't matter whether the Indians were Cheyenne, Arapaho or Hunkpapa Sioux, they all shared a common factor with each other: they were meat eaters and in order to maintain a steady supply of food, they had to hunt for it. Seasonal climatic changes made their prey move from area to another, constantly traversing the Great Plains in all directions and, naturally, the Indians followed them. Occasionally the Indians supplemented their diet with wild corn, berries or fish, but they knew that their tall, erect stature and their incredible strength came from the rich protein diet they obtained from the various animals they killed and ate. Their main supply of meat came from the buffalo, elk, deer and antelope. These animals wandered across this vast sea of grass in enormous herds and wherever they were to be found, hungry tribes were not far away.

The buffalo was a very formidable creature to hunt. It was huge in comparison to the deer or antelope, attaining a height of 180 centimetres at the shoulder; a length of 2 to 3.5 metres (not including the tail); and a weight of up to 1,000 kilograms, with the bulls being larger than the cows. When disturbed it could run for great distances and was ready to turn and charge at the least provocation or short notice. To the warriors who hunted the buffalo it was a huge challenge, testing their skill as much as their stamina and courage. Their ancestors had successfully hunted the much larger mastodon and woolly mammoth, and the techniques the warriors now employed had been inherited from them. Even so, the task of hunting such creatures was extremely arduous and fraught with danger.

Before the introduction of the horse, The Indians hunted on foot with methods customised according to the region they were in. A usual tactic was for the warrior to don the hide of a buffalo and crawl through the undergrowth to a distance from where he could throw his spear or fire an arrow. If his aim was sure he would bring the animal down, however, if it was not he could cause a stampede thus endangering the lives of his fellow hunters as well as his own. With the advent of the horse, hunting the buffalo became a work of art and, although a much easier practice, it was no less dangerous. Indian horses were small, fast and nimble animals, with a high tolerance of endurance, sure footed and highly trained in the art of hunting. A skilled hunter could manoeuvre his horse alongside a buffalo and it would stay there, keeping pace with the quarry while he took aim with his bow.

Other creatures featuring high on the hunter's menu were the common (or Virginian) deer, the black tailed deer, the Rocky Mountain goat and the Big Horn sheep, which were also to be found in the Rockies. The latter were in demand for their horns as much as their flesh, for they were circular in shape and could grow as much as a metre in length on each side of the skull. Animals that yielded little meat, but were prized for their fur, included the coyote, white or black wolf and the racoon. Rabbit and squirrel were low on the list, although they were acceptable when other game was scarce.

Occasionally this catalogue of game was headed by a much more savage beast, the Grizzly Bear. Even when in a good mood this beast was best left alone, as its Latin name *Ursus horribilis* suggests. The Grizzly was also a native of the Rocky Mountains and could grow to a height of 2.5 metres. Solid in build, it could weigh more than 400 Kilograms and would think nothing of dragging a buffalo carcass, weighing something like 500 Kilograms into its lair. All Indians regarded this huge beast with a profound reverence and it was the ultimate test of a hunter's courage and skill to catch one and kill it. If he was successful, the hunter then sought to appease the bear's spirit, often apologising to it or talking to it as though it were a member of his own family.

After the hunt, the game was butchered and prepared for storage. The liver was sliced and eaten raw, for it was a rich source of vitamins and it replenished the organic compounds the Indians had used up during the winter months. Winters could be very hard in this region, so they stored as much meat as they could during the summer months in preparation. They made pemmican by pounding sun-dried meat, mixing it with crushed dried berries and putting the mixture into sacks, over which they poured melted fat. This kept fairly well, as did another method of jerking the meat; cutting it into strips and drying it in the sun. When the buffalo were plentiful, the Indians feasted well. Most of the tribes divided the catch between everyone in their camp, for it was considered a greatness of their manhood to provide for the old and the needy as well as the young.

Once the meat had been prepared, the Indian women began the arduous task of tanning the hides and working the leather to make it soft and supple. The skin would first be scraped and tanned by rubbing it with a mixture of brains, liver remains, sour milk and elm bark. Then it was soaked in water, wrung out and stretched across a frame to dry. Some tribes achieved great fame for their ability in preparing leather. The Crows, for example, made their clothes and tipi of deerskin and buffalo hide so perfectly that when it rained the leather dried out quickly with little or no damage.

If there was one thing the Indians did extremely well, it was in dressing themselves. The men of the Plains tribes usually wore leggings with a breach-clout and moccasins only, leaving their chests bare or covered by a breast plate made of bone. Shirts were only worn by the chiefs, medicine men or warriors of high repute, and then only for ceremonial occasions or when in battle. The women wore one-piece dresses of very soft skins, or a blouse with leggings. All items were carefully stitched by hand and then ornately decorated with beads or quill-work, the Plains Indians preferring geometric designs as opposed to the more complicated floral designs of the woodland tribes in the east. No item was left plain, for it was a passion born within to display their talents in art in any shape or form. Even if their clothing was not furnished with attractive bead or quill-work, then the items were adorned with feathers, embroidery work or heavily fringed. Both men and women of all tribes wore bracelets, necklaces and amulets made of metal, bone and/or fur.

Adornment of the head was a serious matter, often accompanied by a religious ritual. Usually the hair was left to grow long, then braided and bound by leather thongs. However, the positioning of the feathers or strips of fur was governed by important rules and ceremonies, as this was a form of displaying their rank in tribal hierarchy. For example, one warrior may only be entitled to wear one eagle feather, whereas another could wear two and so on. If a warrior was fairly high in rank, then he would be allowed to wear a piece of fur on his head or some other part of the body. The fur could be from an otter, beaver, fox, racoon or any other small animal, the type of fur denoting his insignia of rank. Of course, the most famous of all the Indian head gear was the war bonnet and, perhaps, the most impressive of these were those of the Sioux. Such items were only worn by the elite of the tribe and then only on certain occasions. The war bonnet comprised of multiple rows of feathers, set into a band of bead-work and decorated with lappets that fell onto the wearer's shoulder, these usually being of highly decorated bead-work but they could also be strips of fur.

Cured hides of the buffalo had a much more important use than for clothing. The principal form of dwelling was the tipi. This was conical in shape, with buffalo hides stretched across 20 to 24 poles, supported by 3 or 4 main poles in the centre. A tipi for family use could range in size but was often quite small, whereas the ceremonial tipi (or lodge) was relatively enormous, sometimes reaching 6 metres in height, with an internal measurement of 9 metres across. Such a lodge could take 50 or more buffalo hides to construct it. However, regardless of size, all the dwellings were easy to erect and dismantle. When the camp moved to another location, the poles were simply arranged across the backs of their ponies and dogs to form travois, the tipi or lodge was folded and strapped to them. In summer the lower edges of the tipi could be rolled up to allow the cool air to circulate within and in winter they could be pegged down to keep out the draughts. The fire was always placed in the centre to allow the smoke to exit through the top, where the poles crossed. If prevailing winds blew the smoke back in, the centre pole could be repositioned so the exit was sheltered and the smoke could effectively escape. The hides were always decorated with either religious symbols, the motif of the owner or scenes of great deeds depicting historic actions of the past. Overall, these were the perfect dwellings for all types of climatic conditions.

The inside of the tipi was Spartan, however. The floor was the earth on which the tipi stood, kept scrupulously clean and sometimes covered with furs or skins. Shields and fetishes were hung on the walls, providing the only relief from the plain hide. Other than sleeping robes, the only pieces of furniture to be found (if at all) were the wooden back-rests, which could support a man as he sat on the ground. Indians had little use for all the finery found in the homes of the white men. If it wasn't functional then it wasn't needed.

Family life was a serious day to day concern. The members of the family were very close to each other and a death, whether by natural causes or warfare, was greatly mourned by all. The elders were reverently respected by everyone and cared for extremely well. Children were encouraged to imitate their elders, for it was an important part of growing up. As soon as they were able to walk they began their education in earnest, for daily life to the Indian was a crucial factor of his survival. Small boys fished in the streams with miniature rods and hunted small game with bows and arrows specially made to size for them. The young girls helped their mothers by looking after their younger siblings and generally helping with the daily chores. Thus, by the time they reached puberty they were judged by their elders to be sufficiently mature to marry and start a family of their own.

However, not all daily life revolved around the austere task of survival. Once the hunt was over and the meat had been prepared, it was time to use their energy in playing games. Young and old alike had their own versions of fun and games. For the children there were ball and hoop games, although for the most part boys did not play games with the girls. As they grew older there were more complicated ball games, such as their highly spirited version of lacrosse and games of chance, using variously marked stones to signify dice. Certain occasions called for dances, where all ages of the younger generation could join in leaving the elders to sit and watch. For the warrior class though, the greatest game of all was war. Next to hunting it was their main occupation and, like hunting, it was the excitement of the chase rather than the actual kill that was the name of the game. The skills and techniques that the warriors acquired whilst hunting, were now employed in the great game of war.

A favourite game amongst the Plains tribes was for a party of warriors to sneak up on the camp of another tribe and see how many horses they could run off without being caught. If the catch included a preferred horse of a renown warrior, then the result was all the more honourable, for the horses were usually tethered to the owner's tipi. Of course, the next trick was to retain ownership of the spoils, for it was inevitable that the irate owners would want to reclaim them. An actual physical encounter was frowned upon unless it was to touch the opponent and run. 'Counting Coup' (touching the enemy with a special 'coup stick') was the greatest achievement for a warrior assuming he survived the encounter. Great deeds were made of such actions as the actual risk involved was far more honourable than the ease of a mere killing. With the advance of the white men across the Plains, war became a much more serious business and warriors were just as proficient in the killing game as well.

However, all Indians were individualists and, as such, they could not be relied upon to carry out any specific plan of action. Indeed, plans were rarely if ever discussed before an engagement, as they usually consisted of the same tactics being employed, time and time again, with a few minor alterations according to the circumstances they faced. These were the ambush, the encirclement and the gradual tightening of the circle until the enemy was completely wiped out. Thus, using these as the basis for attack, the tactics were virtually always the same: attack the enemy when they were least expecting it or at their weakest point, and circle them. The ambush never failed to take the enemy by surprise and once begun, the warriors simply whittled away at them until they were satisfied enough had been slain or wounded. The latter was the more common offensive and often left the survivors in a complete state of astonishment that they were still alive! Unfortunately, there was no degree of discipline amongst the warriors and although they may have ridden into battle together, once the initial engagement had been established it was every man for himself. If a warrior felt he had achieved his objective he would simply abandon the fight and return home. There was no shame in that, just common sense, for it was far better to live to fight another day.

Some historians have claimed that the Indians of North America were the greatest cavalrymen the world has ever known, (in particular the Comanche, whose horsemanship and aggressive fighting skills are legendary). Due to diverse conditions and circumstances concerning other ethnic groups around the world, that statement could be a matter for debate. However, most authorities agree that the Indians did possess an uncanny ability to manoeuvre their horses with exceptional adroitness. (Buffalo hunts were extremely good training grounds it seems!) Yet such expertise meant nothing to the warriors if they felt the odds were against them or if they had had enough. As we shall see, George Custer was more concerned that the Indians would withdraw before he could engage them in battle, rather than the overwhelming numbers he would actually face.

The commonest weapons the Indians had at their disposal were the bow, lances, war clubs, (the latter of which are often mistakenly referred to as 'tomahawks') and knives. A warrior's proficiency with the bow was primarily gained from his hunting days since his youth and was second to none. It was their main weapon, with other items being additional or optional. All warriors carried a shield which was made from wood and hide. The shields of the Plains tribes were circular or oval in shape and colourfully painted according to the owner's personal taste. Fetishes, that professed to possess magical powers to protect the warrior, hung around the edge amidst any trophies he may have collected in previous fights, such as locks of hair or fingers. Being customised as they were, it was not unnatural for the shield to be buried with the owner upon his demise. Hand guns and rifles were highly prized trophies, as long as there was plenty of ammunition to go with them. Most rifles were obtained from the agency posts on the reservations, for the specific purpose of hunting and although the warriors never actually stated what they were hunting it was generally presumed to be meat for the pot! Other such weaponry was obtained from slain settlers or soldiers, although any ammunition that was collected soon ran out and the weapons were discarded.

Following the fight with Custer's battalion, on the Little Big Horn, some 590 cavalry carbines and revolvers were carried from the field by the victorious Indians. It was these Springfield carbines that probably wreaked the most damage throughout the duration of the battle, given that they were extremely accurate and had a remarkable range. Examination of the field following the battle showed evidence of forked sticks along the Indians' line of fire, indicating that the hostiles had used the old buffalo hunters' method of steadying their aim with their newly acquired carbines. Recent excavations of the battleground have revealed that the Indians were probably armed with as many as 41 different types of firearms, including Winchester and Henry repeating rifles, in addition to the weapons taken from the fallen soldiers. In contrast, it has also been estimated that only around 500 warriors in the entire hostile force actually possessed repeating rifles. Not many considering the number of the hostiles in action, but if it was true for Custer and his men it was 500 too many! Very few hand guns were kept by the Indians as ammunition was very difficult to obtain. They were used and thrown away. According to a government report, written in the wake of the fight, there were very few hand guns employed apart from those of the military. The most common appear to be the .44 calibre revolvers manufactured by Messr. Colt, Remington and Smith & Wesson, the major manufacturers of the time, of which many, if not all, could have been taken from other white victims. If truth were known there were probably more makes of hand guns used during the battle and subsequently carried away as spoils of war. Custer and many of his officers carried privately purchased hand guns rather than the military issue, many of which were not found on the field.

Much has been said over the years concerning the Indian practice of mutilation of the dead, usually regarding it as an act of brutal savagery. (It should be noted here that the indigenous tribes of North America were not the only ethnic groups to indulge in this practice. The Zulus of South Africa, for example, also mutilated their slain enemies as was observed during the aftermath of Isandlwana in 1879.) Rather than being just an act of brutal savagery or deliberate defilement, a deeper study of the practice reveals it was a cultural phenomenon. Although the Plains Indians had no fear of being killed in battle themselves, they did have an innate fear of being hunted by the spirits of those they had slain, even to the point of being killed by them. In order to avoid this, the Indians practised the application of mutilation whereby certain areas of the deceased body were cut or removed to prevent the spirit from tracking them to take their revenge. Each tribe had their own method of deterring restless spirits. The Cheyenne preferred to cut the muscles of each arm from the armpit the elbow, thus ensuring the spirit could not raise any weapons in anger again. Similarly, the Comanche severed the hands for the same reason. The Arapaho believed that if they cut across the nose, sometimes cutting the nose off completely, their fallen opponent could not use his sense of smell to haunt him. The Sioux, however, made sure their dead enemies were not going anywhere. They cut their victim's throat, sometimes totally severing the head, thus ensuring the spirits could not find their way anywhere, much less do any physical bodily harm. If it is accepted that mutilation of the dead was a spiritual motivated act within the culture of the Indians, it is difficult not to comprehend the ferocious mutilation that was observed on the battlefield of the Little Big Horn after the fight.

A death in the family, whether from natural causes or as a result of a fight, was accepted by the Indians with a general air of impassiveness, save for a brief period of mourning to rid themselves of any grief or responsibility they may have felt for the departed. This period of mourning could last as long as 3 or 4 days, during which time the relatives would wail and sing lamentations. Occasionally they may tear at their hair or slice their arms during this period, but it was not a common practice. Once this ritual was over the Indians resumed their lives and no more was said. Indian burials were simple affairs. The Sioux wrapped the body in a cloth or animal skin and either placed it in the fork of a tree or on a wooden platform. The personal possessions and the extra items the deceased would need in the next world would be placed on the platform or in a tipi erected nearby. Any sacrificial offerings would be put with them and they would be left alone to continue their journey.

The next world, often referred to as 'the happy hunting ground' or the 'land of many tipis' was the only one known to the Indians. Until the appearance of Christian missionaries, these people had not heard of anywhere like Hell, where they could be sent as a punishment for the crimes they committed during their lifetime. As far as they were concerned all Indians had a right to go into the next world; where the sun shone continuously, game was gloriously abundant and life was everlasting with their ancestors. Totally fearless in the face of death the Indians were absolutely terrified of ghosts, so much so that after the burial the living would often adopt another name so the ghost could not find them. No matter how fond they were of the deceased during his or her lifetime, now they were no longer walking the earth and the farewells had been said, the living Indians would not go anywhere near the burial place for fear of disturbing their spirits. In other words once a person had crossed the thin line between life and death, it was best that he remained where he was. Burials that had been disturbed awakened the spirits and they sought to invade the world of the living to seek revenge. Such ghastly beings were considered as evil and cursed, and as such, cast fear amongst the remainder of the tribe. Thus, burial grounds were deemed highly sacred places and any intrusion was severely censured.

The whole world of the Indian was encased by the mysterious aura of the spirits. As well as the evil ghosts and monsters that roamed around unseen, there were also the spirits that governed everything the Indians did and swirled around them everywhere they went. These spirits could be invisible like those who furnished the wind and the rain, or they could take the form of the many creatures who shared their environment, such as the high flying eagle, the grizzly bear, the woolly buffalo or even a wild horse. Mountains, trees and rivers had their own spirits, all of which kept the Indians alive and well. However, these lesser deities, although powerful in their own right, were ultimately governed by a more divine hierarchy to which all Indian tribes looked to for guidance. The Algonquins of the St. Lawrence valley, referred to this supreme being as 'Manitour': to the Sioux it was 'Wakan-Tanka' (or Great Mystery). Wakan-Tanka ruled over everything; the sun, the moon, the Plains, the wild creatures and the Indians themselves. Wakan-Tanka was the ultimate supreme deity. A late 19th century Ogalalla chief, Flat Iron, was to observe:

> 'From Wakan-Tanka, the Great Mystery, comes all power. It is from Wakan-Tanka that the holy man has his wisdom and the power to heal and to make holy charms. Man knows that all healing plants are given by \Wakan-Tanka; therefore they are holy. So too is the buffalo holy; because it is a gift of Wakan-Tanka.'

Thus, the complex world of Indian religion was a serious aspect of their everyday life and was treated with strict observance by all.

Every village had a medicine tipi in which sacred bundles, stones and other mysterious artefacts would be placed for safe keeping. Inside the tipi fetishes, drums and other emblems of the warrior societies would hang from the walls or the supporting poles. It was very important that the fire was kept burning constantly, for this was a sacred fire, lit in dedication to the many spirits who were so powerful in ensuring their welfare. When a religious ceremony took place within the tipi logs were thrown on the fire to create a roaring blaze and aromatic herbs added to create the right atmosphere. Drums were then set to a rhythmic beating and the chosen participants of the ceremony formed a circle around the glowing flames.

Worship of the spirits could be communal or personal. An Indian would often go off on his own to talk with his guardian spirit, generally to request good fortune for himself and his family. In a village, however, he would join in with everyone else and ask that the welfare of all the tribe be taken into consideration. Outside the medicine tipi, communication with the spirits would take the form of singing and dancing, often lasting for quite a few days at a time. The Indians of the Plains had ceremonies dedicated to everything that was entwined with their daily life. Apart from the rituals of growing up, (i.e. the sacred ceremonies of birth, puberty, marriage and death,) there were dances specifically performed for the deities that guided them each day. There was the Bear Dance, the Buffalo Dance, the War Dance and the spectacular but torturous, Sun Dance, to name but a few. The Ghost Dance did not put in an appearance until a later date.

The Sun Dance was celebrated by most of the Plains tribes, each having their own variation on the theme. But nowhere was it performed with such panache than by the Sioux and the Cheyenne, who staged this ceremony in mid-summer when the sun was at its zenith in the sky. During the first 3 days, pre-ceremonial preparations were meticulously arranged; a 'sun-pole' was erected and then a 'sun-trail' was laid that led up to the 'sun-tipi'. (Depending on the tribe concerned, the 'sun-pole' was sometimes placed inside the 'sun-tipi'.) Then the main phase of the ceremony, called 'Okipa', began. This can be compared to a play in which each act tells the story of a warrior's career.

The four acts involved were the warrior's capture, his torture, captivity and final deliverance. These acts not only symbolised his promising career but also the struggle of his soul or spirit to free itself from within and to show him, by some dream or vision, how he was to conduct his life in the future. The volunteer for the Sun Dance was first captured by members of a warrior society and the horrifically tortured. Wooden skewers were thrust into the volunteer's shoulders or chest, who accepted this excruciating pain without uttering a sound. Long leather thongs were then tied to the skewers with the remaining ends being thrown over the crossed bars of the 'sun-pole' and he was raised into the air. The agony of such torture defies comprehension, but it was an important part of the sacred ceremony and accepted as such, for it was believed that the extreme pain that was endured was a prime factor in inducing the vision the warrior sought. Periodically he was lowered to have a brief rest, whereupon women would wipe the blood from his wounds. While he was suspended from the 'sun-pole', those watching the procedure sung songs of captivity to encourage him to be strong. The climax came when the warrior summoned all the strength he had left and tore himself free from the wooden skewers. When the last warrior had achieved this the Sun Dance was over; the special tipi could be dismantled and the 'sun-pole', stripped of all its finery, would be left to the mercy of the sun.

Even though the Plains Indian was basically an individualist, the major ceremonies and the general religious or health and welfare of the tribe was the responsibility of the Medicine Man. All tribes held such a man in complete and utter reverence, respecting his unrivalled powers in healing the sick or wounded and honouring his exclusive gift of being able to communicate directly with the Great Mystery. Indeed, many tribes ranked the Medicine man as second only to their chief.

Due to their deep religious convictions, the Indians believed that sickness was caused by an evil spirit and so the Medicine Man was called upon to exercise his special powers to drive the bad spirit from the afflicted person. Failure to effect a cure could result in his own death and sometimes did, especially if the patient was someone of importance. It was not surprising then that the Medicine man worked extremely hard to ensure a pleasing result. A good Medicine Man was a wealthy one, although they were seldom envied for such wealth. Apprenticeships to become a Medicine Man were extremely arduous and only those that showed a special aptitude for the vocation were chosen. After graduation his personal life was one of solitude, often being forbidden to marry and isolated from the rest of the tribe. His only contact with other people came when he was in attendance at an important ceremony or when he was called upon to heal the sick.

Unfortunately, there were times when even the influential settlers across the Plains brought new diseases which, until then, had never been experienced by the native tribes. One notable example of this was the terrible outbreak of smallpox in 1837. Brought west along the Missouri River by fur traders, the Indians had no resistance to such a contagious disease and very quickly succumbed to it. The Assiniboin, Blackfoot and Hidatsa tribes were severely affected, as were a veritable number of the Sioux. But the Arikara and Mandan tribes were dealt a disastrous blow from which they never recovered. The Arikara lost approximately 2000 people out of a total population of 4000. The Mandan were totally destroyed as a tribe, with only 31 survivors out of an estimated 1600 Indians. All out war between the Indians and the white invaders could not have had such a devastating effect in such a short time.

And so the first seeds of discontent were sown, the first of many that would accrue in the years to come.

Chapter 3

Neither Red nor White

Alienated as the Plains Indians were against the white man, some accepted their way of life and sought the relative security of being clothed and fed on a regular basis by joining forces with them, usually by becoming scouts for the army. This practice had been used by the military for some years and had proven to be highly successful, especially if the Indians employed had some enemies to settle old scores with. The Arikara and Crow are prime examples of this, being long time enemies of the Sioux.

The Arikara had been natural enemies of the Mandan, Hidatsa and the Sioux, participating in numerous skirmishes against these tribes for many years. Similarly the Crows, although distant cousins of the Sioux, had little in common with them and through their earlier contacts with fur traders and white settlers, they had established a permanent relationship them.

Early colonial settlers had found that the employment of friendly native Americans, as scouts or guides, had been extremely favourable both economically and physically. These natives were not only familiar with the land but they were also aware of which of the neighbouring tribes were hostile or not. Their exceptional tracking and survival skills were also additional attributes that were of an enormous advantage to the military, not to mention the fact that they were sorely needed extra able-bodied fighters when the need arose. Both the British and American forces made extensive use of native Americans during the Revolutionary War of 1774 and continued to do so when the hostilities ended. Colonel John Freemont later employed Delaware Indians as scouts during his epic expedition across the Rocky Mountains in 1853. During the Civil War, both Union and Confederate forces enlisted various tribes of Indians, although it was the Southern States that actually incorporated them within the ranks. Approximately 18 regiments were formed from the Cherokee, Choctaw, Creek, Chickasaw, Osage and Seminole tribes to fight for the Confederacy. Perhaps the most famous of these regiments were the Cherokee Mounted Rifles, who served for 4 years of the war. Obviously, those Indians were more than just scouts and records show that their use in warfare did arouse increased savagery amidst the brutality of the conflict. Even so, their effectiveness had been keenly noted, for in later years both Crook and Custer made great use of native Americans as military scouts and both men extolled the tactical advantages these scouts had given them.

By 1866 it was felt that the employment of Indians within government service should be officially sanctioned for the future by an approval of scout service in law. An Act of Congress was finally approved on 22nd June 1766 and Section 1112, of the revised statute of 1873 clearly stated:

> 'The President is authorised to enlist a force of Indians not exceeding one thousand, who shall act as scouts in the Territories and Indian Country. They shall be discharged when the necessity of their service shall cease, or at the discretion of the Department Commander.'

As with most government edicts, especially those that dealt with Indian affairs, the statute is extremely bias and ambiguous in favour of the military, for this meant that the Indians could virtually be enlisted and then discharged at will, regardless of the circumstances at the time. Although it must be said that the majority of army officers, on the frontier, treated their Indian scouts with respect with only the minority abusing the system and then there were some who did not agree with such employment for a variety of reasons.

Whilst commanders in the field, such as Crook and Custer, found their Indian scouts to be irreplaceable, others argued that using Indians within the military organisation took away their individuality. Some critics even argued that the cultural and linguistic differences would inhibit successful campaigns against hostile Indians, thus affecting the efficiency of the units involved. They were obviously not aware that Indian scouts, when on campaign, were usually accompanied by white scouts who were quite accomplished in Indian customs, many of whom had married Indian maidens thus bridging any cultural or linguistic difficulties that may occur.

When in the employment of the military Indian scouts faired extremely well. They not only received the same allowance as the regular cavalrymen they also received a payment for their services which varied considerably according to the area in which they were operating. Indian scouts were also issued with the same clothing, although many invariably embellished it according to their own tastes, much to the chagrin of their commanding officers. By 1890 Indian scouts had been issued with a fulldress uniform designed in the same style as the regular cavalrymen, including a plumed helmet. Not all things were the same though and there were a few striking differences to distinguish an Indian scout from the troopers when on parade.

The blue serge tunic had 9 brass buttons down the front, each button having crossed arrows on them. The collar, shoulder straps and cuff flaps were all white edged with scarlet piping. Scarlet piping also edged the tunic. The 1881 pattern cavalry helmet has a red and white horse-hair plume and sported woven cords, also of red and white. (It should be noted here that the facing colour for the regular cavalry was yellow.) However, all things considered, it was a serious attempt to make the Indian scouts feel equal and the military cannot be condemned for that. For all intents and purposes the Indian scouts were an integral part of the standing army in the field.

There was a formal procedure to be observed before any Indians could be enlisted as scouts. The procedure itself and the duration it entailed varied according to the tribe that was being recruited. The duration of the ceremony could be quite lengthy and often was, after all the Indians had to make it quite clear that the military authorities knew they were the ones who needed the Indians' help! After numerous councils in which army officials (through renegade interpreters more often than not,) put their requests and propositions, the Indians would retire to discuss the matter amongst themselves. First it was the turn of the elders, who rarely approved anyway. Then the young braves put forward their case, most of whom wanted to avenge their ancestors against aggressions of old enemies and taste blood. It was the young braves who usually managed to persuade their elders to agree to the requests from the army and allow them to become military scouts. Colonel John Gibbon, 7th United States Infantry, gave the following description of his own experiences when enlisting Crow scouts for the summer campaign of 1876:

> '....... The next morning the whole number came forward and were sworn into the United States service. This ceremony was peculiar. We wished to bind them to their contract in some way, and in casting around for a method we were informed that the Crow's way to take oath was to "touch with his finger the point of a knife." After this solemn proceeding if he failed to keep his pledges he was a disgraced man; but what was more likely to keep him faithful was the belief that a violation of the oath laid him open to terrible calamities by way of disease and other misfortunes to himself and his family.
>
> All the volunteers were paraded and an officer presented to each in succession a hunting knife, on the point of which each one gravely placed the tip of his forefinger and the deed was done. Thus they became United States soldiers for 3 months and were entitled to a soldiers pay, rations and clothing.'

Amongst those who enlisted under Colonel Gibbon on the Yellowstone were some of the Indian scouts who would accompany Custer on his fateful journey to the Little Big Horn. Show-His-Face was already an old man. He did not enlist to engage in any fighting but to encourage the younger warriors in their obligations. Half-Yellow-Face was so amenable that he became a firm favourite with the officers and men of the Seventh Cavalry and was present during the climatic fight of Reno's battalion on the bluffs. White-Swan was also present at the battle and badly wounded as a result. Curly-Hair was one of the youngest to enlist and accompanied Custer's battalion up to the start of the fight. He claimed to have made his escape from the field by covering himself with a Sioux blanket and riding alongside them. His story is open for debate. In all there were approximately 49 Arikara and 6 Crow Indians employed as scouts in the Seventh, all under the direction of Lieutenant Charles A. Varnum, although many more had been deployed between Terry's and Gibbon's columns. A number of Custer's Indian scouts did survive the battle and it is their testimony regarding the sequence of events, that has been an invaluable source of information for present day historians.

There is no doubt that if the critics had had their way and Indians had never been employed as scouts, the Plains Wars would probably have turned out very differently and dragged on for many more years, with a much higher loss of life. That the army was so effective in the field was due, in no small measure, to the unequivocal service constantly displayed by the Indian scouts.

Perhaps the best epitaph concerning the employment of Indian scouts was written by General George Crook, when he stated:

> "...... that without them the white men would have been outwitted, exhausted, circumvented, possibly ambushed and destroyed......."

He never spoke a truer word!

Chapter 4

Boots and Saddles

Needless to say, in contrast to the Native Americans, the military style of life was totally different in the extreme. The true army of the west bore very little resemblance to the clean-cut image that was created many years later by the actors and producers of Hollywood. In fact, the early western films, when cinema was in its infancy, were much closer to the reality that the west had been. Military posts on the frontier were often under-manned; frequently short of supplies; usually commanded by officers who were either incompetent or misfits within the armed forces; and disgustingly squalid. However, in general the men of this frontier army were extremely hardy and defiant in spirit. Once they had realised that any support or understanding for their perilous position was not forthcoming from the bureaucrats, snugly ensconced in Washington, they gave up all hope of the situation improving and became virtually self-sufficient, ultimately priding themselves on their continuous adaptations to the ever-changing environment.

April 9th 1865 saw the end of the Civil War. The conflict had left countless numbers dead on the bloody battlefields or terribly maimed for life, both physically and mentally; stripped much of the landscape, including valuable arable land; and, changed ideas amongst the populace for years to come. Having utterly devastated the Confederate states, Washington now found itself forced with the daunting prospect of having to rebuild them, combining the manufacturing resources of the north with the natural resources of the south. The capitulation of the Confederate forces also presented the grave prospect of thousands of men who had nothing to return home to, thus many headed west to build a new life for themselves.

At this time the size of the Union army was enormous, having been comprised of both regular and volunteer regiments that were hugely expensive to maintain. To the politicians it made good sense to cull the manpower, thus saving precious government finances. Within a year the army was reduced to 57,000 regular troops, with this being cut even further to 39,000 by 1869. By 1873, with another 4 years of occupation still to be completed in the Southern States and Indian hostilities now increasing on the western frontier, the army had been reduced yet again to s total of 25,000 enlisted men. Predictably, many of the politicians who controlled the military services had little or no understanding of life on the frontier and the troops they sent to the outposts had little or no experience of frontier survival either. The result was a dangerous mixture of ignorance and confusion making the frontier an explosive melting pot.

By now, the western frontier was a hotbed of unrest and lawlessness. Numerous wagon army trains, overflowing with immigrants, were surging into this untamed land in search of a fresh start at an alarming rate. Townships sprang into life along the routes and those who settled in them had no thought that the land might actually belong someone else, be they red or white. Any form of law was non-existent until army posts were established to exact some sort of control, at least until a town marshal or sheriff could be legally appointed. Prior to this, army posts had only been erected to protect settlers and miners from Indian attacks. Now the troops found themselves having to continue the protection of the immigrants and police the townships as well. It was a situation that was not altogether pleasant. Their resources were stretched beyond their capacity and tempers flared frequently between the military and the civilians they were duty bound to protect.

Railroad companies were quick to grasp the advantages, starting to spread their branches and follow in the wake of the land hungry settlers. Wherever a township suddenly appeared, the railroad was quick to follow, its tracks traversing the untamed Prairie in all directions thus presenting the military with another element to protect. These townships were sprouting at such an alarming rate along the old trails the army found it difficult to keep pace and amidst all this rapid expansion and movement the hostile Indians, angry at such terrestrial encroachment of their ancestral lands, naturally went on the offensive to stem the flow. White settlers were attacked and homesteads burnt to the ground, leaving the soldiers to pick up the pieces. Reports of these hostile actions inevitably filtered back to the very politicians who had originally given the troops their marching orders to the frontier. They, in turn, lashed out at the military commanders for failing in their duty and, of course, the lowly outpost received the blame.

The army had been saddled with expectations that were impossible to fulfil. They were expected to patrol an area of approximately 2.5 million square Kilometres with only 15,000 regular troops. Over the following years there was never more than this number of troops on the frontier, which meant that there was one man to every 129.5 Kilometres! An absolutely ludicrous minimal number of men, given the formidable task they had been entrusted with and with all-out war with the Indians just over the horizon it was this small, under-equipped army that would have to face the final consequences. A fact that would not be recognised by the bureaucrats until after the defeat of the 7th Cavalry at the Little Big Horn.

Previous clashes with hostile Indians had impressed upon the military strategists in Washington that the continual use of infantry along the frontier was extremely impractical. The mobility of Indian warfare called for mounted troops not foot soldiers. However, the infantry did have its uses and were occasionally employed in campaigns against the Indians, including the 1876 campaign. They were tediously slow and commanders in the field did their utmost to use them as guards for their supply depots. In general, though, foot soldiers were usually retained on the frontier to maintain the forts and outposts. Thus, the cavalry took pride of place and bore the burden of establishing new forts from which they sallied forth their regular patrols in an effort to keep the peace. The strategy in most cases was theoretically sound but the awesome practicality was not and it took an enormous amount of hard work and sheer courage to achieve even a percentage of their target.

The composition of a cavalry regiment had changed very little since the end of the Civil War. A regiment comprised of 10 or more companies, with 50 or more men in each company. (75 men in a company was the more desired requirement but this was not always achievable.) With the exception of companies C and F, who had 60 and 61 men respectively, the average company complement of the Seventh Cavalry was 50 when on active service. A regiment was ideally commanded by a Colonel with the support of a Lieutenant-Colonel, two Majors, and an Adjutant of any rank, with one Subaltern who acted as a Quartermaster. Unfortunately, once again, this was the exception rather than the rule.

With the formation of the Seventh Cavalry on 28th July 1866, George Armstrong Custer was assigned to it with the rank of Lt. Colonel. The Colonel of the regiment was Andrew Johnson Smith and although he was the overall commanding officer from the formation of the regiment until the 6th May 1869, he was kept away on assignments by General Phil Sheridan and, as such, never joined his troops at all. The succeeding Colonel, Samuel Davis Sturgis, who commanded the Seventh from May 1869 until the 11th June 1886, was apparently away on recruiting duty at the time of the battle on the Little Big Horn. As not much is mentioned of Colonel Sturgis in the histories of the 7th Cavalry, it begs the question as to his whereabouts when the 1876 campaign began. Thus, it can be safely deduced that George Custer was the active Commanding Officer of the Seventh Cavalry from its formation until his death and it was his influence that shaped the regiment into the formidable fighting machine that it was.

The companies, themselves, were usually quite abundant in officers and very rarely fell short of an officer in each command. Each company had a Captain; one or more Lieutenant; a Sergeant for each section and a Sergeant or Corporal who took charge of each squad, consisting of 8 men. The regimental surgeon or assistant surgeon was always given an honorary rank of an officer as befitted his profession, but other specialists such as the armourer, blacksmith, saddler or wheelwright were to be found in the rank and file.

Every fort had a band of some sort or another and whereas the infantry and artillery units used drums to issue commands, the cavalry had buglers. The 7th Cavalry had a 16-piece brass band that were mounted on grey horses. (Many historians state that the horses were white. Pure white horses were a rarity and as such, greys were eagerly accepted.) During the summer of 1874 the band had accompanied the regiment on its expedition to the Black Hills and it was also present during the initial stages of the 1876 campaign. Custer had requested that the band remained with the regiment on its march along the Rosebud, but Brigadier Alfred Terry, the General commanding, would not give his permission. Instead, Chief Musician Felix Vinatiore said farewell to the band's beautiful grey horses as they departed with Custer and the regiment for the last time.

The men who formed the rank and file of these frontier cavalry regiments came from all walks of life. At the time of the battle, the Seventh encompassed men who had previously been employed as goldsmiths, bookkeepers, engineers and printers, as well as farmers, watchmakers and tailors, just to give a few examples. Many of the occupations were established trades and it is interesting to note that the men gave them up to enlist and be posted to the frontier. They enlisted for 5 years at a time for $13.00 a month, with clothing, food, shelter, mounts and weapons being provided by the military. Re-enlisted men received an extra $2.00 per month as they were considered to be experienced soldiers. Company officers did not fare so well as their men in comparison. They received $125.00 per month (depending on their rank,) out of which they had to supply or buy their own food, clothing and raise a family, if they had one. Weapons and mounts were provided for the officers, although many preferred to purchase their own. Unfortunately, the government were not always prompt in paying their military employees, for in 1876 the 54th Congress adjourned without bothering to pass the Appropriation Act for the coming year, with the consequences that the army was not paid until November 1877!

Although uniforms were issued to all regular troops, regardless of rank, they were allowed tremendous latitude in their choice of apparel and, according to numerous photographs of the period, they took full advantage of it. However, it should be noted that this was often born out of necessity rather than personal preference. In posting troops on the frontier came the enormous problem of clothing and equipping them. During the Civil War, civilian manufacturers had fulfilled unlimited government contracts, producing more clothing and equipment than was actually required. Now huge amounts of clothing were lying in massive warehouses throughout the eastern states, idly attracting moths but little else. Shamefully, many of these wartime contracts had failed to reach the required government standards and yet, they had slipped past the inspectors who were already overworked in the post-war chaos. It was not inconceivable then, with government finances at a premium, these uniforms had to be put to use and so they were issued to all new troops right up until 1872. Of course, climatic conditions on the frontier were much harsher than those on the battlefields in the east and these poorly manufactured uniforms quickly fell apart or simply wore out in a matter of weeks. As military supplies were somewhat slow in being delivered, or in some cases failed completely, the troops had no option but to turn to local civilian supplies for their apparel, which was obviously tailored to suit the area and its environment.

In a magazine article written by Captain Charles King, 5th Cavalry, in 1883, the author highlights the discrepancies in the uniforms worn by the members of his regiment:

> '.......throughout the entire command the remarkable fact was to be noted that a company of regular cavalry, taking the field against hostile Indians, had discarded pretty much every item of dress or equipment prescribed.......
>
> ....and had supplied themselves with an outfit utterly un-uniform, un-picturesque, undeniably slouchy but no less undeniably appropriate and serviceable.......
>
> ....you could not have told an officer from a private.'

Civilian bought hats, shirts and scarves, in a variety of colours and styles, were commonplace on the frontier as were the many types of weapons employed. Indeed, many officers of the Seventh Cavalry wore buckskins out in the field, as did Custer himself. In all fairness, it should be pointed out that the military authorities in the east were not totally blind regarding the clothing problem in the west. In July 1871 the Army Clothing Board convened, under the direction of General R.B. Marcy, in an effort to rectify the awkward situation. On 27th July 1872, new uniform regulations were authorised, having re-designed the old Civil War uniforms that had originally been adopted in 1863. Although far from perfect it was a step in the right direction, even though the frontier army uniforms that we have all become accustomed to were not introduced until a few years later. In December 1875, the Army Clothing Board assembled yet again, this time under the direction of General D.H. Rucker. Serious considerations were given to the enlisted men's uniforms, making them serviceable yet relatively smart, and their attention was also focused on the officer's uniforms, laying the foundations for the accepted standard that would out-last the next decade.

The standard issue campaign hat of 1872 was totally useless in the varying climates the troopers had to face. Made of black felt, it had a flat crown around which was a yellow branch-of-service cord and a turned up brim. It offered no protection from the hot blazing sun and became a soggy mound of wet felt, flopping dismally around the head, in the rain. It was hardly surprising that all ranks tended to discard this slouch hat in favour of privately purchased headgear, which were of a much superior quality, or even straw hats. Some even preferred to wear the old Civil War fatigue hats. The fatigue hat or 'bummer' was a shapeless version of the French army kepi and considering its impracticality on the frontier, it surprisingly lasted for quite some time.

The 'sack coat' of 1874 was actually just a modification on the 1872 issue 'blouse'. Approved on 27th February 1874, the coat was made of dark blue wool flannel, with a yellow cord trim on the collar and cuffs, although this trim was often removed when on patrol in the field. Photographs of the period show this coat being worn with and without the yellow trim, however, by May 1883 new regulations had been issued that discarded the branch-of-service trim altogether. A single-breasted garment, it was fastened by 5 brass 'eagle' buttons down the front. Inside, it was lined with a grey twill-flannel mixture, with the sleeves being lined with unbleached muslin.

Rank was displayed in the form of yellow chevrons for all non-commissioned officers. The only exception to this rule were the 9th and 10th Cavalry regiments (the famous 'Buffalo Soldiers',) whose branch-of-service colour was white. Officers had shoulder boxes which were yellow rectangles edged with gold braid, that displayed their rank insignia superimposed within.

The shirt, when worn, was a grey flannel pullover type that had 3 cast-iron buttons, fastening the top part of the front. Recent excavations at the Little Big Horn battlefield have revealed a huge number of these buttons, leaving historians to assume that those shirts were worn by the troopers who fought there. The dark blue version, issued for trial in 1875, were so successful that they led to an authorised full-button pattern to be issued in 1881. Officers were requested to file a report on these 'trial shirts' from which the Secretary of War commented in his 1876 annual report:

> '......It appears that the Army is universally in favour of the dark blue flannel shirts.'

Thus, although originally issued as under-shirts, these popular items of clothing quickly became worn as over-shirts.

Trousers were made of sky blue kersey, a much refined kersey of the Civil War period. They had a canvas or linen lining that was sewn inside the waistband and, for frontier duty, many mounted troops added extra seat and leg re-enforcements of canvas or buckskin. Yellow stripes on the outer seams were only authorised for Corporals (1.25cm in width); Sergeants (2.5cm in width); and Officers (3.7cm in width).

Underwear was constructed of unbleached Canton flannel, with a wide waistband. It was not very popular with the serving troops, who preferred to purchase the more comfortable civilian patterns.

Boots were always a contentious item and one the Army Clothing Board repeatedly overlooked. Made of black calfskin or grain leather uppers, the leather soles were stitched on underneath. They were square-toed with a small Cuban heel, (or sometimes a flat leather heel,) the soles of which were apt to wear out in a matter of weeks. (At least the regimental cobblers were never short of work!) 1872 pattern boots were 38cm high at the front, gently curving to 25.6cm at the side seams and rear, giving the troopers ample room in which to tuck their trousers. Brass rowel spurs with black leather straps were worn with the boots and were standard issue to all ranks.

According to the 1874 regulations, all cavalry equipment was to be made of black leather with brass fittings. This consisted of a waist belt with a brass plate, that could be fitted with removable cartridge loops; a detachable sabre sling; a carbine cartridge pouch; a pistol cartridge pouch; a pistol holster and, separately, a carbine sling. Similarly, all horse furniture was to be made of black leather with brass fittings. The McClellan saddle had been in service for a number of years and it continued to be used throughout the Indian Wars, with slight modifications added periodically. The girth was made of strong blue linen webbing and the saddle-cloth was made of dark blue felt, this being laid between the saddle and the under-blanket when on long marches. Officer's saddle cloths were edged with yellow or gold lace, depending on their rank.

Each trooper was issued with the Model 1873 .45/70 calibre Springfield carbine, with 100 rounds of ammunition; a .45 calibre Colt 'single-action' Army revolver, with 24 rounds of ammunition; and a cavalry sabre. Often referred to by the Indians as 'long knives', the sabre was of little use in the field, for to be an effective weapon a trooper had to be engaged in close-quarter combat with the hostile Indian and very few were prepared to do that! Traditional cavalry charges against the warriors of the Plains were useless and so, by 1876 the sabre had been discarded as a fighting weapon, being retained for parade use only. As the Seventh Cavalry prepared for the 1876 campaign, Custer ordered all their sabres to be returned to the stores. First Lieutenant Charles DeRudio took his sabre with him on the campaign, although it was stored with the pack train and was not used.

The single-shot Springfield carbine, Model 1873, was a simple but sturdy weapon with a fascinating history of its own. It began its career during the Civil War as a muzzle-loader and was so successful that thousands upon thousands were manufactured. By the time the war was over a global revolution in the design of firearms had taken place and breech-loading guns were now in vogue. Northern arsenals bulged at the seams with new muzzle-loading Springfield's that had never been issued. There were literally thousands of them, far too many to scrap. In any event the government could not afford to re-issue their troops with new weapons, even though they had cut the military strength by as much as 50%. So, a means of converting the stockpile had to be found. Erskin S. Allin, Master Armourer at the Springfield Armoury, devised such an alteration and the conversions began in late 1865. With a few periodic minor improvements, the 'Allin-Action' Springfield eventually became the well-known .45/70 firearm that was officially adopted by the army in 1873. Interestingly, the board that approved the adoption of this weapon was presided over by Brigadier General Alfred Terry, (Custer's superior officer on the 1876 campaign,) and one of the members of the board was Major Marcus Reno (one of Custer's officers).

The 'Allin-Action was a simple device. A moveable breech-lock, including a firing pin, was hinged forward at the end so that it could be flipped upwards (trapdoor fashion,) exposing the chamber and ejecting the spent cartridge case. A fresh cartridge could be slid into the empty chamber, the block snapped shut and with the side-hammer cocked, it was ready to fire. Ammunition for the new Springfield Model 1873 was a centre-fire cartridge that housed 70 grains of black powder to charge a .45 calibre bullet. Hence the term, .45/70 calibre.

Military officers who finally selected the 'Allin-Action' Springfield felt that it was the best of all the systems they had to review, especially as it meant they could use up the huge stocks of Civil War firearms by having them economically converted. However, many American and foreign ordnance officers disagreed, believing that the Remington and Peabody breech-loaders were by far superior. Unfortunately these weapons cost money and that kind of commodity was not available. Nevertheless, the Springfield with the 'Allin-Action' served the military fairly well, although it did have a serious fault which appears to have been overlooked or ignored, and that was in the extraction of the spent cartridges. This was not actually highlighted until after the battle at the Little Big Horn, when large numbers of cartridge cases were recovered from the battle debris with their heads torn off, indicating that they had been forced from the breech with a knife after they had jammed. Subsequent tests proved this was so, especially when the breech became heated after prolonged action. However, the frequency of such a failure appears to be relatively low, considering the huge number of engagements these firearms were employed in and they continued to be used by the army right up until the First World War.

The official side-arm of the period was the 'single-action' Army revolver, manufactured by the Colt Company in 1873 and accepted by the military shortly after. Extremely robust in its construction, this .45 calibre weapon was sold by the thousands to military and civilian personnel alike. It's popularity was due to the fact that it was made with a solid frame, which was quite a break though in the evolution of hand guns to date. Until now, such weapons had broken under the impact of coming into contact with an adversary's skull. The ancient art of 'pistol-whipping' being common practice on the frontier! Cavalry models had a barrel length of 19.1cm, as opposed to the civilian model that had a barrel length of 14cm. The revolving chamber was loaded through a side gate on the right and spent cartridges were ejected through the same gate, using an ejector rod situated beneath the barrel. The hammer had to be cocked by pulling it back before each shot could be fired, hence the 'single-action'. This rotated the chamber and lined up the next bullet within the breech. Squeezing the trigger made the hammer fall and the gun fired its charge.

All ranks were issued with these revolvers although personal variations in weaponry appears to be common place amongst the officers. On the day of the battle of the Little Big Horn, Custer carried with him his two double-action Irish Constabulary pistols and his favourite .50 calibre Remington sporting rifle. Needless to say, none of these weapons were recovered from the battlefield.

Troopers had very little training before joining their unit. They were expected to learn all the necessary skills of horsemanship and become proficient in firing their weapons during the first few months after their arrival at an operational outpost. This was not an easy feat to accomplish but by all accounts the raw recruits did their best.

The art of horsemanship was learnt the hard way: a trooper either stayed in the saddle or he fell off! Grim determination and a collection of painful bruises soon helped him overcome any difficulties he may have been experiencing with his mount. However, learning to use weapons with any degree of effectiveness was not so cut and dried. The use of ammunition was severely restricted, with each trooper only being allocated 12 rounds per year for target practice. This was in addition to his normal ration when taking part in any hostilities. Obviously this meagre allocation for target practice was barely enough when many of the recruits were handling a firearm for the first time in their life. Many of the recruits came from the east, where law and order had been firmly established and the necessity of having to carry a weapon for personal protection was virtually a thing of the past. This coupled with the romanticised lure of the wild untamed west, brought many a young recruit to the desolate outposts only to have their fanciful ideas shattered. Life was precious and if you wanted to stay alive, you learnt fast.

Having arrived at his destination, a new recruit would find life within a fort completely different from anything he had previously known. Forts were dirty, dusty, draughty and an ideal breeding ground for any amount of diseases, which were rampant despite the unerring efforts of the medical officers to contain them. Forts were generally constructed from local timber, varying enormously in size and design according to the area they had been erected in. There were very little home comforts to be found within their walls, even though the married women did the best they could to make a home out of what little they had. All married men were permitted to live with their wives, regardless of rank, and their married quarters were usually set apart from those of the unmarried servicemen. Needless to say, with all the best will in the world not everything always works to plan and adultery flourished amongst the officer's set, with 'squaw hunting' being the name of the game for enlisted men.

When not on duty, the main pleasures open to these soldiers were drinking, gambling and fornication. Indeed, the poker games that wore well into the night between Captains Keogh, Yates and Tom Custer, with Lieutenants Cooke and Porter, are legendary in the annals of the Seventh Cavalry. Ales, beers, wines and spirits, (the latter being beyond the financial reach of the enlisted men,) could be purchased from the sutler's store. Here, everything from clothing to supplies of imported luxuries could be bought if they had enough money to pay for it. But the main item across the counter was alcohol. The sutler could offer an enlisted man a daily ration of a pint of beer or a gill of wine, if he could afford it. Unfortunately the majority couldn't. Instead enlisted men usually preferred the 'hog ranch' where the liqueur was cheap, watery and tasteless, entering the stomach as 'rot-gut.' Here were to be found the frontier whores or dance-hall girls, who were only too pleased to entertain the troops and relieve them of their hard-earned pay.

For the most part it was a struggle not to succumb to sheer boredom at these lonely forts. Unless the troops were out on patrol or on duty, finding something to occupy them in the evenings was a persistent problem. Drinking and gambling cost money, as did being entertained by dance-hall girls and whores. A soldier's pay did not last long and many found themselves in debt by the time they reached the next pay day. Post dances were always a success with everyone, the officers holding theirs on separate days from the enlisted men. If there were any theatrically inclined personnel within the ranks, they grouped together to put on shows and plays. Custer enjoyed a spot of acting now and again, lamenting on the fact that there was no-one competent enough to give him lessons. Occasionally, travelling theatres found their way to the forts, much to the delight of everyone, for they were fresh faces to look at if nothing else. Horse racing was also a favourite pastime, but again, this cost money at the end of the day. To relieve the boredom of the daily routine, many officer's wives kept journals and some, like Elizabeth Custer, even wrote books which have given historians of today a unique window into the life on the frontier in the 1870's.

In most cases, when not on campaign or patrol, garrison duty was the order of the day. This was the military term for what could otherwise be interpreted as heavy labour. Trees had to be felled and prepared for the construction or repair of buildings, the remaining wood being cut for fires and stored. Stables had to be cleaned out and the horses exercised, groomed and fed, for these animals could mean the difference between life and death for the troops if they were not properly cared for. Daily rubbish had to be shovelled up and burnt. The laundry was collected, washed and returned. The cook-house was always a hive of activity, with the large numbers of meals they had to prepare each day. There was never any shortage of helpers, being constantly supplied with troops who had found themselves on fatigue duty as a punishment. Then there were the parades, drills and kit inspections, as if to remind the troopers that they were, after all, in the army. This then was garrison duty; hard laborious work and it often came as a relief to the enlisted men to be chosen for a patrol. Thus, whereas the evenings and nights spawned boredom, the days were a hive of activity.

Patrols were sent out for a variety of reasons: hunting, surveying the territory, searching for deserters or law breakers, protecting the trails and the railroads, the latter being particularly hazardous if the Indians were hostile. Hunting wild game to supplement their diet and stock the stores for the winter months was the most popular patrol, but it was also a dangerous one as it often brought the soldiers in contact with Indians who were pursuing the same occupation. In most instances the surrounding country was richly abundant in flora and fauna, and animals such as the buffalo, elk and deer were eagerly enjoyed by the soldiers as much as the Indians. Army supplies usually consisted of salt beef, salt pork, dried fish, beans, rice and hard-tack (large coarse unsalted biscuits), all of which could have been stored for months at the fort before being used. So any fresh meat was a welcome sight. Coffee was served with all meals, if the troopers' stomachs could endure it, for it was reputed to be capable of 'growing whiskers on a cannon ball'!

Hardly one metre of the frontier was left unscathed by some form of military action involving the Indians, whether hostile or not. A few of these campaigns, such as Sand Creek (1864) or the Washita (1868) did little credit to the army. On the other hand the army could be extremely gallant, if not foolish, in action as was shown by the Fetterman Fight (1866) and the deadly Modoc War of the Lava Beds (1873). Indeed, between March 1865 and December 1891, some 420 Congressional Medals of Honor were awarded to military personnel of all ranks, for gallantry in action against hostile Indians, 24 of these being awarded for bravery at the Battle of the Little Big Horn alone.

Military tactics and strategy in Indian warfare underwent a series of radical changes between 1861 and 1891. During the early years of the Civil War the army tried to use standard 'text-book' tactics when dealing with hostile Indians.

It was a big mistake. By sending out expeditionary forces to locate the Indian camps, they hoped to force the Indians to stand and fight. The absurdity of this policy was highlighted by the fact that the majority of the regiments in the field were infantry, who had no hope of keeping up with the meandering movements of a mobile enemy. A perfect example of this was General Sibley's Sirocco Expedition of June 1863. Sibley marched his force of 8 companies of infantry; 3 companies of cavalry; and a battery of mountain howitzers through Indian Territory for four months and during that time his troops only encountered the Indians four times. When they did clash, it was the Indians who had chosen the time and the place, not Sibley. Suffice to say, the campaign was a complete and utter failure. Ever slow to learn, the next expedition that was ordered into the field was another military fiasco. Bearing in mind the mistakes that Sibley had made, Sulley's Expedition to the Badlands in May 1864, consisted primarily of cavalry. This force marched through the Badlands in Dakota for over two months and in that time only had one skirmish with the Indians!

Whether it was just sheer incompetence by the desk Generals in Washington, or just the plain fact that they were a world apart from the frontier style of warfare, is a matter of conjecture. What is plain to see is that although they did try to re-organise their tactics in dealing with hostile Indians, they really did not have a clue what they were doing as, over the years, they continued to perpetrate one tragic disaster after another. One significant change that was authorised, was the use of cavalry rather than infantry and to operate them from a series of forts situated directly within hostile territory. Having ignored the warnings (and the Indians had issued many,) this policy led to the Powder River Campaign commanded by Colonel Henry Carrington, which culminated in the deaths of Captain William Fetterman and 80 soldiers at hands of hostile Sioux and Cheyenne on a cold winter's day in 1866. Military strategists and politicians in the east had been proved wrong yet again. Their revised tactics had resulted in the wasteful deaths of Fetterman, his command and numerous others who tried to journey along the Bozeman Trail. (To be fair, Fetterman's arrogance towards the Indian warriors did much to seal his fate as well.) The uprisings that followed, collectively known as 'Red Cloud's War', left the territory ablaze for the next two years and a tentative peace was not restored until after the forts had been burnt to the ground and the soldiers had been withdrawn from the area.

This was a hard blow for many area commanders to accept, particularly the newly appointed commander of the Western Department, General Phil Sheridan. He was determined that his forces were not going to succumb to threats and he decided to employ new tactics of his own,

> ".......to teach these savage bands of cruel marauders a lesson!"

Based upon the highly successful 'scorched earth policy' of the Civil War, Sheridan's new methods were to seek and destroy the Indian camps during the winter months, when the Indians were least expecting it. Winters were extremely harsh in this region and the Indians preferred to stay in their camps until spring. The main problem with Sheridan's directive is that it did not distinguish between peaceful and hostile Indians. To him they were all the same.

By now the Indians had become masters of the art of guerrilla warfare and hostile camps were hard to locate, regardless of the time of the year, whereas peaceful Indians were easy prey. Thus, on 27th November 1868, a peaceful band of Cheyenne under the leadership of Chief Black Kettle were attacked and murdered while under the protection of the American flag. Within minutes, George Custer and his Seventh Cavalry had killed Black Kettle and 103 Cheyenne, only 11 of which were actually warriors. The soldiers also captured 53 women and children and destroyed the entire camp, along with the pony herd. The military losses were one officer, Major Joel Elliot, and 19 troopers. Custer's orders from Sheridan had been very explicit:

> '.......to proceed south in the direction of the Antelope Hills, thence towards the Washita River, the supposed winter seat of the hostile tribes; to destroy their villages and ponies; to kill or hang all warriors; and bring back all women and children.'

Of course, Custer did exactly as ordered. Upon his return to Camp Supply on the Canadian River, Custer's victory at the Washita was hailed with overwhelming enthusiasm by Sheridan, who publically congratulated Custer for his

> "........efficient and gallant services rendered,"

adding that,

> ".......the only good Indian is a dead Indian!"
> (This quote can be found during the various phases of Sheridan's life. Whether or not he said it more than once at different venues is not clear. What is known is that the phrase is definitely attributed to Sheridan.)

The reaction of the Indians was not so enthusiastic, however, and the appalling massacre on the Washita was seared in their memory for the next 8 years when, at the Little Big Horn, they would claim their revenge.

During the 1870's. the War Department revised their tactics yet again and reverted to the old attempts to force the Indians to stand and fight, but with one crucial difference. Rather than just rely on one expeditionary force to flush the Indians out, several were sent into Indian Territory at the same time, each one from a different direction. The idea being that each force would be strong enough to deal with any hostile Indians it may encounter and if the enemy retreated, they would be caught by one of the other columns in the field. The idea was sound in theory but in practice it was never entirely successful. This complicated manoeuvring consumed months of wasted time, required endless wagons of supplies and, in general, the columns were far too long to move fast enough to keep up with the Indians, who just evaded the soldiers until they were ready to fight. A typical example of this was the Yellowstone Campaign of 1876.

Finally, the army hit upon the strategy they so desperately needed to bring an end to their troublesome and costly Indian campaigns: the use of Indians to locate hostile Indians in the field. Detached units of Indian scouts, who were conversant with Indian methods of warfare, (in fact they were often recruited from the very tribes they were employed to track,) and who would relentlessly chase after a retreating foe, never allowing it to rest, were sent ahead of the army column. They were closely followed by highly mobile cavalry units who remained within distance to offer assistance should the enemy turn and fight. This, in conjunction with the use of the new heliograph and telegraph systems, meant that the troops could be assembled at any given point within a very short notice, weather permitting of course. Eventually the exhausted Indians would stop running and either stand and fight or surrender. Modern technology had finally reached the West!

It was during the early stages of the Indian Wars that the legends of the Old West were born. But it was during the latter stages of the conflict that the cavalry earned its reputation as being one of the finest fighting units America had to offer and there are numerous books, both factual and fictional, that bear testimony to these later tactics.

Despite the harshness of being a soldier on this wild, and often deadly, frontier, there are no records of any major mutinies taking place and there were certainly no disloyal officers within the regiments stationed there. Give or take the odd murder or rape, the major crimes committed by the troops fell into two main categories: desertion and drunkenness.

The rate of desertion within the ranks varied from area to area, but on average it has been estimated that 1 in 5 enlisted men attempted to desert each year. The official sentence for desertion was the firing squad, although this was very rarely carried out. The usual punishment was 50 rawhide lashes on the naked back. The deserter's head would be shaved and the mark of a 'D' was branded on his hip. The regimental band would play 'the Rogue's March' and children would be encouraged to throw rotten fruit and vegetables at him.

Drunkenness was a universal problem within the army. It is estimated that 10% of the soldiers who served time in the guard-house were there for drunkenness or crimes committed whist under the influence of drink.

Court-martials were local events that all the community attended, civilian and military, but they were extremely rare. Sentences to fit various crimes were usually dealt with by the commanding officer of the fort and company officers could order various punishments at their discretion with or without a court hearing. Examples of the types of punishment an enlisted man could be expected to receive from a company officer were as follows:

1) Solitary confinement on a bread and water diet for a set period of days.
2) Being hung by the wrists for a specified period of time.
3) Marching around the parade quadrangle for hours or even days.
4) Carrying a pack full of bricks.
5) Forfeiture of pay or loss of a percentage of it. (This being the most frequent punishment handed out.)

However, despite all the trials and tribulations of being a regular soldier on the frontier, the army's record for fighting and bravery in the face of the enemy was excellent. (In truth, for most cases it was fight or die!) It is testimony to their grim determination to overcome the odds stacked against them that was unrivalled and their efforts certainly paid off in the end. Perhaps a fitting epitaph for this dramatic period in the history of the Old West should be drawn from the address given by General Godfrey, at the Custer Battlefield on the occasion of the 40th anniversary of the engagement in 1916:

> ".......Neither ambition nor glory called us to this field. The sacrifices we then made and the suffering we endured were in our line of duty. I pray that those sacrifices may always be reminders to you to be ready to defend the country we opened up for you to occupy, and may the peace and prosperity you now enjoy be yours forever."

Chapter 5

Nothing is Sacred

On the 4th July 1776, representatives of the newly formed United States of America assembled in the State House, in Philadelphia, for the reading of the final draft of a document that was to shake their fellow colonists into taking decisive action and declaring themselves a nation of free people. The signing of the Declaration of Independence was the first step of many that would lay the foundations of a true United States government and within the opening paragraph of that historic document it clearly stated:

> '.......that all men are created equal, that they are endowed by their Creator with certain inalienable rights, that amongst them are life, liberty and the pursuit of happiness.'

Amongst the signatures to be found on this memorable document are those of John Hancock, President of the Continental Congress and the first to sign; and Benjamin Franklin, Deputy Postmaster General of the Colonies, who warned his colleagues:

> "We must indeed all hang together, or most assuredly we shall all hang separately."

Other signatories included John Adams, who would become the second President of the United States; and Thomas Jefferson, who was destined to become the third President.

Having been oppressed by the British government for so long, there is no doubt that these men firmly believed in the words they had so eloquently written and they had declared to stand for freedom when they signed it, knowing the British would regard their act as treason. Sadly, ideas and circumstances change over the years and, only a century later, those strong words were to mean that all men are created equal, only some men are more equal than others!

Following the final defeat of the British forces in 1781, these same representatives began the monumental task of forming a central governing council that would grow in strength as the nation grew in size. Strangely enough, even at the birth of the nation, the Indian question had not gone unnoticed, for in 1786 Benjamin Franklin wrote to a French friend:

> 'Almost every war between the Indians and the whites has been occasioned by some injustice of the latter towards the former.'

On 17th September 1787, after a lengthy deliberation, the foundations of American democracy were finally laid with the compilation of the Constitution of the United States. Having fought a war for their independence, in defence of their idealistic freedom, these men had the formidable and unenviable task of proving they could build a new kind of democratic system based upon their ideals: that every man has an equal right to live his own life in his own way, so long as he doesn't interfere with the rights of others in doing so. A brave statement, but it takes a very courageous government not only to adhere to it but also to enforce it. So far successive administrations have failed to do either.

Although the Constitution included a statement of these rights, they were not clearly defined and many colonists felt that they should be made much clearer. Thus, in 1791, the Bill of Rights was added to the Constitution, giving a detailed guarantee of the rights of all who inhabited American soil. Over the years numerous amendments have been added to these laws, amendments that have been deemed necessary due to the varying changes in fortune and ideas, but nonetheless important to the security of the American people However, these amendments still expressed the belief of those early representatives, no matter how they are written or why. What is important is how they are interpreted.

The first of these amendments appeared in 1791 and its contents are important enough to be included here, for yet again, less than 100 years later it was to be blatantly ignored by those inane actions it would constrict. Amendment of the Bill of Rights clearly stated that:

> 'Congress shall make no laws respecting an establishment of religion, or prohibiting the free exercise thereof.'

That same year, the most famous of all the amendments was drafted, the 5th. Defining the rights of a person accused of a crime, the 5th Amendment concludes:

> '.......; nor be deprived of life, liberty, or property without due process of law; nor shall private property be taken for public use without just compensation.'

These statements formed the basis upon which the American legal systems were born. They clearly define what the central government could or could not do, in respect to a person's right to life, liberty and happiness. Modern historians can only study and reflect on the events of the past, sometimes passing scholarly judgement on those who created history, be they good or bad. When studying the historical aspects of the Indian Wars there can only be one conclusion, that no thought was ever given to the native population at any time when these documents were compiled and that over the subsequent years, these native Americans were systematically persecuted in the name of greed. And it fell upon the shoulders of the poor bloody soldier to ensure that the politicians were shown to be right and all powerful, whether they were or not. In less than 100 years of those magnanimous words being set to paper, thousands of lives were victimised and wasted, both red and white, but no tears of shame were ever shed.

The motivation behind the policies that instigated the Indian Wars, (a bitter conflict that would span over 30 years of Western history,) can be summed up in just two words: greed and fear. White settlers travelled west in droves to seek a new life, their senses clogged with excitement, fear and apprehension. Excitement is a natural feeling but a powerful drug and their apprehension was the inward worry that their new life would be good enough to support their families. After all they were venturing into the unknown. But the fear concerned the long journey they would have to undertake and, in particular, the Indians they would most assuredly encounter as they crossed the Great Plains. Newspapers and publishers of the 'Penny Dreadful' books did little to allay those fears. In fact they actually fuelled them. Fanny Kelly, a survivor of a wagon-train that had been attacked by Indians, wrote of the encounter:

> 'Mr Sharp was killed within a few feet of me. Mr Taylor, I can never forget his face as I saw him shot through the forehead …….The Indians quickly sprang into our wagons, tearing off covers, breaking, crushing and smashing all hindrances to plunder…….
>
> They filled the air with fearful war-whoops and hideous shouts……..'

Fuelled by such reports, the civilians of the eastern seaboard expressed shock and indignation at such savagery upon innocent settlers. But that is as far as it went, until that is when such attacks became more and more frequent and, more and more brutal. Still the problem remained unaddressed, for the underlying factors were that white Americans had not only hyped themselves into a panic on an issue they knew little about, they also fed their fear of Indians by not understanding them and very few took the trouble to do so. Once again, the Indians appeared to have no rights and the politicians in the east were not the slightest concerned about that.

Having discovered the natural wealth that the Indian Territories abounded with, a strong desire developed amongst the white communities to acquire it for themselves and, thus, the second part of the motivation behind the policies came to fruition: greed. Never ones to miss an opportunity, politicians and business magnates in the east struck swiftly, using carefully planned propaganda to fuel the settlers' basic instincts. After all, they were the legitimate American populace and the Indians not only had no use for such vast wealth they had no right to it, or so the settlers and adventurers were led to believe. (It may be worth noting here that the Indians did not become citizens of the United States until after an Act of Congress, which was eventually passed in 1924!)

Of course, to some extent, fear was also deeply instilled within the various Indian tribes, although greed never entered their minds. The native Indians did not understand the use of money at this time. Their wealth lay in their possessions, such as the number of ponies they owned. They were afraid of the white people because they were steadily encroaching onto their lands at an alarming speed, like a river bursting its banks. Thus, their fear extended only to the fact that they were losing their natural hunting grounds, not to mention their source of food and clothing. They could see their very existence evaporating into the distant mists. In their mind it was not unreasonable to want to retain what had always been theirs; the freedom to live on their old hunting grounds and enjoy their old way of life. Surely, this was precisely what the Declaration of Independence and the Bill of Rights stated? Unfortunately for the Indians, these documents were not written for them or by them and therefore did not make any provision for them.

Early pioneers had described the Great Plains as being desert country, too barren to grow anything of any consequence and so, as the majority of colonists had been farmers, they showed little interest in cultivating the land. As their population increased, they gradually advanced even further towards the west, seeking more land to exploit and a larger area in which to raise their families. But on reaching the edges of the Great Plains, this expansion stopped. Instead, they continued their journey across this vast expanse to settle in the rich, fertile valleys of California and Oregon. During this progressive surge westward, the Indian tribes who had inhabited the areas along the eastern seaboard, were gradually driven from their lands and pushed onto the Great Plains, taking with them many un-nerving tales of white supremacy. Some, such as the Seminole Indians, resisted this violation of their life style, only to be eventually subdued by the military and placed on reservations. In an optimistic effort to deal with the problem, the government set aside vast areas of the Plains and declared it to be Indian Territory. This region included what is now known as the States of Kansas, Oklahoma, Nebraska, North Dakota and South Dakota.

With the discovery of gold in California in 1849, fortune hunters joined the settlers and the great migration from east to west began in earnest, with adventurers of all ages crossing the Plains by the thousands. These wagon-trains left a trail of devastation wherever they went. Wild game was slaughtered for food along the way, (sometimes for sport as well, as the days spent on the trail could become weary and extremely boring,) and precious trees were felled for firewood. The Indians watched in dismay and trepidation as their beautiful lands were laid to waste by these never-ending invaders. It was not long before they began to resist the intrusion. Tempers flared and in 1854, Senator Stephen Douglas, of Illinois, introduced the Kansas-Nebraska Act which enabled Congress to open up these two regions for settlement, thus allowing the wagon-trains a safe route westward. This irresponsible action, by a supposedly learned politician, defies logic. In just 26 years the Indians had lost huge areas of land that had been assumed as being theirs forever. It didn't take the white settlers long to take advantage of the situation by moving into these regions at a great rate of speed and it took an even shorter time for them to realise the full potential of these lands.

By far the greatest threat to the Indian's survival, at this time, was the indiscriminate slaughter of the buffalo herds, ostensibly to clear the way for the oncoming settlers. The Plains tribes had hunted the buffalo since the early days of their ancestors, taking great care not to cull the beasts out of existence. Now with the advance of the white man, these huge herds were moving further away north to escape the guns that could shoot at a much faster rate than arrows. To supplement the loss, the Indians turned to the traders offering small types of high grade hides and artefacts. But the traders' main interest lay in obtaining buffalo hides to sustain the profitable market in the east. Thus, to obtain the much needed supplies that they had become so dependent on, the Indians had no option but to increase their own slaughter of the buffalo.

By the mid 1850's, the Indians of the Great Plains were selling 100,000 buffalo hides per year to the American Fur Company, who quickly established new trading posts to accommodate their willing customers. Due to the difficulty in handling bull-hides, the majority of the buffalo that were slain were the females. Such concentration on the females was a prime factor in the reduction of the natural increase of the herds and, as such, their numbers began to drop dramatically. By 1870, leather factories had devised an efficient method of handling the tougher bull-hides and they were prepared to offer up to $3 per hide to anyone who was willing to supply them. Already the railroads had advanced across most of the Plains towards the west coast, making shipment of the hides considerably easier. To accommodate the demand for more hides, swarms of hunters, eager to make some easy money, armed themselves with .55 calibre Sharps rifles and plenty of ammunition, and drove their wagons on to the Plains in search of their fortune.

The totals of this wholesale slaughter stagger the imagination. Between 1870 and 1880 more than a million buffalo were killed each year by the white hunters alone! The Indians could not hope to compete with such skilled marksmen and their superior weapons, thus they were forced to retire from the field. With the herds rapidly diminishing they even found it difficult to hunt for food and they realised their future looked very bleak.

Their livelihood gone, many tribes were forced onto government reservations and the Indian agencies began to flourish. A few notable Indians, such as Red Cloud, Crazy Horse and Sitting Bull, could foresee that war with the white man was inevitable and they point blank refused to accept reservation life under any circumstances. A Ute Indian, by the name of Colorow, expressed the Indian point of view when he said:

> "Colorow owns this country. Buffalo are Indian cattle. White-men's cattle eat grass, buffalo die……..
> No hunting, no meat, no robes. White-man must go quick!"

Incensed by the persistent invasion, the Indians began to retaliate in earnest. They attacked anything that moved along the trails or stood still long enough to receive the shaft of an arrow. Wagon-trains, settlers and even townships felt their wrath and, before long, public outrage demanded that the politicians in Washington find a solution to the problem, even if they did not acknowledge that they had created it. Unfortunately, not fully comprehending the situation, or more likely choosing to ignore it, the only answer the politicians could come up with was to use military force to quell the troublesome tribes. This was a strange decision considering it would cost government resources approximately $600,000 a year to place a cavalry regiment in the field.

There were very few military establishments in the Department of the West during the post Civil War period. In fact there were none at all in North Dakota or Montana, the nearest frontier post covering these regions was Fort Ridgely, in Minnesota. The main line of forts had been erected further south with Fort's Laramie, Kearney and Leavenworth being the more notable. In view of the dangerous situation within the region, the army did its best to mediate between the two factions and keep the peace. But it was becoming increasingly difficult and there was a limit to just how far they could enforce their jurisdiction, particularly with regard to the civilians.

The key to the whole business seemed to rest in the hands of the Indian agents, in whose sole charge lay the reservations. It was widely known that they openly exploited their native charges for huge personal gains. Being political employees, their superiors let them get away with anything and frequently did, doing nothing to curb their actions which would have helped to relieve the Indians of their abject misery. In fact it only added more fuel to the already explosive state of affairs. One Indian agent, of the Sioux Agency near Fort Ridgely, expressed his view that was shared by many others of his profession when he said:

> "If they are hungry let them eat grass for all I care!"

Andrew Myrick, the agent in question, laughed with the frontiersmen who had overheard his comment. Those who did not find such remarks funny were the army and the Indians. The army watched in apprehension as agents such as Myrick grew rich on the poverty stricken Indians. The Indians watched in anger as their people, young and old, starved to death on the meagre rations the agents distributed. Sooner or later tempers on all sides would be aflame.

By the autumn of 1862, Chief Little Crow and his Santee Sioux had had enough. Well armed and streaked with war-paint, they struck back. Their victims were three German families as they sat together at dinner. Every last soul was brutally murdered in a few minutes of uncontrolled frenzy, after which they were scalped and horribly mutilated. Their emotions pushed beyond any limit of control, the Santee Sioux had committed the first of many such acts on white settlers that would eventually become known as the 'Minnesota Massacres'. Well over 700 white pioneers were to die or disappear before the military authorities even realised they had a serious situation. The result was the 1863 expedition under General Henry Sibley, who eventually managed to engage the marauding Santee warriors at Wood Lake. The use of cannon fire shocked the Indians into submission, reducing their will to fight, and a month later 2000 Sioux surrendered.

Sibley put 400 Indians-those he considered were responsible for the atrocities committed-in irons and actually condemned 303 of them to death. President Lincoln was not so sure that Sibley's actions were in pursuant of the peace that was required. He was convinced that public anger was clouding the army's judgement in this case, for the main culprits of the uprising had escaped across the border into Canada. Lincoln appointed a commission to review the incident and, based upon their conclusions, he set aside the sentences of all the convicted Santee save for 38, who were hung at Mankato in late December of 1863. Chief Little Crow himself had been killed earlier in July as he led another fearsome raid on a ranch.

Although Sibley had successfully quelled the Sioux uprising, tactically his expedition was an utter failure and the military learned a valuable lesson in Indian warfare, the hard way. Word spread across the Plains like a prairie-fire of Sibley's actions in those events and other tribes, uneasy at the treatment they were generally receiving, began to talk of war, total war against the whites. War drums echoed across the vast expanses and by 1864 they could be heard in Colorado and Kansas. It was in this area that the mighty Cheyenne nation resided and it was here, in Colorado, that the first serious blunder by the army occurred, paving the way for the long trail that would eventually lead to Montana.

The Civil War was a difficult time for the Indians, particularly the Cheyenne and Arapaho whose hunting grounds skirted the primary battle zones. Wherever they went the unfortunate Indians ran into Union troops, who were either manoeuvring into position for an attack or searching for Confederate rebels. The whole area seemed to be alive with soldiers wearing one kind of uniform or another. They did not understand the white-man's war and, more to the point, they had no inclination to. They had enough problems of their own to contend with. Their main concern was in feeding and clothing their families and, as such, any clashes with the military were carefully avoided, although it was inevitable that a few minor skirmishes did occur.

In an effort to maintain a peaceful co-existence with the Indians, the army signed a treaty with them at Fort Wise, on the Arkansas River. Amongst those present were Colonel A. Greenwood, the Commissioner of Indians Affairs; Black Kettle, Chief of the Cheyenne; and Little Raven, a Chief of the Arapaho. All appeared to be going well as the talks progressed and peace between the parties seemed assured. Indeed, Black Kettle and his wife were even invited to Washington to meet President Lincoln in person, which they did. Lincoln gave the Cheyenne medals to wear and Greenwood presented Black Kettle with a United States flag to fly above his tipi, assuring the old chief that as long as he flew this flag no soldiers would ever fire upon him or his village. Black Kettle believed every word and upon his return to his people, he proudly flew the flag above his tipi and wore his treasured medal. Unfortunately, neither Greenwood nor Black Kettle were aware that men such as Colonel John Chivington of the 2nd Colorado Cavalry, were in existence.

John M. Chivington was a Methodist preacher at the start of the Civil War. A towering man with a thick barrel chest, his sermons were explosively fiery at the best of times, but his anti-slavery speeches were just short of being fanatical. In his spare time Chivington was a bushwhacker with some of the most deadly border gangs and when Civil War was declared, he refused to join the army as a chaplain, saying:

> "If I go with the soldiers, I am going to fight!"

Incredibly, he was given the rank of Colonel and put in command of the 2nd Colorado Cavalry, (some sources state that it was the 3rd Colorado Cavalry, which is incorrect,) a volunteer State Militia that came under the jurisdiction of the regular army.

In 1864 Colorado was virtually an open State. Harassed in the north by the hostile Indians, it was an easy escape route for outlaws and guerrillas on the run from Kansas, the adjoining State in the east. While many inhabitants sympathised with the Union cause, outlaws such as the infamous Reynolds Gang plundered the countryside in the name of the Confederacy. The Reynolds Gang were led by two brothers, Jim and John Reynolds, who claimed they had been sent to Colorado by General Henry H. McCulloch to attack the Union gold fields and recruit volunteers for the Confederacy. Whether this was actually true or not is a matter of conjecture. The fact remains that the Reynolds Gang did attack and rob anyone who was foolish enough to cross their path, including stagecoaches which were quite definitely civilian.

One such attack on a stage coach ultimately led to the demise of the gang and provided Chivington and his troops with their first taste of blood. On 26th July 1864 the Reynolds Gang robbed the Denver Stage of around $60,000 plus the U.S. Mail. After a lengthy chase by U.S. Marshal Hunt and a posse of volunteers, the gang was finally trapped and following a shoot-out, four members of the gang were captured. The two Reynolds brothers managed to escape. As Marshal Hunt prepared to lock his prisoners in jail, Colonel Chivington intervened, arguing that as they were Confederate guerrillas he had the authority to deal with them as prisoners of war. The prisoners were turned over to Chivington who duly tried them in a military court. However, some protesters claimed that Chivington did not have such authority and so the trial was suspended.

A few days later, Chivington calmly stated that his commanding officer, Major General Samuel Curtis, had ordered the prisoners to be transferred to Fort Lyon, where they were to stand trial for their crimes. Thus, Captain Theodore G. Cree and 100 troopers were directed to escort the prisoners to the fort. No one ever arrived at their destination. Two days after their departure, Captain Cree and his command returned, saying that they had to shoot the prisoners when they attempted to escape. The bodies of the prisoners were subsequently found on the route, still in their shackles and still fastened to the trees, where they had been savagely executed and butchered. It was alleged that Chivington had ordered the executions and, given the Colonel's nature, it is not unreasonable to assume that he did. Suffice to say, no inquiry was ever conducted with regard to the incident.

With increasing unrest amongst the Indians following the Minnesota Massacre, the army was ordered into the field to restore and maintain the peace. Unaware that these military manoeuvres were in progress and with the majority of his warriors out hunting to the north, Black Kettle settled his camp in a horseshoe bend on Sand Creek, some 48 Kilometres from Fort Lyon.

Orders reached Fort Lyon in November 1864 and, accordingly, Colonel Chivington prepared for the march. With his bushy beard bristling and a glint of furious madness in his eyes, Chivington gave a vehement speech concerning the handling of the Indians they were probably going to encounter, ending with:

> "Kill and scalp all Indians! Big and little…….scalp them all, nits make lice!"

Having suitably incensed his command, which included Captain Cree and the troops who had committed murder only a few months previously, Chivington led his regiment into the field to face his savages.

As the morning of Tuesday 29th November 1864 dawned, Chivington and his troops found themselves on a high ridge overlooking Black Kettle's camp of 600 Cheyenne. The camp had not been difficult to find, after all Black Kettle had nothing to fear from the soldiers or did he? Orders were silently passed through the ranks and on a given signal the troopers charged 'hell for leather' down the slope towards the gently smoking tipis.

On hearing the thundering hooves an Indian squaw cried out that a buffalo herd was stampeding their village. Naked Indians, still half asleep, appeared at the openings of their tipis only to be confronted by a cavalry charge in full momentum. The women and children sought refuge with Black Kettle, over whose tipi the American flag fluttered in the morning breeze. But to no avail. Many were cut down in a hail of bullets before they had run a few metres. In desperation, Black Kettle grabbed a white cloth and standing in full view beneath his cherished flag, he frantically waved it at the advancing soldiers. But the blue-coated horsemen spurred their mounts onward, their sabres flashing wildly in the winter sunlight. Men, women and children of all ages were mercilessly murdered as they ran in all directions, panic stricken, to escape the moment of terror.

The barbarity of the soldiers was totally uncontrollable and beyond anything the Indians had ever experienced. The few warriors who were present grabbed their weapons and tried to protect their families. But they were instantly cut to pieces. Women and children who had tried to hide in the banks of the creek were flushed out and mown down, leaving the cold waters of the Creek flowing a dark red. A 6 year old child was sent out from one foxhole by a group of terrified squaws, carrying a white flag in her tiny hands. She was brutally shot as soon as she had been able to stand, along with the squaws she had, unwittingly, exposed to the frenzied troops. Another child, only a few months old, was thrown into a wagon and when it fell out it was left on the ground to perish.

A few Cheyenne, including Black Kettle, managed to escape the blood bath and hide amongst the high banks beyond the bend in the Creek. Here, they stayed until nightfall when Chivington and his soldiers had retired from the scene and his warriors had returned from the hunt. The bodies of the slain Indians had been scalped and hideously mutilated. The soldiers, drunk from whiskey and the sheer violence of the killing spree, had draped various mutilated body parts over their horses and themselves, while Chivington watched and said nothing. In fact his demeanour displayed quite the opposite. With no remorse, he cheered his troopers on, encouraging them to commit even further obscenities and pushed them on into a frenzy. It was only when he was completely satisfied that all available Indians had been killed that he ordered his bugler to sound 'recall.'

This horrific event must be, without any shadow of doubt, the most heinous and shameful in the history of the U.S. Cavalry. The total count for less than a few hours of grisly work was, 105 Cheyenne women and children dead along with 28 men. Of the soldiers, 9 were killed and 38 wounded, the majority of these casualties being the result of 'friendly fire' from their own comrades. It must be emphasised here, that the dreadful actions of Colonel Chivington and the men under his command in no way reflected the Indian policies of Major General Curtis, Chivington's commanding officer, nor the policies of the army as a whole at this time. Chivington had debased himself and the military of his own accord.

Colonel Chivington returned to Fort Lyon with 7 women and children as prisoners. He also had over 130 fresh scalps, which were put on public display in a Denver theatre. He was highly pleased with his achievement but the Denver populace were shocked. Three of his own officers were also deeply disgusted at what they had witnessed. The official reports of Captain Silas Soule, Lieutenant Joseph Cramer and Lieutenant James Conner, together with immense public outrage, eventually led to a hearing being convened to determine the reason for such brutal barbarity within the ranks. Such deplorable behaviour could not be allowed to surface again, besides which it was contrary to military regulations.

The Congressional investigation lasted for a period of 72 days, during which they heard such disturbing evidence that few of those who attended the hearing did not fail to be visibly shocked. The committee eventually condemned Chivington's actions against Black Kettle's Cheyenne village, although the Colonel couldn't have cared less. He believed that he had executed God's will and that he had done it well. However, public opinion was firmly against him. Chivington relinquished his commission in the army and returned to Ohio, where he became a newspaper publisher. Inevitably, his appalling behaviour at Sand Creek followed him like the plague and he died some years later a bitter old man, although he was still preaching his version of the Bible and still believing that the dreadful crimes he had committed had been for the good.

Black Kettle and his survivors were paid a large indemnity for the unacceptable trauma they had endured at Sand Creek. But it did not bring back all those innocents who had been savagely murdered. The old chief took what was left of his village and moved south into Comanche territory, in an attempt to avoid any further contact with the soldiers. After some time he did accept the government's apologies for the massacre, much to his regret. Only 4 years later he was to witness a re-enactment of the grisly scene. This time it involved George Custer and the Seventh Cavalry. This time it would cost him his life!

News of the massacre spread across the Plains like a bush fire. Further north the Sioux, already angered by the passage of settlers and gold hunters through their lands, became incensed. Until now they had watched from a distance as the army steadily moved on to their hunting grounds, ostensibly to guard the many trails along the Platte. By the end of 1865, troops were openly entering the Powder River territory and erecting forts to protect the ever increasing roads, trails and railway lines that were spreading their tentacles westward. Red Cloud, a powerful Ogalalla Chief, decided it was time to call a halt to this invasion. With spirited young warriors such as Crazy Horse and his followers, this grimly determined Ogalalla went on the warpath and set a torch to the frontier that was to burn for the next three years.

The spring of 1866 saw the arrival of Colonel Henry Carrington into the Powder River area, accompanied by the 2nd Battalion 18th U.S. Infantry. Although Carrington had been instrumental in raising the 18th Infantry in 1861 and the regiment had subsequently distinguished itself throughout the Civil War, he had not actually joined his regiment until after the surrender of the Confederate forces in 1865. In short, Colonel Carrington had never seen the hard face of battle, much less commanded a military unit in the field and he knew absolutely nothing about Indians. In his infantile wisdom, the Commander of the Department of the Missouri, General John Pope, issued the following orders to Carrington:

> 'The 2nd Battalion, 18th U.S. Infantry, will constitute the garrison of Fort Reno on the Powder River, and the two new posts on the route between that place and Virginia City in Montana.......
>
> At these posts the battalion will be distributed as follows:
>
> Four companies at Fort Reno and two companies each of the other posts. The Colonel of the Regiment will take post at Fort Reno.'

If the stupidity of this order defies comprehension, it must be remembered that the times reflect the personalities of the period and their actions. Pope knew no more about Indians than Carrington did, but even so it is difficult to understand why he spread his forces so thinly in a dangerous hostile region when there were still plenty of military units available. It appears that the troops were expendable pawns in a deadly game of frontier chess. But Red Cloud had never heard of chess and he was certainly not playing any game.

Colonel Carrington lived by army orders and if the army needed forts along the Powder River, he would make sure they had them. He arrived at Fort Reno on 28th June and immediately began mobilising his forces in order to protect the Bozeman Trail that led to the gold fields in Idaho and Montana. Within a month he had begun the construction of Fort Phil Kearny on a bend on the Powder River and, being an engineer himself, he was an excellent choice for the project. He had intended the new fort to be completed by the winter and his urgency was probably prompted by the continuous reports of Indian attacks along the trail. However, by December, although the fort had been firmly established it was far from being completed and the bitterly cold weather that now engulfed his command, hampered the work considerably.

Throughout the summer, Red Cloud and his warriors had steadily whittled away at the civilian wagon trains and the troops who had tried to protect them, shattering their morale and causing outcries within the civilian communities. Whilst still keeping a watchful eye on the progress of the work at Fort Phil Kearny, Red Cloud had increased his forces, amassing close to 3,000 warriors (although official reports vary on this figure). On the occasions that Red Cloud had talked with the military, he had repeatedly warned them not to enter Sioux lands under any circumstances or face the consequences. The soldiers had ignored his warnings so now he would teach them a lesson. The wily chief watched and waited, biding his time until he was absolutely sure of a victory. His chance came on 21st December, towards the close of 1866.

Early that Friday morning 55 men left Fort Phil Kearny to cut the last of the timber that was needed to complete the construction of the post. By 11 am they were signalling that they were under attack from the Indians. A bugler put his frozen instrument to his lips and 50 men of the 18th Infantry, together with 24 troopers of the 2nd Cavalry, assembled on the parade ground. A fiery headed Captain, William Fetterman, commanded the detachment assisted by Lieutenant George Grummond, another cavalry officer. Carrington gave Fetterman explicit orders:

> 'Just relieve the wood train and drive the Indians back. On no account pursue the Indians beyond Lodge Trail Ridge.'

Carrington repeated the order which Fettermen acknowledged and then the relief column left the confines of the fort. However, for some unknown reason Fetterman led his troops directly to Lodge Trail Ridge and not Sullivent Hills, where the wood train actually was. By now the wood cutters had managed to extricate themselves from the hostiles and on returning to the post they informed Carrington of Fetterman's position.

Beyond the ridge, well out of sight of the fort, the Sioux lay concealed within the very small ravines and gorges waiting to spring their trap. The warriors who had attacked the wood train were only decoys, whose prime function had been to lure the relief column into the hands of the main Sioux attack force. Without question, the plan had worked extremely well. Fetterman completely disregarded Carrington's orders and gave chase. Once the soldiers were out of sight of the fort, the Sioux sprang their trap. For the infantry it was all over in a matter of minutes, but Grummond's cavalry did at least manage to reach higher ground before they were overwhelmed and cut to pieces as well. It was a carefully planned ambush and, for once, the Indians had adhered to it. The blue-coated soldiers never had a chance. Had Fetterman followed orders, the catastrophe may never have happened. He had not and now he lay dead with his entire command, their bright red blood staining the pure white snow beneath them. Fetterman had boasted that he could ride through the entire Sioux nation with just 80 men. He died with exactly that number; 80 men.

The following day, Captain Ten Eyck returned to the fort with the remains of Fetterman and his men. Carrington was visibly shocked by the mutilated bodies and gave a lot of thought to the reasons why the Indians perpetrated such savagery, eventually putting his hypothesis to paper. Had he seen the carnage caused by Chivington's troops at Sand Creek, he would have seen practically the same mutilations, only these had been performed by his own kind, government soldiers.

In due course, Carrington was blamed for the disaster and was dispatched to Fort Casper in the south. He was replaced by Colonel Wessells, who continued to guard the Bozeman Trail to the best of his ability, but it was fast becoming an impossibility. Carrington requested a military court of inquiry to investigate Fetterman's conduct and it took over 20 years to finally absolve the Colonel of any blame.

Although Red Cloud was deemed responsible for the Fetterman Massacre, it was in reality the result of careful planning by one of his young warriors, Crazy Horse. It was Crazy Horse who gave the signal to attack and it was he who led the warriors into the fight, spurring them on with his brave actions. This was the young Ogallala's first taste of battle with the military and it marked the start of a long ride that would find him on the banks of the Little Big Horn some ten years later.

What the Fetterman massacre did reveal was that the frontier army had a real nasty war on its hands. Red Cloud had only just begun his campaign in earnest and over the next 18 months his warriors continued to attack all who dared to enter their territory. On 1st August 1867, the Sioux caught the army yet again, with a surprise attack near Fort Phil Kearny in what has become known as the 'Hayfield Fight'. The following day, the Sioux attacked the soldiers again, but with much more ferocity this time. The 'Wagon Box Fight', as it is referred to, was a hard pitched battle and it has been estimated that Red Cloud lost around 67 warriors and incurred some 120 wounded. The Sioux had lost this fight, but unknown to them they had actually won the Powder River War. The army had had enough.

In the Spring of 1868 a peace commission arrived at Fort Laramie, a frontier post that had been erected near the junction of the Laramie River and the North Platte. They carried orders from the government to obtain a peace treaty with Red Cloud at all costs, even if it meant abandoning the Powder River country. Headed by the new Commissioner for Indian Affairs, Nathaniel Taylor, the peace commission also included Generals William T. Sherman and Alfred Terry. Red Cloud was not the least impressed and refused to attend such consultations with the representatives, preferring instead to remain in the mountains, from where he could keep a watchful eye on the army below. On behalf of the Ogalalla Sioux he firmly stated:

> "When we see the soldiers moving away and the forts abandoned, then I will come down and talk!"

Dismayed and humiliated by their failure, the peace commission returned to Washington where the War Department finally issued the order to abandon the Powder River territory. On 29th July, the army left Fort C.F. Smith and marched south. The following morning, Red Cloud and his warriors entered the stockade and set fire to it. Four weeks later Fort Phil Kearny, the centre of so much bitter fighting, was also abandoned. Fort Reno and the Powder River trails were officially closed. With the military gone and all the forts razed to the ground, Red Cloud finally agreed to meet with official representatives to discuss a peace treaty and on Friday 6th November he rode into Fort Laramie accompanied by all his triumphant warriors. The great chief had rejuvenated the pride of his people and he was their hero. He had won the fight against the white invaders and now he would establish the peace.

The Peace Treaty of 1868 stated:

> 'From this day forward all war between the parties to this agreement shall forever cease. The Government of the United States desires peace and its honour is hereby pledged to keep it. The Indians desire peace, and they now pledge their honour to maintain it.'

This part of the treaty is quite straight forward but the remaining sixteen articles were very ambiguous and controversial, and they would remain the centre of dispute for the next 20 years or so.

Having reached an amiable agreement with the northern tribes of the Great Plains, the army still had to contend with the Arapaho, Cheyenne, Comanche and Kiowa in the south. They had been hostile for the past 3 years and although there had been no major engagement to speak of, they had been periodically attacking the white communities that had settled in the areas surrounding the Arkansas River. Throughout this time, hundreds of lives had been lost and the settlers angrily blamed the army for failing to protect them.

The new Commander of the Western Department was none other than General Phil Sheridan, who was openly ruthless in his policies and a hard man to pacify. Following the Civil War, Sheridan had been given command over Texas and Louisiana where he had been instrumental in the collapse of Maximillian's regime by his support of the Republican Army. However, his brutal treatment of former Confederate soldiers in Maximillian's forces led to charges of 'absolute tyranny' against him and so, within months he was transferred to the Department of the Missouri.

Sheridan decided to enforce a 'scorched earth policy' and whip these troublesome Indians into submission the hard way. This type of warfare had been successful during the Civil War and he saw no reason why it should not work now. He firmly believed that attacking the hostiles in their villages during the winter months would give his forces the element of surprise, thus reducing the number of casualties they may incur. Such a method would also deprive the Indians of their winter supplies, including the forage for their ponies. He was totally unconcerned about the possibility of including non-combatants during the attacks, saying:

> "If a village is attacked and women and children killed, the responsibility is not with the soldiers but with the people whose crimes necessitated the attack."

It is blatantly obvious that Sheridan had very little, if any, understanding of the Indians, or the situation his troops were facing. With snow blanketing the ground and fierce blizzards howling across the hills, he ordered his forces into the field to destroy all Indian villages they could locate and kill all Indians who put up any kind of resistance. Flanked on one side by General Eugene Carr with seven companies of the 5th Cavalry and on the other by Colonel Evans, who had six companies of cavalry, two companies of infantry and four mountain howitzers; the main attacking force that led the field was the 7th Cavalry under the command of Lt. Colonel George A. Custer.

With such a hard winter to contend with, many of the hostile tribes had moved further south and taken refuge alongside the camps of the more peaceful Indians along the banks of the Washita River, some 64 kilometres east of the Antelope Hills in southern Arkansas. By a strange coincidence the principal chief of these peaceful villages happened to be Black Kettle, the same chief who had suffered the appalling massacre at Sand Creek in 1864. In all, these villages contained around 2,000 warriors, although it must be remembered that not all of them were hostile. To the army though, in view of recent events all Indians were to be regarded as hostile and it was their duty to subdue them, place them on carefully selected reservations where they could be contained and eventually re-educate them to live the white man's way.

By Friday 27th November, Custer's column had reached the Washita River and through the early morning mist the soldiers could see 180 tipis along the banks. Unfortunately for Black Kettle, it was his Cheyenne village that Custer now had in his sights. Determined to succeed in his orders, Custer engineered his plan and deployed his troops. Four detachments would encircle the village: Major Joel Elliott, with three companies; Captain Thompson and Captain Meyers, each with two companies; and himself, with the remaining four companies. When the bugler sounded the 'charge' they would attack the village simultaneously from all sides.

In complete silence the soldiers took up their positions, each man cursing the weather, the Indians and their officers-not necessarily in that order. The horses stood in the icy wind, their heads lowered and shivering in unison with their riders. Weapons gleamed in the pale light of dawn as the bugler put the cold metal to his lips and blew.

The sound of thundering hooves pounding the frozen ground aroused the Indians from their sleep, spilling them forth from their warm tipis. Black Kettle could not believe his eyes. It was Sand creek all over again! Accompanied by his wife, he rode out to meet the advancing soldiers as bullets whizzed through the cold air. As he reached the ford a bullet tore into his stomach and as he toppled from his pony, another bullet caught him in the back. Black Kettle was dead before he hit the snow and within seconds his wife lay beside him, several more bullets having found their mark.

The cavalrymen splashed across the ford, riding over the fallen bodies and firing their weapons wildly into the camp. Terrified Indians ran to the river, only to be cut down by the merciless gunfire or torn to pieces by the razor sharp ice-floes in the freezing water. Women grabbed their children and tried to escape the slaughter, only to run into more soldiers as they broke through the mist. Screams echoed down the river as the clear blue water turned crimson.

By mid-morning it was all over. Alerted by the noise, warriors from nearby villages rushed to the aid of the stricken Cheyenne. On observing the approach of these fresh warriors, Custer recalled his command and retreated to Fort Supply. In just a few hours the toll on human life had been incredible. Two Indian Chiefs, Black Kettle and Little Rock, lay dead along with 103 Cheyenne, of whom only 11 were actually warriors! Over 700 Indian ponies had been slaughtered and all their winter supplies had been destroyed, along with most of the village itself. However, it had not been a complete pushover, for the soldiers had incurred casualties as well; 2 officers and 19 other ranks had been killed with others wounded. Captain Hamilton was the only soldier to actually fall within the village. Major Elliott and the majority of his command were killed as they charged into some approaching Arapaho warriors.

At Fort Supply, Sheridan ordered the entire post turned out to review the victorious 7th Cavalry. With the band playing a triumphant welcome, Custer and his command rode through the gates displaying the grisly scalps they had taken and dragging behind them 53 Cheyenne women and children they had taken captive. Sheridan publically congratulated Custer for his

> ".......efficient and gallant services rendered."

In his official report the General wrote that he was more than pleased to have wiped out Black Kettle, adding

> ".......we have a great victory over those savage butchers and their savage bands of cruel marauders."

The fact that Black Kettle and his people were peaceful Indians was never included in the report.

News of Black Kettle's death spread across the land in all directions. The Plains Indians were enraged and vowed to have their revenge, which came as no surprise really. But in the east, military commanders and politicians who had had dealings with the dead chief were appalled and publically denounced Sheridan's policies as nothing short of 'cold-blooded murder'. Sheridan obviously retaliated by calling them

> '.......good and pious ecclesiastics,'

adding that they were,

> '....... Aiders and abetters of savages who murdered without mercy men, women and children.......'
>
> Undaunted, he then ordered the Arapaho, Cheyenne, Kiowa and Comanche to report to Fort Cobb and surrender. Some chiefs duly

> complied with the directive, notably Little Robe, who brought in his Arapaho. Only a few Comanche appeared, however, and when Chief Tosawi arrived with his small band of Comanche, he greeted Sheridan with,
>
> "Tosawi good Indian."

Sheridan retorted,

> "The only good Indians I ever saw were dead!"

(It appears from official reports and statements, Sheridan never tired of using that phrase whenever he could.) Fortunately, Tosawi's understanding of the English language was very limited and he meekly allowed his people to be placed on a reservation. The proud Kiowa gave no sign of reporting to the fort. They had no reason to. With plenty of game drifting south for the winter, they could eat as much as they could hunt and that was far more than any government agent could give them.

Annoyed at this response, Sheridan ordered Custer and his regiment into the field yet again, to force the Kiowa to submit or die. Thus it was, on a cold December day, that Custer arrived at the edge of the Kiowa village on Rainy Mountain Creek. Not really eager for a fight and fearing another massacre like the Washita, Chief Satanta rode out with an escort of warriors to talk. When dealing with the enemy, Custer was a man of few words and it soon became abundantly clear that the talks were not going well. Finally, Satanta understood Custer's curt demand,

> "Surrender your people to Fort Cobb or face destruction by my soldiers!"

Before Satanta could reply, Custer became impatient and ordered his troops to place the chief under arrest. Satanta and his escort would be held at Fort Cobb until his people submitted. The Kiowa had been deceived by treachery and not wishing any harm to come to their chief, they surrendered and gave up their weapons at the fort.

To keep a constant watch on the Indians who inhabited this region, the army erected a new outpost named Fort Sill. Situated midway between the Washita and Red River, it was commanded by General Benjamin Grierson and garrisoned by the 10th Cavalry. Sheridan officially opened the new fort and released Satanta, warning him and his followers to settle down and behave themselves on the reservation nearby.

Having now subdued the southern tribes, Sheridan adjusted his sights to view the mighty Sioux nation in the north. They were relatively peaceful at present. However, the majority of them were still free and not confined under a military jurisdiction. Sheridan distrusted all Indians, after all they had proven themselves to be generally unpredictable and he felt uneasy in the pit of his stomach at the thought of these fearless warriors still being able to roam free to do as they pleased. And, as if that were not enough, one of his finest regiments, the 7th Cavalry, had been temporarily disbanded. The reasons for this temporary disbandment are relatively obscure. It appears they were split to undertake constabulary duty, under the jurisdiction of the Department of Justice, as part of the reconstruction program in the South. In any event, it would be a further four years before the officers and men of the 7th Cavalry would meet again.

Chapter 6

No Man is Equal

From the moment Ulysses S. Grant entered the White House as the 18th President of the United States in 1869, his administration was constantly rocked by one scandal after another. It was a period of discontent and distrust, with numerous Congressional committees hearing endless complaints concerning government officials, many of whom were removed from office and prosecuted as a result. For the national hero of the Civil War, being President was the hardest time of his career. His military skills were worthless in the world of politics and his naivety as a politician was cleverly concealed by his Secretary of State, Hamilton Fish, to whom any of Grant's achievements during his administration must be credited. Incredibly, Grant won a second term of office in the Presidential elections of 1872, even though his position within political circles had not improved. A year later, the U.S. Congress were about to begin an investigation into yet another scandal within his administration and with the possibility of war looming with Panama, Grant also had the opening phases of a general depression on his hands. His only relief came when the Secretary of War, William W. Belknap, wrote in his official report that all hostilities with the Plains Indians had now ceased and that they were gradually settling down to accept a more peaceful existence on the reservations set aside for them.

Unfortunately for Grant, Belknap's report was only partially correct. It was true that Red Cloud and Spotted Tail, two of the most feared of the Sioux chiefs, had brought their people in to the reservations, but it was also true that another two, the most deadly of all the Sioux warriors, were still at large and undeniably roaming free across the Plains: Crazy Horse and Gall. They had both featured prominently in Red Cloud's War and they absolutely refused to capitulate to the white man's will. With a considerably large following of young warriors, they had settled within the sacred Black Hills (known to the Sioux as 'Pa Sapa',) and had continued to practice their traditional way of life in defiance of the government's policy.

For years rumours had been whispered around the frontier towns that gold deposits had been found in the Black Hills. Those prospectors who had found gold and managed to evade the Indians, added credence to the rumours when they showed their haul in the small scattered towns nearby. Having lived a much harder life than those in the big cities, these settlements were being hit hard by the depression that was sweeping the country. Anything had to be better than the poverty they were now experiencing and even the slightest chance of making some money could not be ignored, Indians or no Indians. After all, gold was wealth and wealth meant money. However, there was no positive proof that gold did exist in this area. A handful of nuggets or a bag of dust did not indicate gold in abundance and the majority of those who had ventured into the Black Hills to seek their fortune had either been killed or chased out by the Indians, who would not tolerate such an intrusion.

During 1872 an attempt was made to determine whether or not any truth in these rumours existed. Charles Collins, a promoter who resided in Sioux City, tried to initiate a prospecting expedition into the Black Hills that was led by a miner called T.H. Russell. The idea was quickly abandoned after the army threatened to arrest them both if they set one foot in to the Black Hills territory. Even so, the talk of gold being found in the area, in huge quantities, persisted and many civilians, including Collins, began to get restless, resenting the army's interference. Newly erected forts began to appear in the Dakotas and reinforcements were hastily moved in to strengthen the army's already stretched soldiers. Not only had the soldiers been struggling to maintain some kind of order throughout the region, but they had also been sorely tempted themselves by the lure of easy gold. One of the new forts to be established was Fort Abraham Lincoln and in early 1873 it received its new commanding officer and compliment of troops: Lt. Colonel George A. Custer and the newly reformed 7th Cavalry.

As more and more prospectors poured into the region, lured by the tales of gold just lying on the ground, the soldiers began to crack under the pressure and tempers flared between the civilian communities and the military posts. Clashes became fairly frequent and letters poured into the politicians' offices, most of them complaining of the soldiers' rights of jurisdiction in a civilian matter. Finally, the government decided it had had enough and, without consulting the Indians to obtain the necessary permission to enter their lands, the politicians demanded an official investigation into the prospect of gold in the Black Hills. The War Department was ordered to put the directive into operation immediately, even though they were fully aware that it was a direct violation of the 1868 Treaty. Orders reached Fort Lincoln in the summer of 1874 and on 2nd July the expedition set forth.

Although it was common knowledge that the Black Hills Expedition was to establish the authenticity of the gold rumours, the official reason was far different. It was, so the official statement said, for the exploration of uncharted territory and to record the resources of the area, so that future military posts could be better sited. Still there was no mention of the 1868 Treaty or authorisation from the Indians. Custer was given command of the expedition which comprised of 10 companies 7th Cavalry, Company I 20th Infantry, Company G 17th Infantry, 60 Indian scouts and a number of small artillery pieces that included a battery of 3 Gatling guns. Also included within the personnel were biologists, engineers, photographers and two miners, Horatio Ross and William McKay, who were to study any mineral deposits found on the route. Unfortunately, newspaper correspondents also accompanied the expedition, whose prime function it was to report on the finding of any gold in the Black Hills. The expedition had been well planned and fitted out, with over 100 wagons carrying supplies and scientific instruments. However, it does appear that at least one person had given some thought to the Indians on whose land they would be trespassing. General Terry officially stated that the huge size of the expeditionary force was intended to prevent any trouble with the Indians, although he did not advise Custer of any strategy in dealing with them if contact was made.

After traversing the country for almost two months and surveying an area of 1,939.25 kilometres, Custer led the Black Hills Expedition back to Fort Lincoln. Throughout that time on the trail, gold had been found in small quantities, but the actual wealth of the area lay in the land itself. It was extremely fertile and rich in vegetation and game. Captain William Ludlow, chief engineer for the expedition, wrote:

> 'Whatever may ultimately be determined as to the existence of large amounts of precious metal in the Black Hills, and the evidence gathered on the trip was on the whole discouraging to that supposition-the real wealth and value of the country are, beyond doubt, very great. Utterly dissimilar in character to the remaining portion of the territory in which it lies, its fertility and freshness, its variety of resource and delightful climate.........'

In his official report to the War Department, Custer concurred with Ludlow on the results of the information they had gathered when he wrote:

> 'While I regard the gold discoveries as very important and promising richness, I do not think they have been prosecuted to the extent, or that sufficient information had been obtained concerning them, to warrant an immense influx of gold hunters into that region in advance of a more thorough and deliberate examination............'

Custer clearly knew that such action would provoke a bloody war with the Indians and questioned whether such action was worth it at the end of the day.

As government officials immersed themselves in the various reports, so the newspapers were already going to print. It did not matter on the amount that had been found. The simple fact was that there was gold in the Black Hills!

Gold fever ran riot in all the frontier towns and the army was put under even more pressure to restrain it. According to the newspaper articles, Custer had reported that gold was to be found all over the Black Hills. Gold had been found in the gravel washed by the clear running waters of the streams and it had been found in shallow deposits on the ground, scarcely deeper than the roots of grass! Mining experience was not necessary to become rich. The trails were literally paved with gold! It is evident that the official reports were embellished upon and that the reporters had deliberately written exactly what their readers wanted to see, rather than report the truth. In any event, the newspapers fuelled the fever and the civilians fired their shots directly at the bureaucrats in Washington.

Although Charles Collins, of Sioux City in Iowa, had been ordered by the army to stay out of the Black Hills, he tried again to promote another prospecting expedition in September. If there was gold in the Black Hills, as had been publicly reported, then he was determined to have a share of it. On 23rd December his train of six wagons found considerable deposits of gold on French Creek. After building a stockade to protect themselves against attacks from hostile Indians, the miners set to work extracting the precious metal. However, much to their chagrin, the army finally located them and in April 1875 unceremoniously escorted them out of the area.

Throughout the months of 1875 the military did its utmost to stem the ever increasing tide of gold-hungry prospectors, who poured into Indian Territory. It was an impossible task. If the army had already broken the conditions of the 1868 Treaty, then the prospectors had ripped it apart. The 1868 Treat, that the Sioux had agreed to clearly stated:

> '.......If bad men among the whites, or among other people subject to the authority of the United States will, upon proof made to the agent and forwarded to the Commission of Indian Affairs at Washington City, proceed at once to cause the offender to be arrested and punished according to the laws of the United states, and reimburse the injured person for the loss sustained.'

Clearly these fortune hunters were in breach of the treaty. Not only were they trespassing on Indian land, but they were also guilty of outright theft! (It is worth noting here that the Indians were never reimbursed for the gold already taken, as they should have been. Nor were they offered any kind of compensation.) The army were well aware of these open violations of the treaty and they did arrest as many civilians as they could physically catch. But the stockades were rapidly overflowing and it was becoming increasingly difficult to contain them. Any that were released, or who managed to escape, quickly returned to the Black Hills only to be arrested and confined by the soldiers yet again.

The Indians watched the proceedings with utter distaste. They had never witnessed such a furore of greed and they deeply resented the intrusion knowing their treaty was by now blowing in the wind. Feelings were running high, particularly among the younger and more excitable warriors. News of Custer's expedition into the Black Hills soon reached Red Cloud and Spotted Tail, both of whom had now settled on their reservations. They held lengthy talks with other chiefs to determine what action, if any, they should take against the whites. They also discussed whether any action was realistically viable. In the event, the chiefs refused to retaliate in any way, much to the disgust of the younger warriors. It was these younger warriors who had already made numerous threats towards the army, who they felt had failed to protect them, and it was these younger warriors who left the agencies to join the hostile camps in the north.

Although Red Cloud was visibly angry at the blatant breach of the 1868Treaty, he was pre-occupied with other matters preying on his mind, matters which could have clouded his judgement in protecting the rights of his people. At this time he was more concerned about the quarrel he was having with his Indian agent, Dr J.J. Saville. Red Cloud claimed that Saville was cheating his people out of the proper rations they had been guaranteed under the 1868 Treaty. He had put his mark to that treaty and had kept his side of the bargain. He, quite rightly, assumed that if he kept to the treaty then the white men should as well. Red Cloud also claimed that Saville was not alone in his shady dealings and that the majority of the other Indian agents were also giving their Indian charges a raw deal. So much so, that the Indians on the reservations were generally poor clothed and underfed to the point of starvation. (Remember Andrew Myrick of the Sioux Agency near Fort Ridgely ?) Article 5 of the 1868 Treaty clearly defined the duties of an Indian agent:

> '…….that the agent for said Indians shall in future make his home at the agency building; that he shall reside among them, and keep an office open at all times for the purpose of prompt and diligent enquiry into such matters of complaint by and against the Indians as may be presented for investigation under the previous treaty stipulations.
>
> …….as also for the faithful discharge of other duties enjoyed on him by the law.'

Thus, according to Red Cloud's accusations, agent Saville was not fulfilling his duties as required by law and as laid out in the treaty. Article 10, of the same treaty, also made provisions for the military to be present when the rations were being distributed:

> '.......and the President shall annually detail an officer of the Army to be present and attest the delivery of all the goods herein named to the Indians, and shall inspect and report on the quantity and quality of the goods and the manner of their delivery.'

For the military this was a difficult undertaking. To begin with, they had been asked to make routine patrols and inspections of the agencies and reservations, an area they had very little jurisdiction in as it came under the Department of the Interior and not the War Department. Secondly, the agents and their suppliers were very adroit at covering up their clandestine operations, many of which led all the way back to certain departments in Washington, as will be revealed.

The army knew that these shady dealings echoed down the corridors of power, a route that was way above their heads. Word filtered back to the bureaucrats in the east that the Indians they had thought were settled, under their constraints, were now very much disgruntled with their respective agents. Already hostile Indians were threatening reprisals over the Black Hills problems. It was a certainty that the politicians did not want another Indian crisis on their hands. Red Cloud had been a real problem before the 1868 Treaty had been fully agreed upon and they did not want either Red Cloud or any of the other chiefs abandoning their agreement and joining the hostiles in the north. That could mean a whole lot of trouble they may not be able to control or finance in the long run. But the frontier was already set to explode. The hostile bands were not listening to any more white men's words. They were ready for action. In an attempt to forestall a complete breakdown, a government commission was sent to the agencies, particularly those of Red Cloud and Spotted Tail, to investigate their complaints.

The commission included two Senators, an ex-governor and two other officials, who were said to be experienced in public business, whatever that meant. It does not appear that there were any representatives from the military or the Bureau of Indian Affairs. Starting their investigation in the east, the commission gradually made their way west, travelling through Omaha, Cheyenne and Fort Laramie, until they eventually arrived at the Red Cloud and Spotted Tail agencies on the White River. They collected enough testimonies to compile a book, but they failed to find any legal evidence of fraud within the agencies, or on the part of the contractors who supplied them. This was hardly surprising. The agents and the contractors had devised an extremely complex and ingenious method of growing rich on government money and Indian misery. The Indians knew these fraudulent dealings were in progress and so did many of the army officers, but without positive proof there was nothing the commission could do.

At a later date, one army officer did testify against the fraudulent actions that he positively knew of, concerning the distribution of flour at the agencies he had been detailed to inspect. The low-grade flour was shipped to a warehouse in Cheyenne, in double sacks. As was the custom, each sack of flour was weighed, stamped by the inspector and then wheeled inside the warehouse to be stored. Once inside, the outer sack was removed and the sack of flour was then taken out of the rear door, to be wheeled around the front where it was weighed, recorded and stamped once again. The contractor would be paid for a full shipment when he had only delivered half of it. (Incredibly, other methods of defrauding the government included mixing the flour with powdered clay!) Needless to say, to succeed in frauds such as this there would have to be a financial agreement between the contractors and the freighters, not to mention the agents concerned. This particular case came to light after an army officer had been stationed at the agency as a temporary replacement for the civilian agent. Observing that the shipment of flour was actually 50% less than the bills were stating, the diligent officer refused to accept the goods and promptly reported the freighter in question to his superiors. Having caught the offender red-handed, a conviction for fraud was easily established. But it must be emphasised that successes such as this were extremely rare and some army officers were not as honest as this one.

All shipments were hauled to the agencies by freight companies, who charged the government a set rate per 100 lb per 100 miles. (Roughly 45 kilograms per 160 kilometres.) Yet the exact distance the freighters had to travel had never been properly measured and recorded. During the investigations into the alleged frauds, an odometer was attached to one of the freight wagons to record the distance it actually travelled from the warehouse to the Red Cloud agency. Unfortunately, there is no record that any of the investigators actually travelled with the odometer to ensure its accuracy. At the first attempt the odometer was 'accidently' broken during its travels. Undaunted, the commission tried again and attached another odometer to the freight wagon. On reaching the Red Cloud agency, the odometer had registered a travelling distance so incredible that the officials refused to accept it. Rumour had it that the wagon had been jacked up each night and a teamster manually turned the wheel for an hour or two! After all, the freighter had to protect his interests but he had overstepped the mark and eventually the army was ordered to measure the distance involved. Once again, there was a great deal of suspicious evidence concerning the freight charges but there was no legal proof found to support a conviction.

Perhaps the most unbelievable, but nonetheless true, story to emerge from the investigations concerned the provision of meat for Indian consumption. According to the agents' records there was enough beef being supplied to the Indians that would feed an entire army division at war strength! The Indians, however, insisted this was not the case. They ardently stated that the rations they were being given were so meagre that they could hardly exist on them. They also stated that the meat was so rancid that it was totally inedible. This was the reason, they insisted, that so many of their young braves periodically left the reservation to hunt fresh meat and supplement their rations. If they were to survive they had to eat. (The army knew this was not strictly true, but to the politicians it was at least plausible.) The cost of supplying the reservations with beef was astronomical and with the Indians insisting that they were being cheated in their rations, one way or another, the commission took a great deal of effort in their enquiries concerning the beef contracts.

One after another of the big cattlemen in Texas, including their trail-drivers, were extensively questioned concerning their delivery methods and after examining all the testimonies given, the commission could not reach a definite conclusion that would instigate legal proceedings. The only positive conclusion that the commission could safely declare was, that according to their investigation the cattlemen knew hardly anything of the business they were engaged in! They all assured the investigators that no one could estimate the weight of a steer before it went on the trail, much less the weight it would be on arrival at the agency. Yet, these men were growing exceedingly rich doing just that!

Red Cloud and many other agency chiefs refused to accept the results of the investigation. He angrily pointed to the scales as being proof of the beef frauds. The scales had heavy wooden planks laid across the platform. It was obvious to all, he insisted, that when a steer was weighed on these scales, the weight of those planks was added to the weight of the steer and, as such, the Indians were being cheated out of that much beef each time. The Ogalalla chief showed very little interest in the proven flour frauds. The Indians did not really know how to use flour, he said, and they would much prefer to be issued corn, if it was possible. Another Ogalalla chief, Old-Man-Afraid-of-his-horses, complained that he had never been given the rations that had been due to him as befits a chief. This did not help the Indians' cause much, as the commissioners were rapidly reaching the conclusion that the Indians were behaving like spoilt children, rather than responsible men with legitimate complaints.

As for agent Saville, his books were in such an awful condition as to render them completely indecipherable. Either he had deliberately altered them into such a mess to cover up his unlawful transactions or he was the most terrible book-keeper ever. In concluding the investigation, the commission stated that there was no clear-cut proof that Saville had committed any unlawful actions. There were, of course, plenty of suspicious circumstances, perhaps more so at the Red Cloud Agency than any other, but there was no positive evidence to file a court case against anyone. Thus, the commission returned to Washington; the Indians continued to accept their rations and grumble at the authorities; and agent Saville resumed his post.

In actual fact, despite their complaints against him, the Indians liked Saville. As one army officer put it, Saville had the responsibility and the work to accomplish that was very similar to that of a Major General and yet his pay was only that of a Lieutenant. With all things considered, Saville did a tremendous job under very difficult circumstances and at the end of the day, he did not receive any thanks for it. Saville was, in all probability, an honourable man, but there were many Indian agents who were not and it was these that gave the agents such a bad reputation overall.

While the corrupt agents and dishonest suppliers grew immensely rich operating their questionable schemes, so the politicians involved kept the investigators from finding any evidence within the corridors of power. Many army officers, of all ranks, knew these nefarious schemes were in operation, but they were powerless to do anything about them. The corruption originated from a higher level which was way beyond their reach. In any case, the army operated under the auspices of the War Department, whereas the Indian agencies were controlled by the Bureau of Indian Affairs, which in turn came under the Department of the Interior. The funding for the Department of the Interior was so corrupt at this time, that even direct pressure of public opinion brought through Congress could not curb it. It is a sad fact that the politicians of both parties needed funding for the elections and it was the illicit money that was obtained through these illegal schemes that actually kept the Bureau of Indian Affairs in existence!

Throughout the commissioner's investigations into the alleged agency frauds, government officials were working out legislation to coax the Indians into selling the Black Hills. It was the only solution they could find to curb the antagonism between all parties in the area. The shameful fact is that, once again, no thought was given to the Indians whose land they were conspiring to acquire. Civilian correspondence on the matter had been horrendous and the politicians now wanted it resolved, by whatever means possible. They simply didn't care. So, another commission was set in motion with the objective of visiting the agencies of Red Cloud and Spotted Tail to air the government's proposals for securing the land. On 18th June 1875, the Secretary of State for the Interior, Zacharia Chandler, issued his instructions to the members of the Black Hills Commission. He began by informing them that they were not only representing the government's interests but also the those of the Indians and they were to bear this in mind during the negotiations. He wanted to see a deal secured that was fair to both sides. However, as well as the Black Hills, the government also wished to purchase the Powder River country and the Big Horn lands. Chandler knew the latter would be cause for concern among the Indians and he instructed the commission to be extremely tactful during the discussions. In other words, the Indians were to lose all of their country and only reside on reservations that had been set aside for them. Chandler also asked the commission to remind the Indians that the 1868 Treaty only allowed for four years provisions and yet, due to the benevolence of the government, they were still receiving it. (Here, it must be assumed that Chandler had not read the 1868 Treaty, although he was aware of it. It appears that he quite simply took the word of his advisors, for that last statement was a flagrant lie. The Treaty did not just allow for four years of provisions, it clearly stated thirty years!) Chandler then instructed the commission that when an amount was agreed upon for the sale, they were to deduct a portion of the price to pay for the continuance of the supplies the Indians would receive. The sheer arrogance of men like Chandler and his cohorts defies belief. The enormity of this scandalous scheme must be one of the most derogatory actions this administration had put into operation to date. The fact that Indian lands had already been stolen and that gold had already been taken from the Black Hills, never entered the equation. Neither did the fact that the 1868 Treaty had already been broken nor that the Indians were not the transgressors. Chandler then announced what the government considered a fair offer for all these very desirable lands. He instructed the commission to offer a maximum of $400,000 a year for the mineral rights only or $6,000,000 for an outright sale. It was a proposition that was doomed to fail at the negotiating stage and one that would force the hand of the Indians, enabling the government to win in the end.

With William B. Allison, Senator for Iowa, as chairman, other senior members of the Black Hills Commission included Brigadier General Alfred Terry, Reverend Samuel Hinman and two traders who represented the commercial interests involved, Colonel G. Beauvais and John Collins. Weighed down with the added responsibility of averting an all-out Indian uprising, the commissioners arrived at Fort Robinson, near the Red Cloud agency, on 4th September 1875. Considering that the lands they wished to acquire were already inhabited by Indians who had no inclination to resort to living on reservations, it appears strange that government officials persisted in dealing with Red Cloud, who had already given up his nomadic existence. It was true that Red Cloud was a very respected chief amongst his people; but it was also true that the treaty he had agreed to no longer counted and the hostile tribes to the north now comprised of younger, more resilient and determined chiefs who made their own decisions. It may be that the commission knew that the hostile tribes were in no mood to talk, much less be located and it could take months to find them. Red Cloud, on the other hand, had talked before and was easily located on the reservation. But if the commissioners thought that Red Cloud was a soft touch, they were in for a rude awakening. The wily chief knew how to negotiate with the whites and was to prove he could hold his own when trying to protect his people's interests.

Collins estimated that there were approximately 20,000 Indians camped within the vicinity of the fort and for the next two weeks he watched, with increasing apprehension, as the Indians quarrelled amongst themselves in determining where the talks would be held. Red Cloud wanted them held at his agency and Spotted Tail wanted them held midway between the two agencies, at Chadron Creek. While the arguing continued, the commissioners held numerous discussions with some of the lesser chiefs and their accompanying warriors. It did not take either side long to realise that the outlook for any successful agreement between them was very bleak. Not surprisingly, none of the chiefs they consulted liked the offers they had heard for the Black Hills and they would not even consider the sale of the Powder River country, nor the Big Horn lands. They firmly stated that these were considered sacred lands for the Sioux; that they were traditional hunting grounds; and, in any event these lands were presently occupied by the wilder Sioux bands, who would never accept any proposals they had to offer. They informed the commissioners that messages had been sent to the chiefs of these hostile camps, informing them of the government's proposals. The messengers had returned conveying replies that it would not be propitious for any Indian to even contemplate the offers, in fact it would be downright dangerous for them to do so.

The 1868 Treaty had contained a provision which stated that if the Sioux contemplated ceding any of these lands, ¾ of all the adult males of all the Sioux tribes must give their consent to the agreement. Thus knowing that this was the case and that it was clearly not about to happen, the commission decided to review their position before committing themselves to anything remotely unpleasant. Feelings amongst the Indians were already at fever pitch and it would be just plain stupidity to antagonise them any further. The commission knew that there was no way ¾ of the Sioux now gathered around the fort would agree to their proposals and even less chance that the hostiles would. Crazy Horse had refused to even discuss it, much less attend the talks. In view of such a delicate situation, the commission decided it was probably more prudent on their part to ask for the mineral rights only.

By 17th September, Red Cloud and Spotted Tail had finally agreed to a site that was suitable for them all to gather to discuss the issues laid before them. It was a flat plain on the White River, just over 12 kilometres east of the Red

Cloud agency. Having had enough of all the dithering, Senator Allison had changed his mind by now. Through an interpreter, Louis Richards, he informed the chiefs that they were there to negotiate the outright sale of the Black Hills, the Powder River country and the Big Horn lands only and that the Indians must reach a suitable agreement soon. Clearly angry at Allison's change of plans, much less his attitude, the chiefs asked for time to consider the new proposals and duly returned to their respective camps. Senator Allison was learning the art of procrastination from the masters! The atmosphere was decidedly cool and tempers were rapidly rising. For the commissioners it was a very tense situation.

On 26th September, the commission assembled on the plain once more, in an attempt to continue the negotiations and force the Indians into a settlement. Behind them stood 120 mounted soldiers from Fort Robinson. Gathered around them were approximately 7,000 angry young warriors, all wearing full ceremonial dress and all carrying their weapons. A number of them had even smeared war-paint on themselves and their ponies. They were in no mood for capitulation. Although it was a very tense situation for the commissioners and their small escort, the scene was electrifying. Red Cloud and Spotted Tail proudly approached the commission and firmly informed them that the Powder River country and the Big Horn lands were not for sale and that was an end to it. However, they would be prepared to accept $50,000,000 for the outright sale of the Black Hills, which they considered was a fair price. They added that the money should be put in a bank to accrue interest, so that the Indians would be able to buy all the necessary supplies they needed in the future. Concluding, the chiefs said that the Black Hills was a bank and that the miners had been robbing the bank.

Allison and his colleagues were stunned. There was no way the government would agree to that. Once more he offered $600,000 for the outright sale of the Black Hills or $400,000 a year for the mining rights, but this time with the added proviso that the government reserved the right to cancel the agreement with just two years' notice. Allison's arrogance is confirmed by the fact that he actually believed this proposal was worth considering, let alone accepting! Naturally, the chiefs refused to even discuss the offer and categorically stated that there would be no more talks on the subject. They returned to their agencies amid great jubilation from their warriors. They had won the first round, retaining their prestige. The commission, on the other hand, were utterly dejected. They returned to Washington to write their reports and they knew their words would not go down well.

The matter was far from settled, however, and instead of leaving the Indians happy at the prospect of having retained their lands, the commission had actually stirred up a hornet's nest. Sensing trouble with the military over the failure of the talks and knowing that the white men would not stop until they had every last grain of Indian gold, many young warriors left the reservations to join the hostile bands of Crazy Horse, Gall and another Sioux who was rapidly making a name for himself, Sitting Bull. If the white men wanted Sioux land and Sioux gold they would have to fight for it.

A former member of a very influential warrior society and now the spiritual leader of the Hunkpapa Sioux, Sitting Bull was a truly remarkable man. His war record as a young man was very impressive, having taken part in numerous raids against the enemies of the Sioux since he was 14 years old. Seven years later he fought and killed a Crow chief during individual combat, a fight that had left him with a permanent limp from a wound he had sustained in his left foot. Amongst the Sioux his exploits were legendary, having established himself as a successful warrior and a man of exceptional physical and moral courage. Now, he had turned the glory of being a brave warrior over to the fresh young men who continued to arrive in his camp daily. He was content to have the much-honoured title of 'Spiritual Leader', for Sitting Bull was extremely gifted in this area. When he spoke, people listened and they gathered in their hundreds to hear him.

Sitting Bull had always been against the idea of reservations and he was a fervent speaker at the Council of Elders, verbally attacking the military for enforcing the Indians to accept agency life, much against their will;

> "What treaty that the whites have kept has the red man broken…..? None. What treaty has the white man ever made with us they have kept….? Not one."

Since the end of Red Cloud's war in 1868, he had bided his time, moving from one village to another throughout the Indian Territory, convincing the tribes to resist the unwelcome advances of the white men, whenever and wherever they could. Now he was urging them to stand fast and not only fight for their lands, but for the future of their very existence! At one council meeting, Sitting Bull threw down the gauntlet when he grimly stated,

> "Only seven years ago we made a treaty by which we were assured that the buffalo country should be left to us forever. Now they threaten to take that away from us. My brothers, shall we submit or shall we say to them, first kill me before you take possession of my father's land!"

When asked about the government's proposals for the Indian's land, Sitting Bull angrily retorted,

> "I wish all to know that I do not propose to sell any part of my country, nor will I have the whites cutting our timber along the rivers……….."

In an effort to consolidate all the numerous tribes into action as a combined fighting force, Sitting Bull sent runners to all the hostile villages, inviting them to join him for the duration of the winter months. It would afford them an opportunity to contemplate their next course of action. He knew that, at long last, these warriors were ready to listen and prepare for war. By the Spring of 1876, Sitting Bull was to achieve something that had never been witnessed on the Plains in all the Indian known existence, or since for that matter; the uniting of all the tribes within a single camp under a common objective.

The hot dry summer of 1875 degenerated into the heavy snow falls and the winter of 1875 was one of the worst on record. On the reservations the food rations, already depleted by the shady dealings of the agents, began to run out and the Indians began to starve. Unable to secure extra rations and not wanting an uprising on their hands, the agents granted permission for the young warriors to leave the agencies to hunt for food. The agents duly noted the numbers of all the Indians who took advantage of this offer and the totals of all those who returned. Naturally, the totals differed considerably. Worried by the large discrepancies, the agents sent in their reports to the Bureau of Indian Affairs, notifying them of the situation. However, it must be noted that in all fairness to the Indians, heavy snow falls prevented many from returning and they naturally sought shelter wherever they could find it. Unfortunately, this also meant the villages of the hostiles, a fact ignored by the authorities. At Red Cloud's reservation, even more confusion ensued when agent Saville was replaced by James S. Hastings. Hastings not only had the current problems of poor weather conditions and a shortage of provisions, but in order to carry on as smoothly as possible, he had to decipher Saville's ledgers and records. It was a nightmare, but Hastings did the best he could under the circumstances.

The failure of the commission to obtain the Black Hills and any other Indian lands, only made the hoards of prospectors more determined to take them, using whatever means necessary. They flooded into the region by the thousands and in the end, powerless to stem the rush, the army gave up trying to stop them. In the northern areas of the Black Hills, townships even sprang up; two of the more well-known being Deadwood and Rapid City. Early in 1875, Colonel Richard Dodge had stated that the country would be a good one for settlers as soon as the Indians could be got rid of. His words were now in practice, for although the Sioux and their allies struck back, it was a hopeless effort. The influx of the white men was too rapid for them to handle and so they retreated to the Powder River country to assess the situation.

Upon their return to Washington, the commission completed its report to the Secretary of State for the Interior. Amongst other things, the commissioners stated that it was their opinion that the Indians were extremely hostile to the government's proposals and that the Indians would not change their minds unless they were shown just how powerful the government could be. On the 9th November, E.T. Watkins, a special investigator for the Bureau of Indian Affairs, reported to his superiors that the Indians still residing outside the reservations were well fed and heavily armed; were lofty and independent in their attitudes; and, as such, they constituted a grave threat to the reservation system they [the officials] were attempting to enforce. Watkins recommended that these uncivilised savages should be taught a lesson and that troops should be mobilised against them,

> "..........unless something is done to obtain possession of that section for the white miners who have been strongly attracted there by reports of rich deposits of the precious metal......"

Clearly the region was seething with unrest and the issues at stake could not be ignored.

On 3rd December 1875, the Commissioner of Indian Affairs, Edward P. Smith, sent a directive to all his Sioux and Cheyenne agents ordering them to notify all Indians not residing on the reservations to report to their respective agencies by 31st January 1876 or they would be compelled to do so by the military. In his annual report for 1875 Commissioner Smith wrote:

> 'However unwilling we may be to confess it, the experiences of the past summer prove either the inefficiency of the large military forces under the command of such officers as Generals Sheridan, Terry and Crook; or the utter impracticability of keeping Americans out of a country where gold is known to exist, by any force of orders, or U.S. cavalry, or by any consideration of the rights of others.'

As senior to Terry and Crook, Sheridan would have been furious at this remark and it would have serious repercussions at a later date. Smith was obviously aware that the universal savage beast, commonly referred to as 'greed', had engulfed the moral and ethical reasoning of the white settlers in the region and beyond. He also knew that despite the politicians in Washington shouting orders at the military to contain the 'gold fever', the soldiers could not hope to do so. It was an impossible situation and the ultimatum that had been issued to the hostile Indians could not help to improve matters. On the contrary, it was actually the lit match that everyone knew would appear one day. In accordance with Smith's directive, the agents duly sent messengers out to all the hostile camps, requesting them to come in to the reservations by 31st January 1876 or face the consequences from the army. Then everyone sat back and waited.

PART TWO

'All day it shook the land –
grim battle's thunder tread;
And fields at morning green,
At eve are trampled red.

But now, on the stricken scene,
Twilight and quiet fall;
Only, from hill to hill,
Night's tremulous voices call.

And comes from far along,
Where campfires warning burn;
The dread, hushed sound
Which tells of morning's sad return.

Benjamin Sledd

Chapter 1

The Sound of the 'General'

The importance of the 1868 Peace Treaty cannot be emphasised enough. It forms the basis upon which the causes of the subsequent Indian Wars can be found, for it appears that rather than putting an end to Indian grievances it actually initiated others that were to become far more complex. Military forces on the frontier were the first to experience the backlash the treaty caused, as they were invariably caught in the middle and had to endure a torrent of contempt from all parties involved. In fact, being a soldier stationed in this region during such a period of unrest was not an enviable profession. The establishment of extra forts and the influx of fresh troops helped to reduce the strain on the forces, which had already been stretched beyond their limits. However, the increase of Indian agencies did very little to alleviate their problems. In actual fact, the agencies made matters worse in many instances. Whereas the army had the authority to deal with hostile Indians, they had no jurisdiction over the reservation Indians, unless the Bureau of Indian Affairs agreed to hand over their charges to the War Department, which they were reluctant to do. It was a known fact to all the official departments concerned, that some reservation Indians were openly aiding and abetting the hostile Indians, if not by sending braves to re-enforce them then by their provocative actions against the authorities, actions they relished and took every opportunity to exercise.

It was obvious that the hostile tribes took full advantage of the unstable situation and frequently challenged the army's authority in the western regions. A winter campaign against these obstinate Indians, who flaunted their freedom in the Tongue and Powder valleys, had been the subject of discussion within the military circles for a number of years. The departmental commanders had all agreed that a large scale campaign, during the winter months, would be the only effective way to curtail their activities and restore some self-respect within the ranks. Now, it seemed, the bureaucrats were about to give them the chance.

Commissioner Smith's 'December Directive', instructing all hostile Indians to report to their agencies by 31st January 1876, was ludicrous in the extreme and tantamount to a declaration of war. But then, that was just what it was meant to be, although very few officials in Washington noted that fact. The general consensus of opinion was that these unruly Indians would readily surrender if a military force large enough could be activated in the field against them. (It should be borne in mind here, that the majority of the civilian population in the east, including most of the government, had never even seen an Indian much less fought one in battle. Therefore, they had no concept of the people they were dealing with and, if the truth was known, they didn't care.)

It was becoming increasingly clear that the original reasons for the Indians continued resistance to conform to government pressure, had been completely forgotten. The discovery of gold in the Black Hills had taken precedence over all other matters, thus effectively clouding the issue. The adamant refusal on the part of the Indians to sell their land only made the politicians more determined to acquire it, by any means at their disposal. Any constructive suggestions from other interested parties were simply ignored. If the use of military force was the only way they would get their hands on the gold, then a full scale campaign against these troublesome Indians would have to be set in motion and nothing was going to stop the mobilisation of the troops.

Smith's ultimatum reached the Sioux agencies on or around the 20th December 1875, amidst the most appalling weather conditions that had prevailed to date. Deep snow blanketed the whole country for miles around and as strong blizzards brought more snowfalls to the rolling hills of Montana and the Dakotas, so the temperature plummeted to – 40 degrees. Travel under such climatic conditions was impossible. (In fact these gruelling conditions persisted until May 1876 when the thaw created new problems of its own.) On receipt of the ultimatum, the agents duly sent their most trusted runners to the hostile camps to explain the situation and, hopefully, persuade the chiefs to bring their people in for talks. With such a severe winter against them, even the odds of the runners reaching their destinations within the time limit were extremely thin. Official records of the time show that many of these Indian runners were not able to return to their agencies until 11th February, two weeks after the deadline! A whole village took much longer to travel and in this kind of weather it would have been suicidal for many to have attempted it. Thus, the Indians stayed put.

On 3rd January 1876, agent E.A. Howard, of the Spotted Tail agency, sent in his report to his superiors at the Bureau of Indian Affairs, stating that he had received no word at all from either the runners or the hostile Indians and that he was still waiting for some response. Agent J.S. Hastings, of the Red Cloud agency, reported that Sitting Bull was reputed to have settled for the winter, somewhere in the Yellowstone region and that his runners had been unable to find the exact location. They had, however, been able to locate the villages of Crazy Horse and Black Twin, near Bear Butte, but their replies had been extremely unfavourable. Hastings concluded his report by stating that his runners had continued on to the Powder River region in an attempt to locate the Cheyenne villages, but as yet he had received no further word from them. The runner from the Standing Rock agency did not return until 11th February and although he had not been able to return prior to that date, he had been successful in locating Sitting Bull's camp. Sitting Bull's reply was no different from that of Crazy Horse. No deal!

Some mention must be given to the sheer courage and determination of those agency runners, for they have been sorely neglected by historians over the years. Being agency Indians, hostile tribes ridiculed them as traitors and alienated them from the more notable societies, referring to them as 'women-who-walk-with-the-whites'. Having to face these hostile Indians took a great deal of courage, for at the end of the day they could have been killed by their own people. The hazardous weather conditions on the outward journey was bad enough, but they had miraculously survived the return journey as well. Taking all into consideration, these runners accomplished some of the most remarkable feats of human endurance in the history of the West, a fact that has never been recognised.

The overall excuse the hostiles had given for not complying with the directive, was that the weather conditions were far too severe to move their people. One excuse was as good as another. The snow was too deep, they said, and it was definitely too cold. However, even the agents knew this was not strictly true. It was true that this was one of the worst winters the Indians had experienced, but it was also true that they were used to freezing climatic conditions and knew how to cope with them. Whether the hostile Indians thought that their locations had been compromised or not is unclear. They were only too aware that as agency runners had found them, reports would get back to the posts and then they could be under threat from the army. If this was the case, then why were the runners allowed to return? Whatever the reasons, the severe winter did not hamper the hostiles in moving their villages to other locations once the runners had left. In January, Crazy Horse moved his Ogallala village to the Powder River, which was a much longer distance than the Red Cloud agency in the south. It is also known that Sitting Bull moved his village at least twice between the months of December and March. Clearly these Indians valued their freedom and had no intentions of surrendering it. If the authorities wanted them on reservations they would have to find them first and force them to comply.

The army, however, were not impressed by this blatant display of arrogance and they interpreted the hostiles' refusal as a sign of absolute defiance against an official policy they had been ordered to enforce. In their official report for the period, they claimed that the hostile Indians were taunting them, daring the soldiers to venture from their forts and face them. Of course, this was an exaggeration of the situation, but it does underline the feelings the soldiers expressed at the time and it was enough for the military hierarchy to apply pressure in the east to gain control and take to the field. The Bureau of Indian Affairs eventually gave up trying to retain their regulatory services. They had pursued more peaceful methods in an attempt to resolve the disputes, although it must be said that their efforts were ambiguous and sometimes extremely provocative. On 1st February 1876, the War Department were instructed to begin preparations to put their intended campaign into operation. There was no doubt that war would be inevitable.

Officials within the Bureau of Indian Affairs estimated that there were approximately 3000 hostile Indians to be dealt with and of those, only a few hundred were warriors of any consequence. Indeed, in his report that was sent to the War Department, Inspector E.T. Watkins added that these tribes were totally disunited, being scattered in bands across the region and that they could easily be dealt with in turn by just a thousand trained troops. Why Inspector Watkins said that is a complete mystery and appears to be a deliberate misinterpretation of the truth. Had Watkins actually read the field reports that his own agents compiled for him, with any degree of thoroughness, his report to the War Department would have been very different and the military commanders may have been able to assess the situation more accurately. If Watkins was deliberately spurious in his report, then it was a very treacherous game he was playing and what was his motive for doing so?

However, the blame for this disastrous error of judgement cannot rest entirely with Inspector Watkins. The military echelon completely accepted his report without any arguable comment, even though they were fully aware of the numerous inconsistencies it obviously contained. Mistrustful of civilian departments, military authorities had received their own reports from area commanders, many of which conflicted with Watkins. From their own observations, the army had recorded the periodic exodus of the Indians from their agencies for the past few years. In fact, they knew exactly how many Indians had left the agencies; when this had occurred; and the total number of those who had returned. Therefore, it appears incredulous that the military hierarchy did not question Watkins' report when they knew it was not consistent with the facts and figures they already had. It is also incomprehensible that the Bureau of Indian Affairs did not inform the War Department of the last known locations of the hostile villages. This was crucial information when considering strategy. On the other hand, it could be argued that the military had received the information from their own reports and chose to ignore it. Even though the two departments did not get along with each other, it does seem doubtful that the Bureau of Indian Affairs would deliberately withhold vital information that could determine the success or failure of a major military operation, even though they had been economical with the truth in regard to the number of hostiles still at liberty. Then again, why did the army not question the information they had been sent by Watkins and why did they not examine their own reports more thoroughly? Was it just a huge mistake or was it a deliberate action that would determine the eventual outcome? In other words, was the campaign purposefully planned from the outset to ensure the outcome? What is abundantly clear is that the conflicting reports, from both departments, seem to have directly contributed to what can be said as gross unprofessionalism, which stirred the resulting confusion into a quagmire of increasing blunders. It was not until General Crook and Lt. Colonel Custer had both been soundly defeated, that the army appeared to recognise their mistakes and openly accuse the Bureau of Indian Affairs of deliberately misleading them. Although this could have been planned in advance so as to shift the blame if and when it became necessary.

On 7th February, the War Department authorised General Phil Sheridan, Commander of the Military Division of the Missouri, to mobilise his troops for the impending campaign against the hostile bands. As far back as the 3rd November 1875, President Grant had held a meeting at the White House to discuss the increasing Indian problems. Among those present were Belknap, Secretary of War; Chandler, Secretary of the Interior; Smith, Commissioner of Indian Affairs; and, Generals Sheridan and Crook. Strangely, there is no mention of Sherman being present, considering he was the Commanding General of the Army. This may be due to the fact that he could not bear the presence of Belknap and took great pains to avoid him whenever possible. There is very little information available concerning this meeting, although it is known that two important decisions were reached. First, they would withdraw all their troops from the Black Hills area and allow the miners to flood in. (Interestingly, by the winter of 1875/76 there were approximately 15,000 miners already prospecting in the Black Hills!) Secondly, they would use their troops to force the hostile Indians on to reservations, whether such a move was liked or not. Brute force was the order of the day. Sherman's absence was not a matter for concern. As a friend of Grant and Sheridan, he would approve anything they devised. In this case, Sheridan and Crook were to formulate the offensive. The very fact that Sheridan and Crook, two key players in the unfolding drama, were both present at this meeting is interesting. Subsequent events suggest that these two Generals probably planned a little more than has been allowed to be known.

Thus, pursuant to his instructions, on 8th February Sheridan sent copies of his orders to Crook in Omaha and Terry in St. Paul. They were to begin preparations and commence their operations against the hostile Indians at their earliest opportunity. Their offensive was to concentrate in the general direction of the Powder, Tongue, Rosebud and Big Horn rivers and they were to thoroughly search every river, every valley and hill in their efforts to locate the hostiles. In compliance with Sheridan's orders, the troops stationed in the Platte region were to be mobilised at once, with General George Crook taking to the field himself. Why was it so important that Crook was to go on the offensive immediately? That is another question that is impossible to answer, but one that is important in the chronology of events that were to follow. The troops of the Department of the Missouri did not move however, giving the appalling climatic conditions as their excuse.

Heavy snow was not going to deter Crook from leading his command northwards, along the Bozeman Trail. Disregarding the falling snow and freezing temperatures, Crook left Fort Fetterman in Wyoming on 1st March. His command comprised of ten companies of cavalry and two companies of infantry, in addition to a number of civilian packers, teamsters, scouts and five newspaper correspondents. (Crook was a firm believer in publicity and had newspaper correspondents accompany him on the majority of his campaigns.)

On reaching the site of old Fort Reno, situated at the mouth of the Powder River in the south, he left the infantry companies and his supply wagons there to construct a base camp. Crook then advanced rapidly with his cavalry and scouts to the Tongue valley, where he rested his troops whilst sending his scouts forward to investigate the Rosebud valley. The scouts had been reliably informed that hostile Indians had made their winter camp along the Rosebud, but they found no signs to substantiate this and reported back to Crook. After some deliberation, Crook decided to continue his advance along the Tongue. The weather was extremely cold and his troops were suffering badly.

Not far from the Yellowstone River, Crook and his column discovered the remains of a large Indian village. It was much larger than he had been told to expect and Crook was inwardly startled at this discovery, but he did not show it. He halted the column and encamped, whilst his scouts continued their survey of the immediate area along the Yellowstone. On 15th March the scouts returned and informed Crook that they had found numerous signs of a large Indian village on the move. Its trail was leading towards the Powder River area. Crook was furious. He suddenly realised that he had been led round in a circle and now the hostile Indians were a threat to his supply wagons, which were guarded by just two companies of infantry. He only had himself to blame. With only one army column in the field, it was easy for the hostile Indians to watch its progress and manipulate the direction they wanted it to go. Crook had been under Indian surveillance almost from the day he left Fort Fetterman and advanced along the Bozeman Trail! The General lost no time in rectifying his mistake. He broke camp and began a rapid retreat towards the Powder. He hoped he would not be too late.

As Crook's command approached the Powder, hostile Indians could be observed in large numbers moving around the surrounding hills. They were watching the advance of the meandering column, estimating the number of troops and it was making the soldiers nervous. During the evening, the number of hostiles within the vicinity gradually increased, although they still kept their distance. Thus, Crook ordered his troops to rest for the night. Under the cover of darkness, Crook sent Colonel Joseph Reynolds and six companies of cavalry to locate and attack the hostile village that he was convinced lay nearby.

At dawn, on 17th March, Reynolds attacked an Indian village that he found not 16 kilometres from the Little Powder River. Reynolds had estimated that there were around 100 lodges in the village and he believed he had located the Ogallala village of Crazy Horse. Obviously, neither Reynolds nor anyone else in his command could tell the difference between Sioux Indians and the Cheyenne, for subsequent research suggests that the village was Cheyenne, whose chief was Old Bear. Even so, it was a typical military surprise attack, for the Indians were caught still asleep with no sentries to give a warning. Reynolds thought he had the upper hand.

Dividing his troops into two attacking forces, Reynolds sent Captain James Egan to charge the village in a frontal assault, while he attacked from the rear to cut off any escape route. Unbeknown to Reynolds, the Indians had been watching his movements and the hapless cavalry Colonel was being drawn into an ambush. It is difficult to understand why Crook sent Reynolds on this mission in the first place. If Crook had realised that their movements had been under constant surveillance for days, surely he was not naïve enough to consider that such observance would actually cease for the night.

In preparation, the Indian women and children had fled to the safety of the steep hills that overlooked the river, leaving the warriors to engage the troops in a rearguard action. When the soldiers began their attack, the hostile resistance was so fierce that Egan's troops were effectively repulsed and left without the immediate support of Reynolds, so they fell back. Reynolds sensed an impending disaster if nothing was done and done quick, so he ordered the village to be set on fire to enable his troops to withdraw under the cover of smoke. It was a desperate situation and the fighting was intense. Definitely not what the soldiers had expected. With around 700 captured Indian ponies, Reynolds managed to retreat to Lodgepole Creek, where he briefly halted to take care of the wounded. Unfortunately for Reynolds the hostiles managed to recapture the majority of their ponies during the remainder of the night, although they lost about 200 of them to Crook on the return journey.

Crook was furious with Reynolds. Normally stolid and taciturn by nature, Crook informed Reynolds that he had intended to make use of the Indian village to shelter his troops from the freezing weather and supplement their rations with dried meat from the hostiles' winter stores. The destruction of the village had made that impossible and Crook bitterly blamed Reynolds for this setback in his campaign. (It was a lame rebuke for most attacks on Indian villages resulted in the destruction of the stores and the removal of the ponies.) With his supplies running low and a large number of his soldiers suffering from frostbite, Crook had no option but to abandon his winter campaign and return to Fort Fetterman. A few hostiles followed Crook's retreating column and took advantage of every opportunity afforded them to recover the remainder of their ponies. This irritated Crook still further and he eventually ordered all the ponies destroyed. With little left to gain, the hostiles abandoned their harassment and Crook returned to the fort without any further confrontation. It was obvious to all that the failure of Crook's winter campaign would result in an all-out war.

His winter campaign at an end, Crook set about re-grouping his command and obtaining his much-needed supplies and reinforcements. He was still annoyed with Reynolds for the destruction of the Indian village and for allowing the Indians to escape, thus enabling them to recapture many of their ponies. In fact, Crook actually brought charges against Reynolds for his mismanagement in handling the Battle of the Powder River, claiming that Reynolds' failure resulted in the failure of the campaign as a whole. Reynolds retaliated by saying that the village had belonged to Crazy Horse (of which he had no proof,) and that he had dealt the Ogallala warrior a severe blow. (Actually, Crazy Horse had been camped a few kilometres away to the north-east and it was to his village that the survivors of Reynolds' attack had fled, seeking food and shelter.) Reynolds need not have worried too much about Crook's charge against him, for even Sheridan had recognised the true cause of the failed campaign as being due to the severe weather conditions. For his part, Crook never forgave Reynolds and continued to blame him to his dying day. It is blatantly obvious though, whatever the causes for the failure, the military failed to see that the hostiles were equally prepared to fight, as shown by the stubborn resistance they had put up against Reynolds. There appears to be no mention of this in the official reports.

April saw a lull in any offensive from either side. With Crook back within the confines of Fort Fetterman and with no other troop movements in the region, Sitting Bull saw his chance to take the initiative. Reynolds' attack had left no doubt in his mind as to the current policy the army had adopted. For once the whites were true to their word. They obviously meant every word in Smith's directive and all-out war between his people and the soldiers was destined for the very near future. As the harsh weather conditions gradually abated and the winter snow slowly thawed, Sitting Bull made full use of the army's inactivity. He sent messengers out to all the tribes still at liberty to join him on the Tongue for a council. The tribes readily responded and in early April Sitting Bull presided over the meeting.

Thousands of warriors were present, not just Sioux but also Arapaho and Cheyenne, all of which were angry and ready to fight. Sitting Bull outlined the army's policy as he saw it and ended his speech by firmly stating;

".......If the whites want war, I will give it to them!"

The warriors were ecstatic. It was all-out war and not before time. They had been waiting for this moment for years. Support from all who were present was guaranteed and Sitting Bull began to organise the preparations for the conflict. The magnanimity of this feat defies the imagination. For generations these tribes had waged wars on an independent footing, even against each other at times, and now they had united to share a common cause: the removal of the whites from their lands.

As well as Sitting Bull's own Hunkpapa Sioux, he had been joined by the Santee, Yanktonai, Blackfoot, Sans Arc, Minniconjou, Two Kettle, Brulé and the Ogallala, led by Crazy Horse. Others present at the council were the Arapaho, with the great Northern Cheyenne presently moving north to join them. By the time this immense force had moved to the valley of the Rosebud, it has been estimated that the whole encampment contained roughly 12,000 Indians, of whom at least 4,000 were seasoned warriors. Not a force to be taken lightly.

Throughout the winter of 1875/76 George Custer and his wife Elizabeth (affectionately known as 'Libby' by Custer,) were enjoying the highlights of New York on a long awaited vacation. Whilst there, Custer had met a very influential publisher by the name of James Gordon Bennett, who owned the 'New York Herald'. A curious friendship was formed between the two men, one that was to prove ultimately lethal for Custer. George Armstrong Custer was at the height of his popularity. He had been a national hero during the Civil War and now he was enjoying new-found fame as an Indian fighter. He had become a household name again and everyone plied for his favour. Bennett, on the other hand, was a shrewd businessman who not only had a keen interest in politics, but also the finances to back any likely candidate for the coming presidential election. He saw Custer as a man who could not fail to win.

The elections of 1876 were a stormy affair, reflecting the two terms of office that Grant had served. Being an ex-military officer, Grant should have had better judgement regarding the presidential appointments that he made. He did not and both terms of office were rocked by one scandal after another. Grant's Secretary of the Treasury was happily collecting taxes illegally and his new Vice President, Henry Wilson, had more than just his fingers in a scheme to defraud the government on railroad projects. The Credit Mobilier' railroad scandal was first publicised by the 'New York Sun', who also implicated the Attorney General and the Secretary of the Interior, as well as Grant himself. Huge amounts of money were flying around the corridors of power and many officials were getting extremely rich, with the exception of the armed services.

When he had first taken office at the White House, Grant had gathered his Civil War friends around him for support and they had stayed with him. William Tecumseh Sherman had been appointed the Commanding General of the Army (an office that would later be filled by Sheridan,) and Brigadier William Worth Belknap had accepted the post of Secretary of War. It was not a good working partnership, for both men hated each other and problems began to rise from the onset, many of which were to put a severe strain on Sherman's friendship with Grant. Belknap was an ambitious man and was not content with the position he held. He wanted complete control over all the military forces which, of course, Sherman was not prepared to concede. They had both been instructed that although the two offices were to work together, they would remain separate entities. Belknap had other ideas. He deliberately encroached into Sherman's domain, much to the latter's distaste. Orders were changed and appointments interfered with, all of which Belknap carried out not realising that Sherman knew everything about it. In July 1874, Sherman wrote to his brother:

> '.........my office has been by law stripped of all the influence and prestige it possessed under Grant, and even in matters of discipline and army control I am neglected, overlooked and snubbed. I have called Grant's attention to the fact several times, but got no satisfactory address.'

Nevertheless, Sherman did manage to combine his talents with those of his old friend, Phil Sheridan, and it was this partnership that conceived the majority of the decisions throughout the Indian Wars. With election fever running riot, journalists were predicting Sherman as the next President, but they could not have been more wrong. Sherman detested political life in Washington, moving his headquarters to St. Louis during the early stages of his appointment and even warned Grant against accepting the presidency. However, it is a known fact that friendships forged during the turmoil of war are long lasting, as Sherman and Sheridan were to prove during the shaky years of scandal that shook Grant's personal and political life.

Bennett suspected that even if Grant were to stand for a third term he would probably fail to succeed and even if on the odd chance that he did win, there was a strong possibility that he would not survive the term of office. (In actual fact, Grant was a broken man by this time. By 1876 his health had deteriorated and his finances were severely depleted. He really had no desire to serve again.) Bennett held the view that if Custer was interested in standing for the presidency, he was a much better proposition and he would have someone of his choice running the country. For the present, he would have to groom his protégé whilst at the same time ensure the downfall of the current administration. William Belknap was the key to the ruination of Grant and now Bennett's business acumen came into play. He believed that he had not only picked the right man in Custer, he had also chosen the right moment.

Sherman was not the only army officer to have crossed swords with Belknap, so had Custer not so many months ago and his encounter concerned the very scandal that Bennett was now exposing. During the summer of 1875, Custer had intervened in an argument between his troops and a civilian sutler at Fort Abraham Lincoln. The soldiers' complaint was that the post sutler, Robert C. Seip, was charging them much higher prices for the same items that could be purchased for less in Bismarck. Custer investigated the complaints and found that, not surprisingly, Seip's annual profit was in the region of $15,000. $3000 of which was his, with the remaining $12000 being sent to various individuals in the War Department. Custer asked Seip to lower his prices and when the trader refused, Custer instructed his officers to purchase any supplies needed in Bismarck and then re-sell them to the troopers at cost. Naturally, Seip became angry and he bitterly complained about Custer's actions to the Secretary of War, Belknap, who ordered Custer to stop the practice immediately. Angered at Belknap's response, Custer had no choice but to comply. However, he publicly accused Belknap of favouritism and accepting bribes from the dubious sutler's racket. This was the second time that Belknap had come under suspicion, a fact that not gone unnoticed by Bennett in New York. The first accusation had been made by Colonel William B. Hazen, who had angrily accused Belknap of being a corrupt politician. For his trouble, Hazen had been posted to the remote Fort Buford, situated in the middle of nowhere towards the north-west region. Custer, on the other hand, was a well-known figure across the country, a celebrity and, as such, a similar fate was out of the question.

At the end of the summer, Custer would again challenge the authority of the Secretary of State for War. When Belknap paid a visit to Fort Abraham Lincoln he was openly snubbed by Custer. There was no official welcome as there should have been and Custer refused to greet him, waiting for Belknap to enter his office instead. Seip sent some champagne across from his store, as his contribution for the reception. Custer duly returned it. Belknap was far from being amused. This impertinent post commander would pay dearly for these deliberate insults one day. Of course, these events had come to the attention of Bennett, who was quick to realise that Custer was the man he needed to spearhead his campaign. Custer, on the other hand, believing that Bennett was sincere in his friendship, was only too willing to fuel the scandal and thus, fell headlong into the wily publisher's scheme.

Bennett had played a leading role in numerous press attacks against Grant and his dubious administration. To him, Belknap was just another notch on the printing press. On the 10th February 1876, Bennett published an article in the 'New York Herald' implicating Belknap in possible discrepancies connected with post sutlerships. It was the foundation for a Congressional Committee Hearing at which Custer would testify. Custer had previously written lengthy protests to his superiors concerning the activities of post sutlers', which had not received any positive results. It was now time to join forces with Bennett in publishing his opinion on the irregularities, forgetting that he should have gathered positive proof before attacking those in higher positions. Except for his own experience with Seip, most of the accounts he would relate at the hearing was hearsay. Bennett paid no attention to that little flaw. He was jubilant with Custer's support and he continued to apply pressure on the shady politicians.

Congress set the hearing for the spring of 1876 and Custer, who had by this time returned to Fort Abraham Lincoln, was called to Washington to testify. With military operations against the hostile Indians set to begin as soon as the inclement weather eased, Custer would have preferred to remain with his regiment and oversee the preparations. Bearing this in mind, he wrote to the chairman of the Congressional Committee, Heister Clymer, enquiring if it was possible to give a written testimony and should any questions arise, whether he could answer them by mail. Considering the time delay this would cause, thus increasing the overall cost of the hearing, it is not surprising that Clymer refused. Custer reluctantly travelled to Washington to give his evidence.

In his eagerness to return to his regiment, Custer hurried his testimony and in doing so, sealed the fate of his military career. He testified that, to his knowledge, post traders on Indian reservations and frontier forts were paying 'back handers' from their high profits to ensure their positions. These payments were being made to a man called Hedrick, who just happened to be Belknap's brother-in-law. As if that was not enough, Custer accused Belknap himself of profiteering from army supplies that had to be re-channelled through various commercial companies the Secretary owned. Actually, Custer had very little evidence to support the last statement and although he must have known that he was treading on thin ice by now, he went one step further. Custer accused the President's own brother, Orvil Grant, of using his influence with the President to receive payments in lieu of this continued silence concerning the nefarious dealings!

Bennett was ecstatic. This was political dynamite! Belknap was stunned. Where had Custer got his information from? (It appears obvious that Belknap should have been more discreet if Custer's allegations were actually true. Belknap had invoked a law that had been passed in 1870, giving the Secretary of War the sole responsibility in appointing post-traderships, an act which in itself may have been relatively harmless, but would later serve as the foundation for the accusations.) President Grant was absolutely furious with Custer. Using his friendship with Sherman, he ordered Custer's immediate suspension from duties. Custer had been effectively castigated and he was forbidden to return to his regiment. The public, however, clamoured for more and the leading newspapers, including the 'New York Herald', readily complied. Custer was the champion for an honest government they cried, and Bennett led the charge, promoting his protégé at every opportunity. As far as Custer was concerned, he had given his testimony and that was the end of it. He either could not or would not see the campaign that Bennett had succeeded in accomplishing. His only concern was in returning to his regiment in time for the impending campaign against the hostiles. There he had a problem. Grant would not reverse his decision and he would not consent to an audience with the hapless commander either. Custer was stuck in Washington while his troops prepared for war.

By now, however, there had been a new twist to the unfolding saga. Sensing an impeachment on the horizon, Belknap resigned his appointment in an attempt to avoid the disgrace and he hoped that in doing so he would put an end to any further scandal. It did not. In fact, it was seen by many as an admission of guilt. Belknap was impeached on five accounts, the main charge being that he had promised to appoint Caleb P. Marsh of New York, to arrange and maintain trading posts at the forts within Indian territory. The charge also stated that Belknap would receive a certain amount of money for his favours. It is not specifically clear whether this sum of money was actually paid to Belknap or his wife, although there is no denying that the contract was actually entered into. What the evidence did show was that Marsh had appointed John B. Evans as his representative after he and Evans had entered into a written contract. Evans would pay Marsh an annual sum of money in proportion to the number of troops stationed at the forts. This contract was put into practice with the full knowledge and consent of Belknap, as Secretary of War, and, what was more damaging, that it was subsequently proved that Evans paid the monies to Marsh as agreed. Marsh, in turn, gave a larger portion of the monies to Belknap. What actually astounded so many people was the fact that this agreement had been going on from the 10th October 1870 until the 2nd March 1876. A total of 6 years without the conspirators being found out and that during that time Belknap had received a staggering $24,4450 from Marsh. Ironically, had Custer's letters that he had written over the years concerning just these irregularities, been given the attention they duly deserved, this shameful conduct would have been exposed much sooner.

Although clearly guilty of misusing his office, Belknap escaped conviction due to a technicality. Throughout the hearing, Belknap had been represented by Mathers Carpenter, Montgomery Blair and Judge Jeremiah Black. They pleaded that as Belknap had resigned his office as Secretary of War before the articles of impeachment had been drawn up, neither the Senate nor Congress

From this additional communication it is evident that Terry considered Grant's order to be based upon personal petulance rather than military protocol. A dangerous assumption for Terry to reveal during this period. However, Terry was not the only one to realise the truth. In the east, the newspapers had followed the unfolding events with great interest. In one leading journal the arrest of Custer was headed as 'Grant's Revenge', stating that Custer had given an honest testimony at the hearing, that his evidence had been upheld by others who had also testified and that Grant was misusing his power to wreak revenge. Actually, by now it did not make any difference what decision Grant made concerning Custer. His administration had been shaken to its very foundation and torn apart, and the presidency had been pulled down with it. Everyone knew that the officials were corrupt, even Grant's private secretary had been skimming the liquor taxes!

On 7th May, Sheridan received a dual communication from Custer and Terry. In accordance with military convention he forwarded them to Sherman, with an additional endorsement of his own:

> 'The following dispatch from General Terry is respectfully forwarded. I am sorry Lieutenant Colonel Custer did not manifest as much interest by staying at his post to organise and get ready his regiment and the expedition as he does now to accompany it. On a previous occasion in eighteen-sixty-eight I asked executive clemency for Colonel Custer to enable him to accompany his regiment against the Indians, and I sincerely hope if granted this time it will have sufficient effect to prevent him from again attempting to throw discredit on his profession and his brother officers.'

The very careful use of wording in this endorsement is interesting. In the first instance, Sheridan is admonishing Custer for not showing the same enthusiasm for his regiment when he left it to testify. Yet, as Departmental Commander, Sheridan would have been aware of Custer's reluctance to testify in person. The Colonel's letter to Clymer would have had to have passed through his office before reaching Clymer. Therefore, Sheridan knew that Custer had been ordered to Washington. But it is the last part of the endorsement that purports to encrypt a more sinister meaning when he wrote;

> '............and I sincerely hope if granted this time it will have sufficient effect to prevent him from again attempting to throw discredit on his profession and his brother officers.'

Sheridan would have been aware of the contents of the reports from the frontier posts, as well as those received from the agencies. Having known Custer since their Civil War days, Sheridan would also have been aware that Custer could be impetuous in the field. It was a known fact that Custer had recently committed a gross insubordination. The question was, could he be relied on to do it again? Sheridan was a close friend of both Grant and Sherman. Was this friendship above his military duty? In other words, was Sheridan suggesting that to allow Custer to accompany his regiment against the hostiles, was in some way an answer to Grant's prayer? Cryptic messages were not new in conspiracies, they had been used for thousands of years. But would Sherman get the message?

Sherman duly took the correspondence to Grant and what followed can only be reviewed as a matter of conjecture, for no positive proof of their discussion is forthcoming. What is known for certain is that the two old friends had a lengthy discussion behind closed doors, a discussion that lasted some hours. The question is, did Grant and Sherman read the same connotation in the last few lines of Sheridan's endorsement? The subsequent chronology of events suggest that they did. From the information the War Department has collected, not only from the Indian Bureau but their post commanders, they knew the vicinity in which the hostiles could be located. Their own forthcoming campaign had been based on that information. They were also aware that the number of hostiles at liberty was considerable, perhaps a few thousand or more, and they also knew that the hostiles were heavily armed and ready to fight. Custer could be the catalyst, if he followed to form, and that being so their scheme would work admirably.

It was a simple scheme and a brilliant one, yet it had been prompted by Sheridan's letter. Of course it is possible that Sheridan had discussed the matter with Sherman at an earlier date, in which case his letter was really asking for permission to put the scheme into operation. All they had to do was to allow Custer to accompany his regiment and if he were to be detached on his own once in hostile territory, the chances were that he would find the hostiles end engage them. If Custer were to emerge victorious, (a doubtful scenario,) then the Indian problem would be solved and Custer would remain on the frontier out of the way. Paperwork following an engagement would see to that, not to mention the 'mopping up operations'. However, if Custer were to be beaten or even killed, then he was out of the way forever and the Indians would be blamed for his demise. Either way, Custer would be dealt with and the Indians would be subdued. The gold in the Black Hills would be freely available to all and their problems, it seemed, could be solved with one stroke of the pen. It all depended on Custer remaining true to form and the odds were that he would.

Grant and Sherman could only see one flaw in the plan and that was the newspaper reporters. Custer was still very friendly with Bennett and he was sure to invite newspaper reporters along on such an important campaign. Grant had suffered enough adverse publicity at the hands of newspaper reporters of late and he had had enough. They decided to specifically instruct the commanders that under no circumstances were any reporters to be allowed to accompany the troops in the field. On 8th May, Sherman wrote to Terry in St. Paul:

> 'The dispatch of General Sheridan enclosing yours of yesterday toughing General Custer's urgent request to go under your command with his regiment has been submitted to the President who sends me word that if you want General Custer along he withdraws his objections. Advise Custer to be prudent and not to take along any newspaper men who always work mischief, and to abstain from any personalities in the future. Tell him to confine his whole mind to his legitimate office, and trust to time. That newspaper paragraph in the 'New York Herald 'of May 2nd compromised his best friends here, and almost deprived us of the ability to serve him.'

It is interesting that Sherman made no mention of the letter he had also received from Sheridan. It appears that Sherman obviously regarded Sheridan's letter confidential or he may have felt that Terry could not be directly included in the conspiracy as he would never deviate from his military duty.

In any event, Terry passed Sherman's telegraphed message to Custer, who had eagerly awaited a reply. Custer was jubilant and immediately left for Fort Abraham Lincoln, his beloved regiment and his date with destiny.

Chapter 2

A Gathering of Forces

Major-General Philip Henry Sheridan, military commander of the Missouri, was 45 years old in 1876 and a seasoned warhorse. He had been born in Albany, New York, of Irish parents and when he graduated from West Point in 1853, he had amassed quite a number of disciplinary actions, as his academy records reveal. During the Civil War he had risen rapidly through the ranks, being promoted to Brigadier-General in 1863 and Major-General by the end of the war. Like Sherman, he had served under Grant during the hostilities and it was during this time that all three had established a strong, long lasting friendship.

It is interesting to note that George Custer had been one of Sheridan's most trusted division commanders, securing numerous victories from the battles he fought. So much so, that following Lee's surrender at Appomattox, Sheridan threw down $20 in gold for the small pine table on which Grant had prepared the surrender document and gave it to Custer as a present for his wife:

> 'I respectfully present to you the small writing table on which the conditions for the surrender of the Army of Northern Virginia were written by Lt. General Grant-and permit me to say, Madam, that there is scarcely an individual in our service who has contributed more to bring about this desirable result than your gallant husband.'

A reward for service was one thing, but Sheridan's views on Custer do not seem to have elevated to sincere friendship.

Contemporary accounts describe Sheridan as very short, (he was only 1:52 metres in height) and stout, with abnormally long arms and a massive oddly shaped head, the latter being a problem when having to wear a hat. He had dark piercing eyes and a thick black moustache that rarely revealed a smile, although whilst in Chicago he did enjoy the social life it afforded him. He could be extremely witty and convivial at the gatherings, even though his barrack-room language often let him down and left the ladies swooning in shock. However, swearing came natural to Sheridan, especially when he was annoyed.

His brilliance as a commander in the field was often overshadowed by his frigid, and at times hostile, attitude towards his subordinate officers. When irritated he would fly into intense rages, being quick to censure but slow to forgive, making his victim suffer prolonged discrimination, as Colonel Hazen discovered to his chagrin.

His friendship with Grant and Sherman ran deep and if the President had been offended by Custer's testimony, then so had he. Custer's experience in dealing with Indians may have been beyond reproach but his insubordination was not. Grant and Sherman relied heavily upon Sheridan's expertise during the Indian Wars. His strategy had been sound these past few years and so had his tactics, even if they were a little unorthodox. Working with his commanders in the field, Sheridan believed he knew Indian warfare well and that he could surmount any problems the frontier posed. Hard on his troops, Sheridan showed little or no regard for Indians at all, if indeed he ever had any thoughts concerning them, contemptuously stating;

> "It is absurd to talk of keeping faith with Indians."

Sheridan's directive, issued on 8th February 1876, had not produced the results he had wanted and he was furious. Terry had not moved his troops at all, giving the adverse weather conditions as his excuse and even though Crook had taken to the field, he had been forced to abandon his campaign, again due to the inclement weather. Sheridan firmly believed his commanders had failed to do their duty, letting him down, which did little to subdue his temper. Knowing the nomadic character of the Indians, he knew they would have to act swiftly and take them by surprise,

> "…….unless they can be caught before the early spring, they cannot be caught at all!"

If Custer were to engage them, it had to be soon. Sheridan blamed Crook for the Powder River disaster and Crook, in turn, blamed Reynolds. It did not matter who was at fault. What did matter was the fact that the hostile Indians now knew the soldiers were moving against them and they would be ready when contact was made. Sheridan must have realised this and, together with the reports he had, he must also have been aware that Custer's chances of a victory were pretty slim. It was obvious to all that the Plains Indians had a renewed will to stand and fight, plus a growing determination to win. Of course, the Indians could not possibly hope to win in the long run, but if they dealt with Custer in the meantime, Sheridan would allow them their day of victory. Equally, Reynolds' retreat had shown that the soldiers could be beaten, giving the hostiles added confidence in their attitude to wage a more aggressive war, especially on the own ground.

Sheridan does appear to have overlooked the fact that Colonel John Gibbon had complied with the February directive. On the same day that Reynolds attacked the Indian village, 5 companies of infantry left Fort Shaw and braved the appalling weather to march 294.5 kilometres to Fort Ellis in the south of Montana. Simultaneously, another company of infantry left Camp Baker and literally dug its way through deep snow drifts to reach the same fort, where Gibbon was stationed. All of these soldiers reached Fort Ellis towards the end of March amidst the most terrible snow storms imaginable and they were foot soldiers! Knowing Crook was already in the field, it was decided to keep the infantry on the move heading towards the General. On 1st April, Gibbon left Fort Ellis with 4 companies of the 2nd Cavalry. He had assumed that the cavalry would quickly catch up with the infantry and overtake them. The trails proved heavy going, being intersected by streams and awash with mud. Wagons became bogged down and horses slid on the slippery stones. It took the column four days to reach Shield's River, a distance of only 45 kilometres, during which time they had been hit by furious winds that whipped up the drifting snow. The troopers were cold, wet and tired. By now Gibbon had received news of Crook's fight and fearing the hostiles would flee north (as it was generally assumed they would), it now became imperative that his troops were in position to intercept them. Thus, Gibbon continued to march along the Yellowstone, following the north bank as ordered. On 21st April, Gibbon's column reached Tullock Creek where, according to Terry's orders, the troops remained in camp until the 9th May. It was a remarkable feat of endurance, a fact that is often overlooked.

Sheridan's professionalism may have been clouded by Grant's personal problems with Custer and it may have alluded to his decisions being made in haste. He was already angry with Crook and Terry, now he had the added responsibility of ensuring that Custer, as one of his subordinate officers, was dealt with. If the overall plan was to succeed, he would have to ensure that his field commanders, Crook and Terry, were given careful instructions, a precept that would have to be adhered to explicitly and one that was so ambiguous as to leave himself in the clear should there ever be an enquiry. Grant and Sherman had both placed their trust in him and he was determined not to let them down. In getting Custer restored to his regiment, Sheridan had completed the first phase of the plan. Now he had to ensure that Crook and Terry fulfilled their duty and followed his orders, although they would not be privileged to know why. History has recorded Sheridan's plan for the summer campaign, but it is how he actually wrote the orders to Crook and Terry that counts and these specific orders are not available to be scrutinised. The evidence has been cleverly concealed, leaving much to conjecture.

Sheridan's plan was a three-pronged attack that would eventually converge on the last known location of hostile activity, the valley of the Little Big Horn River. Brigadier-General George Crook would lead a column from Fort Fetterman, in Wyoming, with the purpose of driving the Indians towards the north. (This manoeuvre was based on the assumption that the Indians would turn and run, rather than confront such a large concentration of troops.) Brigadier-General Alfred Terry, who had never actually fought Indians before, would lead his troops west from Fort Abraham Lincoln, in Dakota, to trap the enemy between himself and Crook. Colonel John Gibbon was ordered to march his column from Fort Ellis, in Montana, along the Yellowstone to stop any hostiles from fleeing north, possibly over the border into Canada. (Had Sheridan read his commander's reports, he would have known that Gibbon was already in position. Obviously he had not.) To the eyes of the casual observer, the basic outline of the campaign appears sound, however, it also reveals that Sheridan, at least, knew exactly where the hostiles could be found. (He had read some reports then!)

While the soldiers mobilised in the north and Sheridan flashed his orders over the telegraph, the hostile Indians had also been busy. The Ogallala Sioux, under the leadership of Crazy Horse, and the Northern Cheyenne had arrived at Sitting Bull's camp that lay to the east of Gibbon's troops at Chalk Butte. As Gibbon settled his troops into camp at Tullock Creek, the hostiles moved west and established a new camp at the mouth of Sheep Creek. Whilst they were there, news of Crook's attack on the Powder River reached them and the word quickly spread to other villages in the vicinity. On 20th April, Spotted Eagle arrived at the camp with his Sans Arc and by 26th April the whole encampment, by now becoming seriously large, had moved to the Powder River area where they were joined by the Santee Sioux. By 5th May the hostiles had moved yet again. This time to the Tongue, where they were joined by Kill Eagle and his Blackfoot Sioux. It was a very formidable gathering of the tribes and they all meant business. However, for the present, Sheridan was right. The hostiles were continuously moving across the region and it would prove fairly difficult to track them down very quickly.

Gibbon had not been idle either. While his troops camped at the mouth of Tullock Creek, he sent out regular patrols in an effort to locate the Indians, all of which had resulted in little success. On the other hand, the hostiles did find him and for the next 3 weeks the unlucky Colonel suffered continuous harassment from the aggressively resolute warriors, although no actual hand-to-hand fighting actually occurred. On 27th May, Gibbon sent a report to Terry informing him that although his patrols had sighted a few war parties, they had not been successful in locating any enemy villages. In actual fact, Gibbon failed to give Terry an accurate report of the situation, for his own account of the events states that the area was literally infested with Indians, which in retrospect, was probably true.

At Fort Abraham Lincoln, preparations for the impending campaign were almost complete. As the Seventh Cavalry enjoyed the warmth of their barracks, the remainder of Terry's forces had been brought together and were now braving the weather under canvas at Cannon Ball Creek, a few kilometres away. On 14th May Terry had issued the first of his field orders, designating his staff:

> 'The Department Commander hereby assumes, in person, the command of the force organised for field operations. The following named officers will act upon the staff:
>
> Captain E.W. Smith, Acting Assistant Adjutant General.
> Assistant Surgeon J.W. Williams, Chief Medical Officer.
> Captain O.E. Michaelis, Ordnance Officer.
> First Lieutenant H.J. Nowlan, Seventh Cavalry Quartermaster.
> First Lieutenant Edward Maguire, Corps of Engineers.
> Lieutenant Nowlan will discharge his duties upon the staff of the Department Commander in addition to those of Regimental Quartermaster.
> The Indian scouts will report to Lieutenant-Colonel Custer, Seventh Cavalry, for duty with his regiment.
> All interpreters, guides and other civil employees in the pay of the Quartermaster's Department will report to Lieutenant H.J. Nowlan, Quartermaster of the forces in the field, to be by him assigned to duty under the direction of the Department Commander.'

The logistics of supplying Terry's column were horrendous and by the time his forces were ready to move out, the wagon train consisted of 114 six-mule teams, 37 two-mule teams and 35 pack mules! Nonetheless, all was ready by 17th May and Terry gave the order for the column to depart for the Yellowstone. At 5 o'clock in the morning, a bugle call spurred the troops to make ready to move and by 7 o'clock, the Seventh Cavalry were mounted and passing in review around the parade ground of Fort Abraham Lincoln to the tune of 'Garryowen'. Their smart, formidable appearance and general air of confidence was intended to ease the anxieties of those loved ones who had to stay behind. Despite this impressive show of bravado, many wives could not bring themselves to venture out of their quarters to wave farewell. Those who did could not hold back the tears as their loved ones proudly rode past. For many it would be the last parade. As the troops rode past the Indian quarters, the old men and squaws, some kneeling on the ground, sang age old lamentations to their departing warriors, the intrepid scouts.

The band, all mounted on grey horses, struck up 'The Girl I Left Behind Me' and the Seventh Cavalry passed through the gates. (Some accounts say the band was mounted on white horses, which may be correct, but white horses were not in abundance on the frontier, so they were probably a collection of varying greys.) Elizabeth Custer, together with her sister-in-law, Mrs Margaret Calhoun, accompanied the regiment as they departed. Custer had allowed them to ride with the column on the first day's march, which would be as far as the Little Heart River, where the regiment would make their first camp. As the column meandered across the sprawling prairie, a strange opaque mist descended giving the troops a surreal appearance. As the mist lifted, the early morning sun broke through creating a magnificent rainbow and as it rose higher into the sky, the mist seemed to mirror the troops above them as they wound their way west. This incredible mirage appeared to envelop half the column of cavalry and to some it was a genuine premonition of an impending disaster, one of whom was Elizabeth Custer, who later wrote:

> 'As the sun broke through the mist a mirage appeared, which took up about half of the line of cavalry, and thenceforth for a little distance it marched equally plain to the sight on the earth and in the sky.'

This peculiar phenomenon was observed by many on the march that day, including newspaper reporter Mark Kellogg, who wrote of Custer;

> 'A man respected and beloved by his followers, who would freely follow him into the jaws of Hell!'

Little did Kellogg know, that was exactly where they were heading!

Contrary to Sherman's explicit order not to allow any newspaper men to accompany him on this campaign, Custer had allowed Mark Kellogg to do so. Perhaps Custer believed that as Kellogg was not a professional reporter, Sherman's order did not apply to him. At 40 years old, Kellogg had a youthful appearance, although his hair was starting to turn grey. A former telegrapher, Kellogg was employed in a Bismarck law office, during which time he had written a few articles that had been published in the 'Bismarck Tribune'. Thus, when the 'Tribune's' editor, C.A. Loundsberry, declined to accompany the expedition (for reasons unknown,) he had suggested that Kellogg found himself in Terry's column as an unofficial reporter for the 'Bismarck Tribune'.

By early afternoon Terry's column had reached the Little Heart River, some 20 kilometres from Fort Abraham Lincoln. Once across, the troops made camp and during the evening the regimental paymaster made his disbursements to the soldiers, so that any outstanding debts could be settled between them. The following morning Elizabeth Custer and Margaret Calhoun left their husbands and returned to the fort, accompanied by the paymaster. It was their last farewell. As he watched the ladies depart Custer turned to his orderly, John Burkman, and remarked'

> "A good soldier has two mistresses. While he is loyal to one, the other must suffer."

For the march Custer had divided the regiment into two battalions, officially designated as the right and left wings. Major Marcus Reno was placed in command of the right wing, with Captain Frederick Benteen commanding the left. However, progress towards the Yellowstone was laboriously slow due to the unaccommodating terrain over which they were travelling. The huge wagon train could not make some of the river crossings or pass through the smaller gullies and alternative routes had to be found on numerous occasions, thus making the march longer and far more strenuous than it might have been. By the time the column had reached the Little Muddy on 20th May, they had only covered a distance of 37 kilometres. Grazing was scarce, although there was plenty of water available, and it was certainly not the kind of country that anyone would have wished to be alone in. Custer appeared to thrive on the hardship and thought that everyone else should too, but the march was beginning to take its toll on the men. Already three soldiers had been excused duty and were riding in ambulances, and two mules had been lost. By 23rd May they had reached Young Men's Buttes, after covering a distance of only 12 kilometres that morning. Knowing they would have a much longer march the following day and the grazing there was good, Custer ordered them to make camp and take advantage of the rest. For many it was a welcome relief. The next day they covered a distance of 30 kilometres and during the evening the first rations were issued to everyone. Thus it was, in a steady march the winding column gradually edged towards the west until, by 29th May they had entered the 'Badlands', an area of which General Sully had spoken of in 1864;

> "Gentlemen, it looks like the bottom of Hell, with the fires out!"

That same day, 29th May, Sheridan wrote to Sherman:

> 'Brigadier-General Terry moved out his command from Fort Abraham Lincoln in the direction of the mouth of the Powder River

> on the 17th instant. The total strength of his column is about nine hundred men exclusive of a force of three companies in charge of the supply camp at Glendive Creek, the old supply station on the Yellowstone. Brigadier-General Crook will move from Fort Fetterman with a column about the same in size. Colonel John Gibbon is now moving down north of the Yellowstone and east of the mouth of the Big Horn with a force of about four hundred, all but four companies of which are infantry.
>
> As no very accurate information can be obtained as to the location of the hostile Indians, and as there would be no telling how long they would stay in one place if it were known, I have given instructions to Generals Crook and Terry, preferring that they should do the best they can under the circumstances, as I think it would be unwise to make any combinations in such a country as they will have to operate in, as hostile Indians in any great numbers, cannot keep the field as a body for a week, or at most ten days.
>
> I therefore consider, and do Terry and Crook, that each column should be able to take care of itself, and to chastise the Indians, should it have the opportunity. I presume the following will occur. General Terry will drive the Indians towards the Big Horn valley and General Crook will drive them back towards Terry; Colonel Gibbon moving down on the north side of the Yellowstone, to intercept if possible such as may want to go north of the Missouri to Milk River. The result of the movements of these three columns may force the hostile Indians back to the agencies on the Missouri River to Red Cloud and Spotted Tail agencies.'

In other words, after outlining the basic plan of operations, Sheridan is giving Crook and Terry a free hand in the field and by informing Sherman of this decision he is absolving himself of all consequences should the campaign produce any adverse results. However, subsequent actions on the parts of Crook and Terry do strongly suggest that these commanders also received orders from Sheridan, which were either destroyed or lost over time. On the same day that Sheridan wrote to Sherman, Crook left Fort Fetterman with his troops and began his march northwards.

The weather had not been kind to Terry's column as it pushed on towards the Yellowstone. The troops had had to endure strong winds, intermittent rain and even the occasional thunder storms, with the annoying result that for the first two days of June the entire column was confined to camp due to snow storms! This was hardly spring weather and the soldiers became despondent. On 3rd June, Terry received the report that Gibbon had sent on 27th May and he used the same riders to return with his reply. Taking advantage of a slight break in the weather to press on, Terry's column covered a further 40 kilometres that day before making camp at Beaver Creek.

Having received no further word from Gibbon by the 8th June, Terry rode ahead of this column in an effort to locate him, leaving Custer in command. Unbeknown to Terry, the dispatches he had sent to Gibbon had never arrived due to the increased activities of the hostile Indians, who were now believed to have concentrated around the Powder or Tongue rivers. Terry had previously arranged for the steamers 'Far West' and 'Josephine' to carry their much-needed supplies to the mouth of the powder and so his column marched on, making camp much later that day. Terry had not been successful in finding Gibbon and felt some concern. Once again, continuous rain impeded any progress the following day, so Terry took the opportunity to travel up the Yellowstone on the 'Far West', this time successfully finding Gibbon and returning later that evening. Colonel Gibbon later wrote of his meeting with Terry:

> 'The existence of any large camps of hostile Indians in this region was now more than ever a matter of doubt; for General Terry had discovered no traces of any on his march from Fort Lincoln to the Powder river, which he had reached at a point twenty-five miles [approximately 40 kilometres] above its mouth.
>
> He informed me that he had heard nothing from General Crook, and he intended on his return to Powder river to send a cavalry command on a scout up that river and across it west to the Tongue and Rosebud. If no Indians should be discovered then the only remaining chance would be higher up the Yellowstone, where from my observation there must be some Indians, and if General Crook should strike them from the south, it would be all the more necessary for us to guard the line of the river and prevent any escape northward.
>
> He therefore instructed me to retrace my steps and await his arrival at the mouth of the Rosebud, and as dispatch was now of more importance than ever I agreed to start the cavalry part of my command that afternoon.'

On 10th June, Terry issued special field orders, number eleven, to Major Reno:

1) The Quartermaster of the expedition is hereby ordered to purchase, for public use, two Mackinac boats, at a price not to exceed twenty-five dollars a piece.

2) Major M.A. Reno, Seventh Cavalry, with six companies (the right wing) of his regiment, and one gun from the Gatling battery, will proceed, at the earliest practical moment to make a reconnaissance of the Powder river from the present camp to the mouth of the Little Powder. From the last named point he will cross to the headwaters of Mizpah Creek and descend that creek to its junction with the Powder river; thence he will cross the Pumpkin Creek and Tongue river to its junction with the Yellowstone-where he may expect to meet the remaining companies of the Seventh Cavalry and supplies of subsistence and forage.

Major Reno's command will be supplied with sustenance for twelve days, and with forage for the same period, at the rate of two pounds of grain per day for each animal. The guide, Mitch Bouyer, and eight Indian scouts, to be detailed by Lieutenant Colonel Custer, will report to Major Reno for duty with his column. Acting Assistant Surgeon J.E. Porter is detailed for duty with Major Reno.'

Of course, in dictating these orders to his adjutant, Captain E.W. Smith of the 18th Infantry, Terry must have accepted the fact that mistakes were bound to occur. First Lieutenant James E. Porter was an officer serving Company I, Seventh Cavalry, under Captain Myles Keogh, and not a surgeon. The correct name of the Acting Assistant Surgeon to whom Terry refers was Henry R. Porter, which Terry and his adjutant should have known.

In accordance with Terry's orders, Reno left with Companies B, C, E, F, I and L to scout the Powder and Tongue areas. His eight Indian scouts comprised of:

Arikara	Forked tongue
	One Feather
	Young Hawk
	Tall Bear
Sioux	Bear Waiting
	Buffalo Ancestor
	Caroo
	White Cloud

The reasons for Terry selecting Reno to command the scouting patrol rather than Custer, are not clear. Some historians have speculated that it was a chance for Terry to exercise his authority over Custer, while others believe that Terry needed Custer to maintain discipline within the column. It is more likely that Terry felt fairly sure that Reno would not run into any serious trouble with the hostiles this far north and, possibly acting on Sheridan's instructions, he was saving Custer for the fight he knew would eventually materialise. Whatever the reason, Terry did not expound upon his decision and Custer could only stand and watch as Reno departed, no doubt furious at being left behind.

A few days earlier, on or around 5th June (the exact date is unknown), the Sioux and Cheyenne held their annual 'Sun Dance'. By now the hostile tribes had encamped along the northern reaches of the Rosebud, where they would remain for the next few days. During the ritual, Sitting Bull sacrificed no less than 50 pieces of his flesh before lapsing into a spiritual trance. At 45 years old, this Hunkpapa Sioux had long relinquished his status as a distinguished warrior and was now a much respected prophet, although many also regarded him as a divine revealer or tribal teacher. When Sitting Bull regained consciousness he told everyone of his vision; of seeing many soldiers falling into his village upside-down. Of course the younger warriors took this as a spiritual prophecy; that Sitting Bull was assuring them of a great victory over the white soldiers. After all, had not some of them already beaten the soldiers in a fight earlier that year? Older warriors welcomed the vision as well but knew that such a victory would not be won easily. Word of Sitting Bull's vision spread rapidly through the region and as the huge camp slowly moved along the Rosebud, more Indians joined the cause, believing in Sitting Bull's great 'medicine'. The Indian agents based on the reservations had no way of knowing just how powerful Sitting Bull's influence over the many hostile tribes really was. They certainly had no way of knowing how many eager young bucks had gathered around him. Later reports would estimate no fewer than at least 4,000 seasoned warriors alone!

As Reno and his command disappeared from view down the Powder valley, Terry marched his remaining troops along the Yellowstone to where he and Gibbon would establish a supply camp, arriving on 11th June. The following day, the steamer 'Far West' arrived and the much-needed supplies were unloaded. Captain Grant Marsh then took his steamer back along the river to collect more supplies, returning to Terry's camp a few days later. Being of senior rank, Terry now took command of Gibbon's forces as well and determined to conduct his field operations from this point. (This change in command was not detailed in Sheridan's basic plan of operations, at least not the one that has survived, and we will never know if these changes made any direct impact on the final result.)

At first Reno meticulously followed his orders, travelling south along the Powder river and then turning north along the Mizpah and Pumpkin Creeks. He found no sign of any hostile Indians and the patrol was rapidly developing into a tedious extension of their previous march with Terry's column. Therefore,

Reno decided to deviate from his orders and swing northwards again to investigate reports of a large deserted Indian camp on the Tongue. On arrival at the site, Reno was amazed at what he saw. Together with Mitch Bouyer, he counted over 400 abandoned tipi sites. This was obviously no ordinary Indian village. His Arikara scouts also discovered the trail the hostiles had taken in their move towards the Rosebud. After he had sent a dispatch to Terry informing the General of his find, Reno disobeyed orders yet again and led his patrol to follow the trail along Rosebud Creek. As he advanced he found more

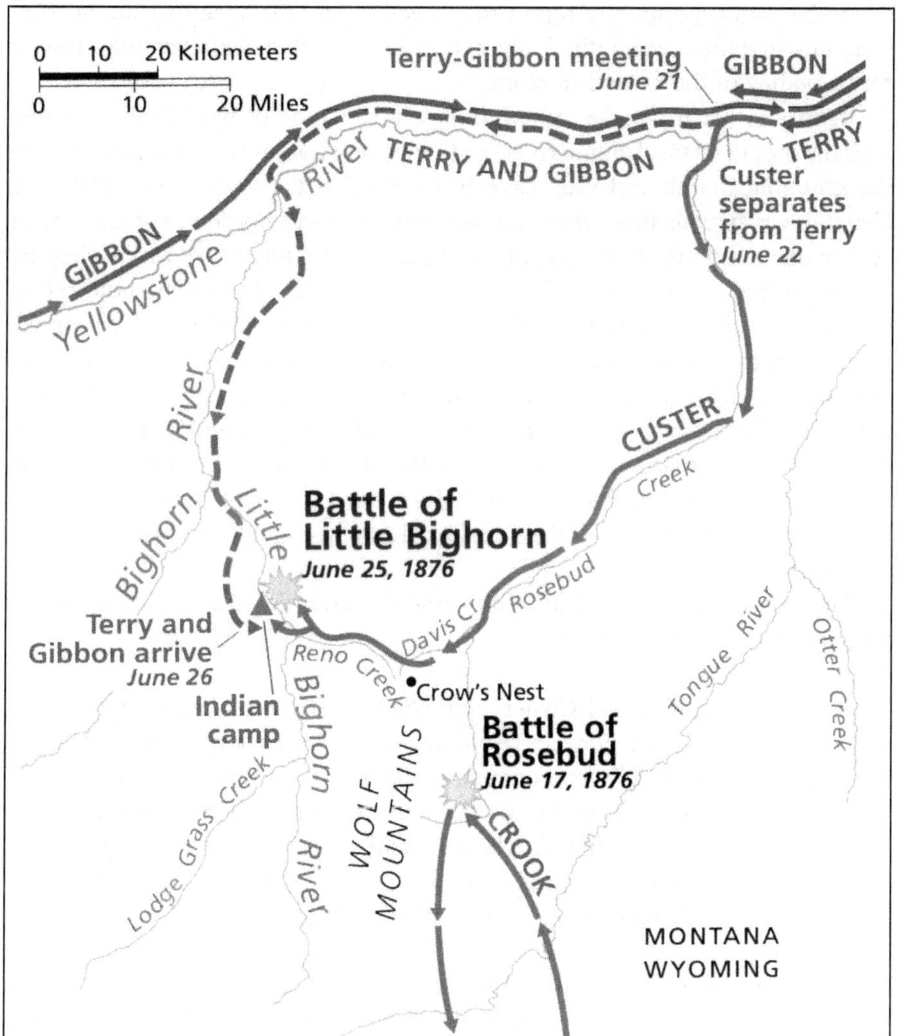

Military Campaigns of 1876. (Kind courtesy of the National Park Service)

signs of Indian habitation, each discovery being more recent than the last and he sent his scouts on ahead to follow the trail. The scouts followed the signs towards the Rosebud for about 32 kilometres before they turned back to report to Reno. Had they but known it, they were only a day's march behind the moving hostiles and they were extremely lucky not to have been discovered themselves. In actual fact, on 17th June, Reno was only 64 kilometres away from Crook's fight with Crazy Horse at the southern end of the Rosebud! If Reno had continued his patrol along the Rosebud he would probably have been caught up in the battle. However, he turned back towards the Yellowstone where he would accurately report the direction and distance that the hostiles were moving; there was little doubt in his mind that they were heading straight for the valley of the Little Big Horn.

Reno and his troops re-joined Terry on 19th June at the General's camp near the mouth of the Tongue river. Both men and horses were exhausted from the gruelling march and they eagerly revelled in the well-earned rest. The General was furious that Reno had blatantly disobeyed orders, but his temper cooled on reading Reno's report. Reno offered Terry no excuse for disobeying his orders and Terry took no further action. After all, Reno's splendid report concurred with the reports of Gibbon's scouts, who had observed smoke from large fires in the direction of the Little Big Horn. But the major was not aware of that. It was obvious to all that there were no hostile Indians in their immediate vicinity, a conclusion that must have produced a sigh of relief from Terry. It was also clear that they could now narrow the search to specific areas that included the Rosebud, Big Horn and Little Big Horn rivers. They had the troops and they had the supplies. Terry just had to be careful how he used them.

The following day, 20th June, Terry issued Custer the first of his orders that would open up the campaign:

> 'Lieutenant-Colonel Custer, commanding Seventh Cavalry, will proceed without unnecessary delay, with the Headquarters and six companies of his regiment, the Indian scouts, and the Gatling battery now at his camp, to the point occupied by the camp of Major Reno's command, where he will assume command of the force there assembled, and tomorrow proceed with it to the mouth of the Rosebud river, where he will await further orders.'

It appears from this order that Terry is placing Custer in position without disclosing the purpose. Of course, it could be that Terry is only re-uniting the regiment, but it does look as if Custer is being deliberately manoeuvred like a knight on a chessboard. Custer duly followed his orders without question and crossed the Tongue to join with Reno and assume command. After receiving supplies from the 'Far West', Custer then marched his regiment to the Rosebud where Gibbon was now waiting. Terry arrived at the Rosebud on 21st June and called a meeting of his officers aboard the 'Far West' that evening. Those who attended the conference included Colonel Gibbon, Major Brisbane (commanding officer of Gibbon's cavalry,) Terry and his staff officers, and Lieutenant-Colonel George Custer. A few hours later prior to the conference, Terry had sent a preliminary report to Sheridan, which ended with;

> '..........I only hope that one of the two columns will find the Indians. I go personally with Gibbon'

It is not clear whether this final phrase refers to Crook or Custer, bearing in mind that Terry had still received no word from Crook. However, from his subsequent actions and surviving documents, it does appear that Terry was not too enthusiastic on encountering the Indians himself, so it may be assumed that Terry was referring to Crook and Custer. That being so, he had placed Custer in command of a column on his own, contrary to his statement to Sherman on 6th May. Or was he simply following Sheridan's orders?

The conference lasted some hours. In fact, Custer did not emerge from the steamer until after sundown. He appeared to be depressed and, as the conference has not been fully documented, it is not clear why. Gibbon later wrote a brief explanation of the conference:

> '..........led to the belief that the Indians, if overtaken at all, would be found somewhere on the Little Big Horn.
>
> ....It was therefore arranged that General Custer should start the next day with the whole of his regiment, take up the trail of the Rosebud, and follow it; that my command should march to the mouth of the Big Horn
>
> ....there to be ferried across the Yellowstone, and march from there to the valley of the Little Big Horn and up that stream to co-operate with Custer's command.
>
> An examination of the map showed that the course of the Rosebud approaches that of the Little Big Horn nearest the point about as far distant from where we then were as the mouth of the Big Horn was from us. Were then Custer, whose command was exclusively of cavalry, marching with pack mules, to follow the trail directly into the valley of the Little Big Horn, he would probably strike the Indians long before I could be anywhere in the vicinity with my command, part of which was infantry............'

Gibbon is clearly sceptical concerning the plan of operations. He knew that as it stood he would not be able to support Custer if he ran into trouble. Custer was well aware of this too. More importantly, it is conclusive evidence that the military knew where the Indians were to be found and that Custer was being deliberately placed in an unacceptable position.

Custer was accompanied to his tent by Terry and Gibbon, where a further discussion took place. It is possible that Custer could see the dangers of the plan, after all Gibbon could. Did these two commanders try to dissuade Terry from his plan of action? If so, they did not succeed. Terry confirmed his displacement of Gibbon's troops and added that from now on he would be directing the campaign from the 'Far West'. Was Terry more wary of his superior officers than his subordinates?

Once Custer and Gibbon had begun mobilising their forces, Terry would navigate the steamer as far down the Big Horn as possible, hopefully to where it converged with the Little Big Horn and await their arrivals. Taking into consideration that Terry was fully conversant with all the reports so far gathered, including Reno's, that not only detailed the correct direction of the Indian movement but also the alarming prediction of the size of the village, it seems strange that he would split his command in such a manner unless he had been ordered to do so. Gibbon was not expected to engage the Indians during his march, but Custer clearly was. Terry knew that Crook was in the field, but having no communication with him, the General's actual whereabouts was unknown. With such a large concentration of hostiles between Crook and Terry, it was not impossible for the two Generals to communicate with each other but it was somewhat difficult. The point is it appeared that neither tried to do so. Crook could not be relied upon to support the two columns, a fact that Terry must have known. It is evident then, that Terry was working to another plan. Perhaps one that Sheridan gave him in confidence should the location of the hostiles prove favourable. What is certain is the fact that Terry's plan gave no thought for the safety of the troops he was sending into the field and he was adamant that the plan would be adhered to.

Once Terry and Gibbon had left, Custer ordered 'Officer's Call'. Having assembled, Custer briefed them on Terry's orders for the march. Each man was to be supplied with 100 rounds of carbine ammunition and 24 rounds of pistol ammunition, which was to be carried on his person and in his saddle-bags, along with 5.5 kilogrammes of oats for his horse. The pack-mules were to be loaded with 15 days rations of hard bread, coffee and sugar; 12 days rations of bacon; and 50 extra rounds of carbine ammunition per man. In conclusion, Custer recommended that the addition of some extra forage should be considered to be carried by the pack-mules. The majority of the pack-mules had only just returned with Reno and they were not in much of a condition to undertake another march of this scale. Captain Moylan, commanding officer of Company A, and Captain Godfrey, the officer commanding Company K, explained the plight of the mules to which Custer replied:

> "Well, gentlemen, you may carry what supplies you please; you will be held responsible for your companies. The extra forage was only a suggestion, but this fact bear in mind, we will follow the trail for fifteen days unless we catch them before that time expires, no matter how far it may take us from our base of supplies; we may not see the supply steamer again."

Custer moved towards the entrance of his tent, then turned to face his officers, adding,

> "You had better carry along an extra supply of salt; we may have to live on horsemeat before we get through."

It is obvious that Custer was disconcerted regarding his orders. Perhaps he felt an air of disaster swirling around him. We will never know, although the answer is now history.

The meeting over, Custer's officers left to instruct their companies for the march in the morning. Preparations had to be made and supplies procured. It was already evident that all ranks in the Seventh Cavalry felt uneasy at Terry's orders. Those who were able to write, wrote letters to their wives and families, giving them detailed instructions as to their personal property should anything happen to them. There seemed to be an aura of impending doom settling over the camp. The jaunty air of confidence appeared to drain into the night. For the rank and file this was normal when they were about to march against the Indians, but this time the officers could sense something was not right and some of them wrote their wills, hurriedly scratching the paper as though it was for the last time. For some it would turn out to be the case. Custer wrote to Elizabeth:

> '...........I am now going to take up the trail where the scouting party turned back. I fear their failure to follow up the Indians has imperilled our plans by giving the village an intimation of our presence. Think of the valuable time lost, but I feel hopeful of accomplishing great results...........'

It was the last letter that he wrote and Elizabeth would cherish it until the day she died.

A short time later, as he returned to the 'Far West', Custer met with Major Brisbane who offered him 4 companies of his 2nd Cavalry. Custer thanked him for his offer and shaking his head, he replied,

"The Seventh can handle anything it meets."

Not long before this, Custer also refused an offer from Lieutenant Low to take all or part of his Gatling gun battery, believing that the guns were too cumbersome and would hamper the rapid progress his cavalry were expected to make. It is obvious that Brisbane and Low had ominous feelings about the campaign as well. However, Custer did accept the offer from Terry to take Mitch Bouyer, the mixed blood Sioux interpreter, much to the annoyance of Gibbon who was now left without a guide.

As the hustle and bustle of the preparations gradually died down and the soldiers began to settle for the night, Mark Kellogg was still very much awake. It was his first campaign in the field and he was with Custer no less! The man of the moment and he could hardly contain his excitement, even though he felt a little apprehensive. In the last part of his message to the 'Bismarck Tribune', Kellogg wrote:

> '..........tomorrow, June 22nd, General Custer with twelve companies will scout from its mouth up the valley of the Rosebud until he reaches the fresh trail discovered by Major Reno, and move on that trail with all the rapidity possible in order to overhaul the Indians whom it has been ascertained are hunting buffalo and making daily leisurely short marches. Gibbon's part of the command will march up the Big Horn valley in order to intercept the Indians if they should attempt to escape from General Custer down that avenue.'

Kellogg's interpretation of the orders seems remarkably clear, although he had no way of knowing that Gibbon was uncertain of giving Custer any support. It is interesting to wonder here whether Kellogg had any time to reflect on this report when he was in the thick of the fighting, probably not. He may have asked where Gibbon's support was, but he would not know that as he folded his report. All he knew at this moment was that he was going to witness a battle between Custer and the hostile Indians. He did not know that he would never follow up on the story.

Chapter 3

The trail of the Rosebud

Over the passing of the years, Crook's fight with the Sioux at the lower end of the Rosebud has been overshadowed by the events that followed it on the banks of the Little Big Horn. Most literature of Custer's epic battle only mentions the battle on the Rosebud in passing, if any notice is placed on it at all. Yet, what happened to Crook and his forces played a very significant role in the unfolding drama.

At 1.8 metres in height and broad across the shoulders, Brigadier-General George Crook was an impressive man. Born in Ohio in 1828, he graduated from the Military Academy at West Point in 1852, where he had become friendly with a young Irish cadet by the name of Philip Sheridan. Throughout the civil war, Crook had a distinguished military career, being appointed Brigadier-General at the close of hostilities for his services rendered. (It is interesting to note here that although Crook served in the Union forces, his daughter, Flora, married Confederate General J.E.B. Stuart who was killed at Yellow Tavern in May 1864.) In the field he displayed a Spartan simplicity, preferring to wear old shirts and trousers to his officer's uniform and he had a stoic indifference to hardship, suffering the same uncomfortable conditions as his men. He was an avid hunter and, like Custer, loved the outdoors, preferring to ride a mule on his expeditions even though he looked as if he was born to the saddle. Crook was a firm believer in publicity, posing for photographs whenever the opportunity presented itself and if he did show any eccentricity, it was in braiding his huge beard with ribbon or string.

His campaigns against the Apache in the south had created his reputation as being one of the most foremost Indian fighters of the day. But the Sioux were not the Apache and it appears that Crook made the mistake of believing that all Indians were the same. He based his field tactics and strategy on his first-hand knowledge of the Apache, a mistake that was to slur his reputation as a result. Some historians have mistakenly confused Crook's expertise in regard to Indians with an underlying sympathy for them. The truth is very much different. In his unfinished biography he states that although the prime causes of the Indian insurrection were due to avarice on the part of the whites, he also states that the Indians in general were,

> '.........filthy, odiferous, treacherous, ungrateful, pitiless, cruel and lazy.'

Crook's encounter with the hostile Indians on the Powder river in March, should have shown him that these Plains Indians were very much different from the Apache and that they were confident in their ability to fight and very aggressive when engaged in battle. If he did notice these facts, he did not pass his observations on in his report. It appears that the only lesson that Crook learnt from the encounter was that his pride could be scarred and he was determined to exact his revenge for that. In actual fact, Crook was very similar to Custer when in the field and there is little to distinguish between them. Both were eager to be the first to strike at the enemy and both would suffer defeat. Crook would outdo Custer on both counts.

Upon his return to Fort Fetterman, Crook lost no time in re-organising his forces. He would ensure that he had a stronger contingent of troops and that they were more than adequately equipped. Life at the fort was exceedingly dull, for both officers and men, and as such they were all eager to prepare for another campaign, if only to break the monotony. By the time Crook's column left the fort on the 29th May, his troops were impatient for some serious action and as the force was fairly large, their confidence was running high. Lieutenant John Bourke of the 3rd Cavalry, serving on Crook's staff, wrote in his journal:

> 'The long black line of mounted men stretched for more than a mile [1.6 kilometres] with nothing to break the sombreness of colour save the flashing of the sun's rays back from the arms of the men. A long moving stretch of white told us our wagons were already well under way and a puff of dust just in front indicated the line of march of the infantry battalions.'

John G. Bourke was a seasoned campaigner, having served with Crook during the Apache campaign in the south. He regularly kept a journal during the Rosebud incident, which has been invaluable in unravelling the course of events. Under the same entry in his journal, Bourke lists the officers and companies that were on the march, the total compliment being just over 1,000 men; comprising of the 2nd and 3rd Cavalry, with the 4th and 9th Infantry. Lieutenant-Colonel William B. Royall, of the 3rd Cavalry, being in command of the mounted troops and Major Alex Chambers, of the 4th Infantry, being appointed to command those on foot. With the majority of the command being cavalry, Crook had assembled a fighting unit to chase the Indians wherever he found them. The Infantry would stand their ground and press forward. At least that was the idea. Crook had also been promised the assistance of Crow and Shoshone scouts, who had yet to put in an appearance, but he was confident they would. Both tribes were age-old enemies of the Sioux and Crook felt sure they would not miss an opportunity to have a strike at them. If it was one thing he had learnt from his years on the frontier, it was that the most effective way in dealing with Indians was to use Indians. The addition of these Indian scouts would bring the strength of Crook's column to around 1,300 armed men.

As Crook's forces neared the ruins of the now abandoned Fort Reno on the Powder river, lying in the shadow of the Big Horn Mountains, it was discovered that one of the drivers in the supply train was actually a woman. Truth will out eventually and her sex was revealed after she had gone for a swim with some mule skinners. Martha Jane Cannary, better known as 'Calamity Jane', was already a legend along the frontier and the subject of discussion at many a sutler's store. Neither her features nor her build resembled anything feminine and dressed in buckskins she could easily be mistaken for a man. Calamity Jane was a skilled rider, could handle a mule team or a wagon with ease and curse, drink or shoot as well as any man. In later life she claimed to have fought Indians throughout the campaigns of the 1870's and although there is no evidence to support this, she was certainly a friend of Wild Bill Hickok as she claimed to be. Calamity Jane was placed under arrest and kept under guard at the supply camp for the duration of the battle on the Rosebud, being returned to Fort Fetterman with the wounded, much to her chagrin.

By 5th June, Crook's forces had crossed the Powder, left the ruins of Fort Reno behind them and reached another old abandoned post, Fort Phil Kearney, where they made camp along the Big Piney. Their location was not far from where Captain Fetterman and his troops had been killed by Crazy Horse in 1866. Crook's troops now knew they were definitely in hostile territory and although the excitement of a possible engagement was still running high, they were acutely aware of what could be waiting for them over the next hill or around a bend in the river. Rumours had spread through the column that Crazy Horse and his warriors were somewhere in the vicinity west of the Rosebud, but nothing was known for certain. Crook had received no word from Terry or Gibbon (on the other hand he had not sent any communications to them,) and his Indian scouts had still not arrived. He was virtually marching blind. He needed those scouts and he needed them now!

On 9th June Crook and his forces were camped on the southern banks of the Tongue. On the opposite bank Crazy Horse had scratched a line in the soil warning the troops not to cross the river or they would have a fight on their hands. Crook regarded the warning as a symbolic gesture of defiance, but if the Ogallala warrior wanted a fight he would be only too pleased to oblige him. Crook should have realised that, once again, the Indians knew his movements and as such had a distinct advantage over him. Whereas Crook could only guess as to the exact whereabouts of the Indians, Crazy Horse now had Crook and his troops firmly in his sights. Crook did not have to wait long to discover that Crazy Horse was a man of his word. Disregarding the warning, Crook crossed the Tongue and immediately the Sioux and Cheyenne attacked, taking the soldiers completely by surprise.

After driving off the pickets from the high ground, the Indians settled themselves amidst the rocks to shoot at the soldiers below. Bourke described the attack in his journal:

> 'The Indians did not wait for a moment, but moved up in good style, driving in our pickets and taking position in the rocks, from which they rained down a severe fire which did no great damage but was extremely annoying while it lasted.'

The attack ended as quickly as it had begun, after Captain Anson Mills of Company M, 3rd Cavalry, led a charge to clear the heights. The Indians disappeared leaving two soldiers wounded, one in the leg and the other in the arm, and the remainder of the column shaken from their idyllic misconception of the campaign. They were not on an afternoon picnic and fighting hostile Indians was not a pleasurable game.

Crook appears to have been momentarily shaken by this sudden outburst from the Indians, but he also knew that this attack was only a show of aggression designed to slow his progress. He probably had an idea that the village was not far away and the Indians needed time to move it out of harm's way. On the other hand, it is also possible that the Indians enforced their warning quite simply because they were in a position to do so. Crook braced himself for the next encounter, one he was determined to win. It is evident that Crook had no idea of the large number of hostile Indians in the area and he failed to recognise their confidence or aggressiveness En masse.

The General also had another problem that needed his urgent attention. He was in the wrong place. Having reached the Tongue, he realised he was not in the area that he thought he was. From his campsite by the ruins of Fort Phil Kearney, he had intended to follow Little Goose Creek to its confluence with Big Goose Creek. Instead, he had taken another valley and followed it north-east, thus arriving at the Tongue. Even without the aid of Indian scouts, Crook must have had maps with him, however crude. Either he did not know how to read them or he had not consulted them. What Crook did next defies explanation. He turned the entire column to march in a south-westerly direction, towards Big Goose Creek. It can only be assumed that he was trying to rectify his mistake. If he had continued in his northerly direction he may not have met with Crazy Horse on the Rosebud, although as the Indians were fully aware of his movements they may have preferred to deal with his column anyway. Alternatively, if Crook had not changed direction he may have met with Terry's forces and the engagement on the Little Big Horn may have had a different result. (An alternative that was not within Sherman's plan.) Of course it is also possible that Crook may have believed that the Indians were now preparing to attack his troops in earnest and in turning his column he may have been trying to gain precious time for his Indian allies to boost his command. He just may have been trying to confuse the enemy at the end of the day. Like many frontier commanders, including Custer, Crook did not communicate with his subordinate officers on a regular basis and his reasons for this odd manoeuvre may never be known. In any event, after a few days' march, his column had reached the junction of Big Goose Creek and Little Goose Creek, where they settled into camp.

June 11th brought Crook some relief when the Crow and Shoshone scouts finally joined his column. The Crows were under the leadership of Chief Alligator and Chief Stand Up; while the Shoshone were led by Chief Washakie. Upon their arrival, all the Indian scouts were placed under the command of Captain George Randall, 23rd Infantry. Altogether, the Indian scouts numbered over 260 armed warriors who were extremely excited and spoiling for a fight. Bourke described the appearance of the Crows:

> '.........somewhat fairer than the other Indians about them. They are all above medium height, not a few being quite tall and many have a noble expression of countenance. The dress of the members of the tribe consists of shirt of flannel, cotton or buckskin; breach clout, leggings of blanket, moccasins of deer, elk or buffalo hide, coat of bright coloured blanket, made with sleeves and hood and a head-dress fashioned in diverse shapes, but most frequently formed from an old black army hat, with the top cut out and side bound with feathers, fur and scarlet cloth.
>
> Their arms were all breech-loaders.........Most of them calibre .50 with occasional .45. Lances, medicine poles and tomahawks......'

The following day, Crook talked to the scouts and formulated his plan of attack. It is obvious that both Crook and his troops were over confident in the abilities to tackle the hostiles. The Crows were not impressed and solemnly informed Crook that the Sioux were,

"...............numerous as grass."

Or to put it more plainly, the strength of the enemy was massive. Foolishly, Crook did not pay much attention to this information. After all, most Indians possessed the ability to exaggerate when necessary. He needed to enhance his reputation as an Indian fighter and now that his allies had arrived, he was ready to go on the offensive. He wanted the column ready to move out on the 16th June and they were heading north once more, towards the Rosebud.

Around the 14th June, the hostile camp was at Reno Creek, only 7 kilometres east of the Little Big Horn. Crazy Horse had known about the presence of Crook and his soldiers long before his warning shots were fired on the Tongue. He was not impressed by the soldiers' apparent contempt for either his warriors, whose numbers grew daily, or his own ability to fight. Three days later on the morning of the 17th June, Cheyenne scouts galloped into the camp with the news that Crook and his blue-coated soldiers were nearing the divide between the Tongue and the Rosebud valleys and they were only stopping for short breaks. The Council of Chiefs advised caution, preferring to wait for the soldiers to attack. Crazy Horse had other ideas. He was not prepared to let the soldiers get anywhere near the village. Images of Sand Creek and the Washita were ingrained in his memory. He was not Cheyenne but he had seen the aftermath. Crazy Horse had decided that they would hit these soldiers before they could get into a position whereby they could attack the village. They would initiate the offensive as one large body and fight as a whole, not individually. That same evening, the hostiles were on the move and ready to fight. Sitting Bull rode with them, urging his warriors on and encouraging them to be brave. As he was still recovering from his active participation in the recent Sun Dances, he was too weak to do any more.

At 3 o'clock on the morning of 17th June, Crook gave the order for the trumpeter to sound 'Reveille' and within three hours the whole column was on the move, with the cavalry and mounted infantry forging ahead of the cumbersome supply train. He had mounted the infantry companies on mules so they would keep a better pace with the cavalry, to the concern of the supply train. But Crook wanted to cover ground at a fast pace, considering he had lost enough time already. He gave no thought to the supply train being left virtually unprotected, assuming they would catch up when the troops went into camp. He had a hunch that the village of Crazy Horse lay ahead and to prove his theory, he sent some of his Crow scouts ahead to locate it. The sky was blue and the early morning sun was already melting the last of the snow, making the Rosebud swollen with swift running water.

At 8 o'clock Crook gave the order for the columns to halt. They had already marched for five hours and if the men did not need a well-earned rest then their mounts did. The horses and mules were unsaddled and the men prepared coffee. John Finerty, a newspaper correspondent for the 'Chicago Times' wrote:

> 'At about eight o'clock, we halted in a valley'.........
> The hills seem to rise on every side, and we were within easy musket shot of those most remote.'

It was obviously not a good location for the column to take a rest. If Finerty, a mere civilian, had noticed that fact why had Crook failed to do so. Finerty added that the valley was,

> '.......a dark, winding and narrow defile.'

Finerty was exaggerating somewhat, as the bottom of the canyon is much wider than a narrow defile, being never less than roughly 400 metres wide at any given point. The surrounding hills, where most of the subsequent fighting occurred, rise gently in a series of rolling folds, separated only by the small streams as they meander their way into the Creek. Overall, the whole area is quite open, affording little or no protection to either an attacking force or a defending one.

As whiffs of thin smoke rose from the camp fires, the supply wagons were just starting to make an appearance in the valley. The drivers were dry and hungry, and as they drove the wagons on they could see the smoke lazily rising from the fires and almost smell the coffee. Up on the bluffs, pickets patrolled the heights keeping a watchful eye for any hostiles. All was quiet and calm, when hardly half an hour later the Crow scouts burst over a hill and galloped towards the camp shouting,

> "Lakota! Lakota! [Sioux! Sioux!]

Subsequent evidence suggests that the Crow scouts had inadvertently stumbled upon the Sioux scouts, who had been reporting on Crook's movements to Crazy Horse.

Crook put his men on the alert, keeping them undercover while he put out extra pickets at the foot of the bluffs to the north. But nothing happened. All remained quiet and after half an hour had passed, the soldiers began to relax again. Officers sprawled on the grass, idly smoking and chatting. Crook himself settled down to a game of cards with some of his officers. Other ranks continued to drink coffee and chat, with one or two even breaking into a song. The young Crows took the opportunity to race their ponies against those of the young Shoshone, causing much hilarity among some of the soldiers. It was as though the whole camp had lapsed into an idyllic recumbency, totally unaware of the dangers that awaited them. Or was it an act of blatant contemptuous confidence? It didn't last very long. Suddenly, painted warriors appeared along the northern ridge driving the pickets back to the camp and without further ado, they began to swarm from the small hills in the west. Crook's column was definitely under attack this time!

With Crazy Horse leading the assault and Sitting Bull spurring them on, the warriors believed themselves to be invincible and the ferocity with which they attacked, the soldiers certainly thought they were as well. Gone was the old method of hovering at a distance, circling the enemy and taking as few life-threatening risks as possible. Gone also was their old method of luring the soldiers into a trap and, what was more alarming, these warriors were fighting as a whole unit and not individually as they had done in the past. They were charging the bewildered soldiers with their ponies at full gallop, often breaking through the lines and engaging the soldiers in vicious hand-to-hand combat. These warriors had changed the rules. They were not out to 'count-coup', they were out for the kill!

At the rear of the column, Captain Randall rallied his Crow and Shoshone scouts and led a charge straight into the attacking Sioux. He clashed with the hostiles on the plateau, just north of the camp and for the next twenty minutes or so, some of the most ferocious fighting occurred. Randall and his scouts held the enemy at bay giving the soldiers enough precious time to get themselves organised. Had he not led the charge to repulse the attack, the death toll of Crook's column would most certainly have been much higher. It was due to the sheer courage of the Crow and Shoshone scouts that averted what would have been a complete disaster for Crook and his troops.

At the first sound of battle, Crook was unable to see what was actually happening, so he rode up the nearest hill to assess the extent of the fighting. At the same time, Captain Mills rode towards a hill further south to appraise the situation there. Crook ordered Mills to hold the bluffs where he was, but no matter what the soldiers tried the Sioux were definitely gaining the advantage. Mills could see that his troops were grossly outnumbered and that his position was very precarious, to say the least.

Crook had never experienced such a brutal attack from hostile Indians. The Sioux and Cheyenne were openly aggressive and confident, displaying no fear at all and he had never encountered such a huge mass of unified tribes that were now attacking his column with all the fury they could muster. (It is worth noting here that the unification of the Plains Indians during the insurrection of

1876, was the first and only time it would ever happen.) The General had been caught napping and he had been unprepared. What was worse, he had totally underestimated his adversary, both in strength and in strategy. He should have listened to his Crow scouts. It did not take a military genius to realise that, once again, he was heading for a defeat at the hands of the hostiles and if he was to extricate his command from an impending disaster, he was going to have to act fast. Very fast.

By now, the oppressed soldiers had managed to organise themselves to meet the onslaught. Captain Van Vliet was sent to the south to protect the rear of the column. As he reached the crest of the bluffs he met another force of angry hostiles and by sheer determination he managed to drive them back. Two companies of the 9th Infantry were ordered to hold the bluffs to the north, with the addition of four companies of dismounted cavalrymen to support them. The remaining companies of the 4th and 9th Infantry were sent to the plateau in the north to form a skirmish line. However, the battle that was raging there was anything but a skirmish, with the Crow and Shoshone fiercely attempting to hold the advancing hostiles at bay.

Some time had now passed since the initial attack and hostile reinforcements were now arriving on the scene. First to join the affray was American Horse and his fresh Cheyenne warriors. It was a perilous moment for Crook and his forces. Captain Nickerson, of the 23td Infantry who was attached to Crook's staff, later wrote:

> 'When we reached the crest of the plateau, there appeared in our front a formidable band of those justly celebrated Sioux and Cheyenne warriors, magnificently mounted, and in all the splendour of war-paint and feathers. Every hill appeared to be covered with these swarming legions, and up from every ravine, and out of every little vale, more seemed to be coming.'

The fight was seriously intensifying on all sides. The Sioux cleverly attempted to outflank the soldiers, but they were driven back by heavy volleys of fire. Again and again they charged forward, the air filled with their wild demonic whoops and yells, while bullets and arrows seemed to whiz from every direction. The Sioux and Cheyenne were gradually gaining ground with every surge, no matter how valiantly the soldiers fought. Amidst the confusion an order was issued for the soldiers to pull back and regroup. As they did so, the Indians pressed forward, confident they were beating the hated blue-coats. While rallying his men, Captain Guy Henry, Company D, 3rd Cavalry, was shot in the jaw, the bullet piercing both cheek bones, smashing his nose and destroying one eye. For a short while he tried to remain mounted issuing orders to his troops with blood gushing from his mouth. As he tried to lead another charge, he fell from his horse and, on seeing this, the Indians counter-attacked, very soon passing the spot where he lay. A few warriors stopped to 'count-coup' or scalp him, but the Crow and Shoshone were having none of that. They courageously charged the hostiles, regaining the field of combat and protected Henry from any further injuries. It was only after the soldiers had rushed forward to support them, that it was found that Henry was still alive!

Crook could see that his command was in great danger of collapsing altogether. His troops were fighting almost to the point of exhaustion and there seemed to be no end to the number of hostiles. He desperately needed to create a diversion. The question was where? He was still convinced that Crazy Horse and his warriors were fighting with such ferocity because they were protecting their village, which meant it must lie over the hill to the north, even though his scouts had not reported finding it there. Thus, he instructed Captain Mills to form his troops into columns of twos and charge the position that he believed was the location of the village. However, before Mills had advanced very far he was recalled to the scene of the battle where his services were more urgently needed. Subsequent research has revealed that if Mills had continued over the bluff, he would have run straight into an ambush that Crazy Horse had already planned. It appeared that Crazy Horse was outflanking every order Crook was issuing. In his report Captain Mills later wrote:

> '........the hostiles were charging boldly and rapidly through the soldiers, knocking them from their horses with lances and knives, dismounting and killing them, cutting off the arms of some of them at the elbows in the middle of the fight and carrying them away.'

On his return from the bluff, Mills led a counter-charge against the hostiles, which although it was not an easy accomplishment, did prove effective. Continuing his report, Mills wrote:

> 'We met the Indians at the foot of the ridge, and charged right in and through them, driving them back to the top of the ridge. These Indians were most hideous, every one being painted in most hideous colours and designs, stark naked, except for their moccasins, breech-clouts and head gear, the latter consisting of feathers and horns; some of the horses also being painted and the Indians proved then and there that they were the best cavalry soldiers on earth. In charging up towards us they exposed little of their person, hanging on with one arm around the neck and one

General William T. Sherman 1820-1891. General of the Army and a close friend of President Grant and Lt. General Phil Sheridan. His word was law. *(Kind courtesy of Brady–Hardy photographic collection (Prints & Photo Division) Library of Congress)*

Lt. General Philip Sheridan 1831-1888. General Commanding the Department of the Missouri. He had no love for any Native American and is quoted as saying "*The only good Indian I ever saw was dead.*" *(Kind courtesy of Brady-Hardy photographic collection (Prints & Photo Division) Library of Congress)*

Brigadier General George R. Crook 1828-1890. General Commanding the Department of the Platte. His native nickname was 'Nantan Lupan' or Grey Wolf. He failed to continue to march north after the Battle of the Rosebud, sealing Custer's fate. *(Kind courtesy of Brady-Hardy photographic collection (Prints & Photo Division) Library of Congress)*

Lt. Colonel George Armstrong Custer 1839-1876. Commanding Officer of the 7th U.S. Cavalry at the Little Big Horn. His various native nicknames included Long Hair, Yellow Hair and Son of the Morning Star. He died at the little Big Horn with his battalion. *(Kind courtesy of the Library of Congress/Public Domain)*

Right: **George Custer (seated) with his wife Libby and brother Tom.** Taken during the American Civil War in which George Custer became a Brevet Major General of Volunteers and his brother won two Congressional Medals of Honour. *(Kind courtesy of the Library of Congress// Public Domain)*

Below: **Lt. Colonel G. A. Custer with fellow officers of the 7th U.S. Cavalry.** Taken on the steps of Custer's quarters at Fort Abraham Lincoln. Many would not survive the 1876 Campaign. *(Kind courtesy of Denver Public Library Special Collections. (B-423))*

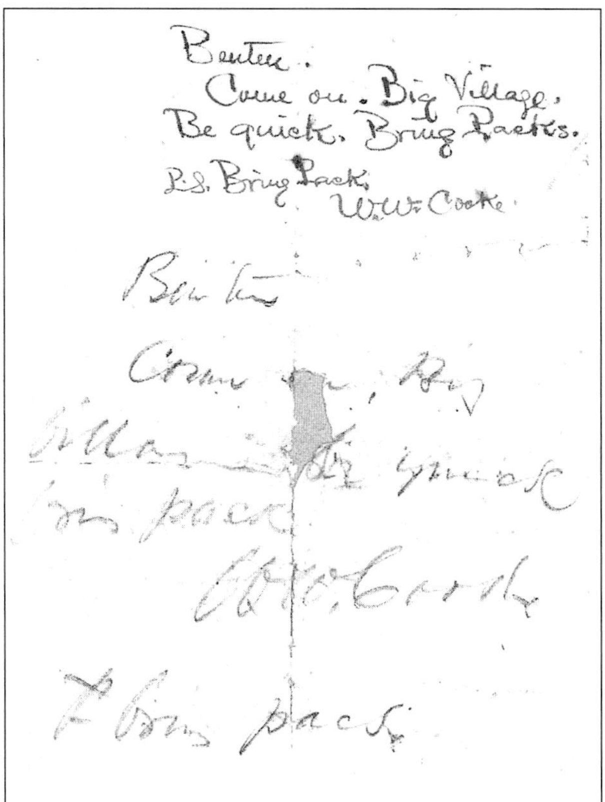

Benteen.
Come on. Big Village.
Be quick. Bring Packs.
P.S. Bring Pacs.
W.W. Cooke

Above left: **Major Marcus A. Reno 1834-1889.**
Lt. Col. Custer's Second in Command at the Little Big Horn. Chased back across the river, most of his battalion survived the fight. *(Photo by D. F. Barry. Kind courtesy of the Denver Public Library/Public Domain)*

Above right: **Captain Frederick W. Benteen 1834-1898.**
Commanded the third battalion at the Little Big Horn. He had no love for G. A. Custer after the death of Major Elliott at the Washita and failed to obey Custer's final order for assistance. *(Kind courtesy of Library of Congress/Public Domain)*

Left: **The Final Message from Lt. Col. Custer to Captain F. Benteen.**
The message was written by the Regimental Adjutant First Lieutenant W. Cooke and carried by Sergeant D. Kanipe of Co. C. *(Kind courtesy of the West Point Museum Collection, U.S. Military Academy)*

Graves of unknown soldiers of the 7th Cavalry on the field of battle at the Little Big Horn.
(Kind courtesy of the National Archives/Photo No. 111-SC-82965)

The Presumed grave of Lt. James Sturgis, Co. E, 7th U.S. Cavalry.
The son of the actual Commanding Officer of the Regiment, he was killed during the battle with Custer's battalion. *(Kind courtesy of the Little Big Horn National Monument/Photo No. 111-SC-82972)*

Left: **Where Custer Fell.** This photograph was taken by John H. Fouch in July 1877 and clearly shows the dreadful carnage of the battle. *(Kind courtesy of the University of Oklahoma Press)*

Below: **Comanche, a survivor of the Custer fight at the Little Big Horn.** Comanche was the faithful horse belonging to Captain Myles Keogh of Co. I, who died with Custer's command. Other horses were also found on the scene but were too severely wounded to save. He was nursed back to health and died in 1891. *(Photo by D. F. Barry 1878. Kind courtesy of Custer Battlefield National Monument. Photo No. NPS-LIBL00011-07119)*

50th Anniversary of the Battle of the Little Big Horn, 26 June 1926.
The scout, White-Man-Runs-Him stands beside General E. S. Godfrey with the marker for the proposed monument for the battle. *(Kind courtesy of the National Archives. Photo No. 111-SC-82968)*

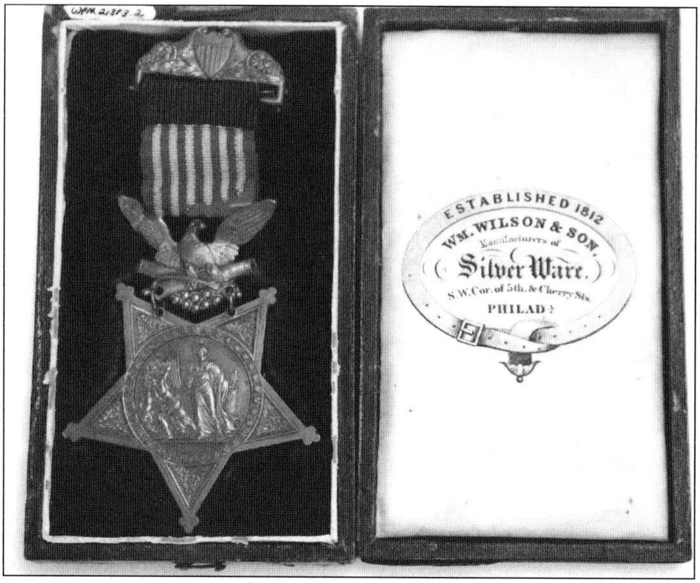

Above left: **Congressional Medal of Honour 1862-1896 issue.**
The highest award that can be bestowed for bravery in the United States, it was instigated during the American Civil War. *(Kind courtesy of West Point Museum Collection, U. S. Military Academy)*

Above right: **Indian Wars Campaign Medal.**
Awarded for the campaigns against hostile American Natives between 1865 and 1898, it was not authorised until January 1905. *(Author's Collection)*

East Side of Battle Ridge, looking south toward's Calhoun's position.
(Kind courtesy of Sam Cahoon)

Reno Crossing on the Little Big Horn. *(Kind courtesy of Sam Cahoon)*

Marker of First Sergeant James Butler, Co. L, 7th U. S. Cavalry.
When his body was found there were numerous empty cartridge shells beneath him, indicating that he died courageously and sold his life dearly. This photograph is looking west into Medicine Tail Ford. *(Kind courtesy of Sam Cahoon.)*

Marker of Acting Assistant Surgeon James M. DeWolfe. *(Kind courtesy of Sam Cahoon)*

Marker of First Sgt James Butler, Co.L. *(Kind courtesy of Sam Cahoon)*

Medicine Tail Coulee.
A clear photograph of the terrain, although four horses abreast would struggle between the coulee sides. *(Kind courtesy of Sam Cahoon)*

Custer Battlefield looking west to the Little Big Horn where part of the Indian Village was located.
(Kind courtesy of Sam Cahoon)

Confluence of the Big Horn and Little Horn Rivers.
(Kind courtesy of Sam Cahoon)

"Total Involvement" [of the Last Stand].
A painting by Harold von Schmidt. *(Kind courtesy of Colonel Charles Custer, a descendant of G. A. Custer)*

> leg over the horse, firing and lancing from under the horse's neck, so that there was no part of the Indian at which we could aim. Their shouting and personal appearance was so hideous that it terrified the horses more than our men and rendered them almost uncontrollable before we dismounted and placed them behind the rocks. The Indians came not in a line but in flocks or herds like buffalo, and they piled it upon us until I think there must have been 1000 or 1500 in our immediate front, but they refused to fight when they found us secured behind the rocks, and bore off to our left. I then charged the second ridge, and took it in the same manner and fortified myself with horses protected behind the large boulders and the men behind the smaller ones.'

By midday, Crook realised his position was in serious trouble. He was having great difficulty in keeping his battalions together, while trying to co-ordinate the battle and he was failing miserably at both. He admits these failings in his official report, written on 20th June, although he gives the rough ground as his reason and not the severe intensity of the battle. Well, he chose the campsite so he only had himself to blame. Each charge made by his troops had been cleverly met by a counter-charge and every time his soldiers were re-deployed, the Indians took full advantage of the move. However, there is little doubt that Crook was causing some of the problems himself. He had not assessed the situation correctly when the battle had begun and he had seriously underestimated the Indians' tactical ability. He constantly issued orders and then countermanded them before his troops could carry them out and he persisted in positioning his men in skirmish lines, just as he had during the Civil War. It was as though he expected the enemy to respond with similar movements. But this was not the Civil War and the Indians did not play the same game as Crook, they had their own rules.

Crazy Horse had reformed his warriors into a very formidable fighting force. He would attack one flank and then another, gradually weakening his opposition. When the soldiers grew weary of this and charged, as he knew they would, he divided his forces and feigned retreat. When the soldiers followed, hoping to consolidate a victory and slowly drifting from their formation, Crazy Horse carefully assessed his foe and attacked at the weakest point. The wily Ogallala had been very careful not to attack the infantry en masse, as these blue-coated foot soldiers were proving very accurate with their rifles. Instead he teased them until they broke their lines and advanced. What was more to the point, the hostiles were fighting whilst still mounted on their ponies, while the majority of the soldiers were dismounted. This gave the Indians speed and manoeuvrability, thus enabling Crazy Horse to switch his attacks from flank to flank. It is not certain whether Crook's officers observed the new tactics employed by the hostiles, however it does appear the Crook definitely had not.

As morning became afternoon the bitter struggle continued, with neither side willing to concede defeat. However, all was not lost yet, for when Mills turned his troops he had inadvertently manoeuvred his command behind the enemy. On discovering they were now threatened from the rear, the hostiles decided to break from the fight. Mills led another charge and the Indians abandoned the field. It was around 2:30 pm in the afternoon and both sides had been involved in the brutal conflict for over six hours. Now, the valley assumed an eerie silence and the scent of roses, growing along the banks of the creek, could be smelled mingled with the acrid smoke of the gunfire. The fight had ended as abruptly as it had begun.

Crazy Horse retired to his village, sure in the knowledge that he had beaten the soldiers and Crook withdrew from the field, finding safety in his wagon train. He was certain that the victory was his as the Indians had left the field of battle. The plain truth was that if anyone had been victorious that day, it was certainly not Crook. Crazy Horse had set out to stop the soldiers marching any further northwards and this is exactly what he had achieved, although he did not know it at the time.

According to Crook, his soldiers had suffered 10 killed and 21 wounded. Frank Grouard, Crook's chief of scouts, estimated the casualties were more around 28 killed and 56 wounded. Lieutenant Bourke stated that their losses were more likely to be around 57 killed and wounded. In all probability, Grouard was the most precise, although whoever was correct the overall totals were minimal considering the intensity of the fighting. By contrast, it has to be admitted that Crazy Horse's casualties numbered some 36 killed with a further 63 wounded.

On his arrival at the wagon train, Crook assessed the situation. He was seriously low on ammunition and supplies. He had a few wounded to be taken care of and he had just barely survived the battle himself. He therefore decided he would send the wounded back to Fort Fetterman with requests for fresh supplies and reinforcements. Crook's decision not to continue the march at this time was a crucial factor in the events that were to follow. There is no doubt that the General had experienced a difficult engagement, but that does not excuse the blatant mistakes he had made and was still continuing to make. Throughout the entire battle he had never managed to take the initiative and considering the size of his command, his casualties were extremely light. Certainly not heavy enough to warrant a tactical retreat. In his book, 'Crimson Prairie', Brigadier General S. Marshall wrote of the 1876 campaign:

> 'But Custer need not have become the victim of the campaign had it been in other parts properly conducted. The whole operation proceeded as if, rather than hunting Indians, the army was seeking a memorable catastrophe.'

How true those words seem to be, for on 21st June Crook sent some wagons back to Fort Fetterman with the wounded and within a few hours of their departure, the Crow and Shoshone scouts abandoned the column and left for home. They were convinced that Crook was no longer active in the campaign.

While Crook awaited his reinforcements and supplies he busied himself hunting and fishing in the streams that ran from the Big Horn mountains. Hardly the actions of an effective field commander who had openly declared his eagerness to strike at the hostiles. He was only 32 kilometres south of the point on the Rosebud where Custer would depart the creek and head towards the Little Big Horn. In hindsight, it is easy to criticise and say that Crook compounded one mistake with another, yet for a renowned Indian fighter that is exactly what he did. He failed to exact a defeat on the hostiles and now he was failing to move north to support Terry and Gibbon. His failures reflected on the rank and file, the majority of whom reviled him for his inert actions during the Rosebud fight. Sergeant John Howard, Company B, 2nd Cavalry, said that he thought the fight was,

> "…….poorly conducted. The soldiers have lost all confidence in General Crook"

However, Crook was to commit the worst failure of all when he neglected to send word of his defeat to either Terry or Gibbon. From what he should have observed and noted, the information concerning the Indians' methods of fighting would have been priceless to either of the other field commanders, not to mention that he was no longer supporting them. This dreadful neglect of duty cannot be attributed to an oversight. He was a seasoned campaigner and would have fully understood the protocol involved. Nor could it have been as a result of battle fatigue or shock, for he was leisurely hunting and fishing in camp after seeing the wounded off to Fort Fetterman. No evidence is readily available to explain any of Crook's actions up to this point. Of course it is possible that Crook may have received other instructions from Sheridan that had ordered him to make those fatal decisions. Crook may have been instructed to delay his juncture with Terry and Gibbon. If that was so, he had certainly complied, not only with his detour during the march but now in his refusal to resume the march in support of the other forces. He may even have been instructed to go no further than the Rosebud until told to do so, after all Sheridan was very adept at covert communications. Historians will never know the truth behind the battle at the Rosebud or the reasons for Crook's numerous counts of dereliction of duty during this period.

Not all the official reports seem to portray an accurate account of the engagement either. In his official report, Captain Henry Noyes, Company I, 2nd Cavalry stated:

> 'The amount of ammunition expended averaged about 12 rounds per man.'

With so many hostiles attacking the troops from all directions, this estimate does seem to defy plausibility. So long as the soldiers had ammunition, they could continuously fire at the enemy until they were to stop. If no check was kept on the amount of ammunition distributed, it is little wonder that Crook found his supplies low after the fight. That in itself was bad management. Nevertheless, even reports that are open to scrutiny, such as Noyes', allow the modern historian an insight into such engagements on the frontier.

However, there is always a brighter side to most disasters and the fight at the Rosebud did produce heroes to be proud of. The simple fact was, that despite Crook's apparent inability to conduct the battle some of his men showed they were more than capable of doing so. For their gallantry in action during the Battle of the Rosebud on 17th June 1876, four members of the 3rd Cavalry were subsequently awarded the Congressional Medal of Honor:

First Sergeant Joseph Robinson	Company D
First Sergeant Michael McGann	Company F
First Sergeant John Shingle	Company I
Trumpeter Elmer Snow	Company M

No mention was made in any of the official reports concerning the superb efforts of the Crow and Shoshone scouts during the fight, whose courage and defiance in the face of the enemy had saved the soldiers on more than one occasion from being overrun. There is certainly no doubt whatsoever that these scouts saved the life of Captain Henry, just to mention one episode. History has sorely neglected them. Their courageous deeds were not even preserved in the ledgers or official reports, but Henry must have been extremely grateful for their actions.

Chapter 4

'Sufficient Reason'

On 22nd June, at the other end of the Rosebud, Custer received his final orders from General Terry:

> 'The Brigadier-General Commanding directs that, as soon as your regiment can be made ready for the march, you will proceed up the Rosebud in pursuit of the Indians whose trail was discovered by Major Reno a few days since. It is, of course, impossible to give you any definite instructions in regard to this movement, and were it not impossible to do so, the Departmental Commander places too much confidence in your zeal, energy and ability to wish to impose upon you precise orders which might hamper your actions when nearly in contact with the enemy. He will, however, indicate to you his own views of what your action should be, and he desires that you should conform to them unless you shall see sufficient reason for departing from them. He thinks that you should proceed up the Rosebud until you ascertain definitely the direction in which the trail above spoken of leads. Should it be found (as it appears almost certain that it will be found) to turn towards the Little Horn, he thinks that you should still proceed southwards, perhaps as far as the headwaters of the Tongue, and then turn towards the Little Horn, feeling constantly, however, to your left, so as to preclude the possibility of the escape of the Indians to the south or south east, by passing around your left flank.
>
> The column of Colonel Gibbon is now in motion for the mouth of the Big Horn. As soon as it reaches that point it will cross the Yellowstone and move up at least as the forks of the Big and Little Horns. Of course its further movements must be controlled by circumstances as they arise, but it is hoped that the Indians, if upon the Little Horn, may be so nearly enclosed by the two columns that their escape will be impossible.

> The Department Commander desires that on your way up the Rosebud you should thoroughly examine the upper part of Tullock's Creek, and that you should endeavour to send a scout to Colonel Gibbon's column, with information of the result of your examination. The lower part of the creek will be examined by a detachment from Colonel Gibbon's column.
>
> The supply steamer will be pushed up the Big Horn as far as the forks if the river is found to be navigable for that distance, and the Department Commander, who will accompany the column of Colonel Gibbon desires you will report to him no later than the expiration of the time for which your troops are rationed, unless in the meantime you receive further orders.'

These are the most controversial orders that Terry was to issue throughout his entire career and they have been the topic of serious debates throughout the years that followed. Reno's reports had been very explicit in defining the direction the hostiles were travelling. There was little doubt that they were heading towards the valley of the Little Big Horn, yet Terry is sending Custer and his regiment directly to that very location, with no immediate support. What was more, he was giving Custer a free hand as he saw fit! In saying that he does not want to hamper Custer's 'zeal, energy or ability' with precise orders, it appears that Terry is actually telling Custer to attack the hostiles should he locate them! It is also apparent that Terry was fully aware that Custer would rather fight the Indians than lure them into a trap. It must be remembered here, that Terry had never fought Indians before and Custer, of course, had. Even so, this inexperience should not have clouded the fact that he was an experienced field commander and his judgement should have been more appropriate to the campaign as a whole.

It is interesting to note that Terry makes no mention of General Crook. If, as we are supposed to believe, Crook was to make his way northwards so all the columns would converge, why was this fact not mentioned as a reminder to Custer? It must also be remembered that neither Terry nor Gibbon had received any word from Crook at this point and, as such, had no knowledge of Crook's fight on the Rosebud or of Crook's subsequent decisions. However, one glaring anomaly stands out above all else in the ambiguous orders and that is the omission of Terry's name. Throughout the document he is referred to as the 'Departmental Commander' and he did not sign it either. The latter, of course, was not unusual for the time. Orders were often written by a staff officer and signed by them on the commander's behalf. These orders had been written and signed by Captain E.W. Smith, of the 18th Infantry, who was serving on Terry's staff. This now poses a question, are these the orders that Terry had devised or are they a re- write of instructions that he had received, to be used when the time was right ? Of course, secrecy was of paramount importance, so in all probability this question will never be answered. However, if there was a conspiracy, cleverly orchestrated by Sheridan (and approved by Sherman), then the final result can only by construed as an act of cold blooded, pre-meditated murder!

Unaware of the conspiratorial forces that were swirling around him, Custer took a brief moment to finish his short letter to Elizabeth. He told her of the trail that Reno had discovered, which he was about to follow, and of the arrival of his Crow scouts:

> 'They are magnificent looking men, so much handsome and Indian like than any we have seen, and so jolly and sportive; nothing of the gloomy, silent red men about them.'

It was obviously an attempt to brighten the letter and make her feel more at ease, perhaps even to alleviate his own tension.

At 12 o'clock, on the morning of Thursday 22nd June, at the sound of the bugler the Seventh Cavalry rode out of the camp in columns of fours, under the critical gaze of their commanding officer, together with General Terry and Colonel Gibbon. In an article written at a later date, Gibbon describes the regiment as it passed in review:

> 'The regiment presented a fine appearance, and as the various companies passed we had a good opportunity to note the number of fine horses in the ranks, many of them being part-blood horses from Kentucky, and I am told there was not a single sore-backed horse amongst them. General Custer appeared in good spirits, chatted freely with us, and was evidently proud of the appearance of his command.'

With the regimental colours proudly unfurled and their guidons gaily flapping in the wind, the troops rode past the officers. There were no sabres glinting in the sunlight this time. Custer had ordered that all sabres were to be packed in wooden boxes and left at the Powder river depot. They were noisy and Indians could spot the flashes of sunlight reflecting off the polished steel from a long distance away. First Lieutenant Edward Mathey had disobeyed Custer's orders and had stowed his sabre in the pack-train, where it was to hand should he need it to kill snakes. First Lieutenant Charles de Rudiio also claims to have retained his sabre, although there is no evidence to substantiate this.

Sitting astride his favourite sorrel gelding, Vic, Custer was dressed in his familiar buckskins and wore a pale grey, broad rimmed hat which he had pulled down to shield his eyes from the glare of the sun. His golden hair, which he usually wore fairly long, had been cut short by Second Lieutenant Charles Varnum and was hardly visible beneath the brim of his hat. Buckskin jackets had also been chosen by a few of his officers, including his brothers Tom and Boston. Others such as Reno and Benteen preferred to retain the blue army-issue blouse. As the last of the regiment returned the salute, Custer spurred his mount into a canter to take position at the head of the column. Seeing Custer move forward, Gibbon called out to him,

> "Now don't be greedy Custer. As there are Indians enough for all of us, wait for us!"

Custer wheeled his horse around and waving a hand at the Colonel replied,

> "No. I will not!"

Terry and Gibbon watched Custer's command mount the bluffs in the distance, the guidons fluttering in the breeze and then the column was gone.

From the moment of their departure, the progress of Custer and his troops was beset with problems. They were not major problems, more in the way of niggling annoyances and they sorely needed to be sorted out. The main concern was the pack-train. Badly packed, the mules began losing their cargo before they had barely left the camp and they continued to do so along the march, straggling behind and causing valuable time to be lost, while the civilian packers stopped and re-adjusted the supplies.

Custer was well aware of the problems the pack-train was causing and he resolved to deal with it when they stopped for the night. Right now he had another issue on his mind, one that he considered more important and one that he felt could have a profound effect on the campaign as a whole. He knew he had a very real weakness in his regiment and that weakness was his own officers. Since the fight at the Washita in 1868, he had never commanded the total respect and loyalty of all of his officers, which ultimately made his command of the regiment all the more difficult. In fact the regiment's senior Captain, Frederick Benteen, had even written a letter to a prominent newspaper condemning Custer for having abandoned Major Elliot and his command to their fate. The result was an ever widening gap in the professional relations between the two men. Custer's present relationship with his senior officer, Major Marcus Reno, was not too healthy either. Being abstemious of all forms of liquor, Custer did not approve of Reno's persistent use of it. He even went so far as to caution Reno of what the consequences would be if he ever saw the Major under the influence of drink whilst on duty. It came as no surprise then that in order to refrain from any further conflict with his officers, Custer remained estranged from them as much as possible and preferred to surround himself with his immediate family and those he regarded as close friends. However, professionalism should have prevailed above all else and these differences of opinion should not have precluded any communication between Custer and his senior officers while on campaign. Evidently it did, as the unfolding events were to prove.

After travelling for about 3 kilometres, the column reached the mouth of the Rosebud and crossed to the west side of the river from where they continued their journey into the valley. Here the river was approximately 10 metres in width and less than a metre in depth, affording a relatively easy crossing for the horses and mules on the gravelled bottom. Once again, the pack-train proved troublesome and the slow advance of the column was annoying Custer. They were starting to follow the Indian trail previously discovered by Reno and if they were to have any chance of finding the hostiles, they would have to move at a faster pace than this or the trail would become cold.

By about 4 o'clock in the afternoon Custer had had enough. The column had hardly covered just over 19 kilometres and the march had been slow and laborious. Having crossed to the left bank where there was an abundance of wood, water and good grazing, he ordered the regiment to halt and make camp. Before resting himself, Custer sought out Lieutenant Mathey and directed him to report his annoyance concerning the civilian packers to Captain Thomas McDougall, the officer commanding Company B whose duty it was to escort the pack-train. He curtly informed Mathey that he was to report to him at the end of each day's march on the efficiency of the packers and the pack-train. Custer also stated that the troops were to inspect the packed mules before the day's march began and any packers who failed to carry out their duties properly would be replaced by soldiers, who could be relied upon. It is clear that Custer was furious at his advance being impeded in such a manner and after addressing Mathey as he did, the efficiency of the pack-train improved and the irritating delays diminished.

As the sun began to set behind the surrounding hills casting a red glow across the sky, Custer ordered Trumpeter John Martin to sound 'officer's call'. The officers duly assembled in Custer's tent to find a different, more subdued commander than the one they were used to dealing with. This seemed to affect everyone present and as Custer began to speak, they all became aware of the sombre atmosphere that was engulfing them.

Custer informed his officers that until further orders to the contrary, no trumpet calls would be sounded except in an emergency. He continued by telling them that they were all experienced officers and that they knew what to do and when to do what was necessary for the troops in their companies. He would tell them when to move out or make camp. But the day to day running of their respective companies would be left to their judgement and it would also be left to their discretion to ensure that they all were to keep within supporting distance of each other. Any change of orders would be directed by himself. Then his tone changed slightly and speaking much quieter, Custer went to great lengths to impress upon his officers that he was relying on their judgement and loyalty to ensure the campaign was a success. This was out of character for Custer which did not go unnoticed by his officers. Clearly his thoughts during the march that day had made an impression upon his own ability and with the absence of his wife to re-assure him, he needed the strength of his officers to take her place. It appears that Custer was deeply concerned about this campaign. It may be possible that he had realised that he was being sent to his death and there was nothing he could do about it. If so, his concerns were reflecting on his actions even now. If they detected a flaw in his character his officers did not disclose it, but they were all moved by his speech.

Custer then became his old self once more and continued by informing them that the reports he had been given from the Commissioner of Indian Affairs, had shown that the number of hostiles they would probably encounter had been estimated at around 1500. (This number had been based on reports from the agencies, which were grossly inaccurate and continue to be controversial to this day. Sheridan had more accurate reports which were never given to Custer.) Custer also let it be known that he had refused an offer of Gatling guns as they would have impeded the pace of the march. (An ironic statement considering the trouble he had had so far with the civilian packers!) Then he proudly announced that he had also turned down an offer of a battalion from the 2nd Cavalry, on the grounds that the Seventh could handle anything it came up against and if it couldn't then no other regiment in the service could. His officers made no comment concerning that remark.

Finally, Custer informed all those present that it had come to his knowledge that his past actions had been severely criticised by some of his officers, to the department's headquarters more directly to General Sheridan. He informed them that as their commanding officer he was willing to accept recommendations or suggestions from the most junior officer, providing they were presented through the proper channels. Custer reminded them that Army Regulations gave precise instructions concerning such matters and should, therefore, be adhered to. He added that any future offences of this nature would be severely dealt with. Captain Benteen, who had been a close friend of Major Elliott, asked Custer to be a little more precise in regard to his last remarks, to which Custer replied,

> "Captain Benteen, I am not here to be catechised by you sir, but for your information I will state that none of my remarks have been directed towards you!"

Clearly their differences were still smouldering, although Custer does appear to be taking what appropriate action he saw fit in an effort to ensure loyalty from his officers however crude his methods might be. In conclusion, Custer stressed his dependency on his officers' ability and loyalty once more and after issuing his standing orders for repelling any Indian attacks, the meeting drew to a close.

There is no doubt that the officers were all perplexed by Custer's uncharacteristic manner. In his narrative of the campaign, First Lieutenant Edward Godfrey states that when all the officers retired from the meeting, he walked the short distance to his tent with Second Lieutenant George Wallace, who turned to him and said,

> "Godfrey, I believe General Custer is going to be killed."

Alarmed at this remark, Godfrey asked him why he should think that, to which Wallace replied,

> "Because I have never heard Custer talk that way before."

It had been an eventful meeting and, for Godfrey, the evening was not yet over. Leaving Wallace to attend to his duties, Godfrey returned to his company and relayed the standing orders. As he went to check their horses were secure, he came across Mitch Bouyer, the half-breed interpreter, who was in conversation with Bloody Knife, chief of the Arikara scouts, and Half-Yellow-Face, chief of the Crow scouts. On seeing Godfrey approach the party, Bouyer asked him if he had ever fought the Sioux before. Godfrey replied that he had. Bouyer then asked him how many hostiles did Custer expect to encounter, to which Godfrey replied,

> "It is said that we may find between one thousand and fifteen hundred."

Bouyer thought for a moment and then enquired whether Godfrey thought they could 'whip' that many. Godfrey said he thought they could. Bouyer then translated the conversation to the scouts and then concluded,

> "Well, I can tell you we are going have a damned big fight!"

If Godfrey was a man to be unnerved by all this fatalistic talk he had heard that evening, he did not show it. After all he was an officer and an officer should not disclose their thoughts or feelings, especially while on campaign. However, he was also a mortal man and he must have mulled his thoughts over in his mind before settling for the night. Everything was pointing to a disaster and there was nothing he, Edward Godfrey, could do to prevent it.

At 5 o'clock, on the morning of 23rd June, Custer mounted his horse and started up the Rosebud. He was followed by two sergeants, each carrying the battle standards, which flapped noisily in the breeze behind them: one carried the regimental standard and the other displayed Custer's personal banner. (Being a brevet General he was entitled to his own standard and many an old campaigner still referred to him as 'General'.) This was the signal for the column to move out and slowly the long lines of blue-clad soldiers began to stretch along the banks of the Rosebud. The bluffs were ragged here and the column was forced to cross to the right bank and resume the march. Actually, the rough terrain was not very accommodating on either side of the Rosebud and the soldiers were forced to cross back and forth as the river wound its way through the valley. In fact, whilst covering a distance that was little short of five kilometres, the column crossed the Rosebud no less than 5 times!

After marching for approximately 12 kilometres, the advancing column came across the first sight of the abandoned Indian villages they would find that day. In fact they passed numerous abandoned camp sites and at each location a halt was made to assess the information they yielded. While the scouts interpreted the many tracks and other signs, others were busy counting the abandoned lodges and noting the various artefacts they found. There was little doubt in all their minds, regardless of rank or creed, that these huge camp sites indicated a very large concentration of hostile Indians in the region, probably many more than they had been led to believe. The trail was exceptionally large and very easy to follow. Huge furrows had been cut into the soft earth by the trailing lodge poles as the ponies dragged them along the ground, giving the appearance of a freshly ploughed field. Amid these furrows were the imprints of a great number of ponies and Indians, who were travelling on foot. On making the discoveries of the abandoned villages, Custer naturally assumed he was following the movements of one camp as it moved along the Rosebud. He could not have been more wrong, for all the abandoned camps showed the same signs of ageing and therefore, all the individual sites he was passing were actually the camps of the numerous bands that made up the hostile population. He was, in fact, viewing the one huge village and mistaking it for just one sprawled out before moving on. Even Custer should have realised that however slow the Indians may move, they would travel more than a few kilometres between sites. It is also strange that his scouts did not discern the different tribes that had been present or if they did they did not say anything.

A little after 2 o'clock in the afternoon Custer and his troops had reached the point where Reno had turned back on his scouting foray. Spurred on by the increasing signs of hostile activity around and before him, Custer set a gruelling pace for his command to maintain. He was sure that the hostiles were not too far ahead of his command and he was determined to catch up with them before they could make a run for it, assuming they would as usual. As the sun glared down from the clear sky overhead so the heat intensified, making the air dry and dusty, choking horses and riders alike. Blisters formed and broke on many trooper's legs and clouds of dry dust burnt their eyes, which were already swollen from the incessant attacks of swirling gnats. Their horses were also suffering considerably. Apart from the numerous insect bites, sores caused by the accumulation of sweat beneath the saddles were festering in the heat, but there was very little their riders could do to relieve the pain. Even if they had been allowed to rest and recuperate there was very little grazing to be had. The Indian ponies had already cropped all the patches of grass to their roots, thus proving once again that there was very little time between the hostiles' departure and the soldiers' arrival.

By 5 o'clock, having covered a distance of about 53 kilometres, the exhausted column finally ground to a halt and made camp. Once the horses had been unsaddled and rubbed down, the troopers were too tired to eat and many just fell asleep as soon as they sat on their blankets. Amongst the rank and file conversation was practically non-existent, but for many of the officers conversation was paramount, with the increasing fresh Indian trails being the prevailing topic for the evening. It had been an extremely long day, but an exciting one.

Unbeknown to Custer (although, once again, his scouts should have informed him of the signs,) the command had actually reached the site of the huge village where the hostile Sioux had spent 6 days celebrating their victory over Crook. During this time the village had grown in size with the arrival of many other tribes eager to join Crazy Horse and Sitting Bull in their stand. It has been estimated that there were at least 1,500 to 2,500 warriors gathered there, all predominantly belonging to the Sioux or Northern Cheyenne. Over the next few days more would arrive thus increasing the number of warriors further still. With vast pony herds already depleting the surrounding foliage, it was decided to move on to the banks of the Little Big Horn where the grass was plentiful. By now the hostiles were growing more aggressive and more confident as each day passed. A fact that Custer was totally unaware of.

Saturday 24th June brought no relief for the exhausted men and horses. The march was resumed at 5 o'clock that morning and within the hour the Crow scouts had returned with reports of fresh Indian signs, although these tracks had not indicated large numbers of Indians. (These were, in all probability, the trails left by smaller bands of Indians seeking to join the hostile camp.) Stopping momentarily to consult with the scouts, Custer then rode on ahead escorted by two companies, while the remainder of the column slowly continued the advance, all the while keeping to the right bank of the river. As they rode further south the Indian signs became more and more frequent and fresher. It was obvious to everyone that they were right on the heels of the hostiles and many began to speculate as to when they would actually engage them.

At one o'clock in the afternoon, the column was halted and the troops were allowed to brew some coffee, although the horses remained saddled. Custer obviously knew he was getting dangerously close to the enemy and he probably suspected that they knew he was on their trail. He therefore took no chances, not wanting to be caught by a surprise attack. (Why did he allow the troops to brew coffee then? That takes fire, the smoke from which could be seen for many kilometres around.) Custer sent some of his scouts on ahead and sometime later they returned, reporting evidence of another abandoned village situated at the fork of the Rosebud. All were of the opinion that the hostiles were no more than about 48 kilometres away. A mixture of apprehension and excitement rippled through the ranks, for some of the troopers had never fought the Plains warriors and they had no conception of just how vicious the fighting could be.

The command recommenced the march around 5 o'clock, after crossing to the left bank of the Rosebud. Again they passed through numerous abandoned camp sites, each trail getting fresher by the hour. Around two hours later, having travelled 45 kilometres that day, Custer ordered the column to halt. Allowing the troops to rest once again, sending his scouts on ahead to ascertain which direction the hostiles had taken as there was more than one creek in the vicinity that they could have followed. The scouts duly returned an hour or so later and informed Custer that the hostiles had definitely crossed the divide and had moved towards the Little Big Horn river. They were now very close indeed.

So far Custer had conducted an orderly campaign. He had methodically sought out the location of the hostiles, protecting his column from any sudden attacks and he had rested his troops at every given opportunity. He had also made strenuous efforts to maintain a supporting distance between each of his companies and his scouts, thus all points considered it belies later claims that he had made a mad, reckless dash to confront the Indians. Custer had also stuck to Terry's orders so far and had actually intended to do so. Whilst in camp that evening, he informed Godfrey and other officers that,

> "........he was anxious to get as near the divide as possible before daylight, where the command would be concealed during the day, and given ample time for the country to be studied, to locate the village, and to make plans for the attack on June 26th."

It was clearly evident that if Terry's directive, as he understood it, was to be successful he had to remain cautious and wait for the arrival of Terry and Crook, both of whom should be somewhere in the area to support him. If all the columns were on schedule they should converge as planned on 26th June, in the valley of the Little Big Horn.

In actual fact Terry's progress had been extremely slow, for which no satisfactory explanation has ever been offered. Terry has claimed that his own tactical ineptitude and the lack of good guides led his forces to becoming diverted through some extremely inhospitable terrain, thus putting him behind schedule. Rather than advancing along Tullock Creek, the General had altered their course through the almost impassable Big Horn valley, with the result that Custer found himself engaged with the hostiles on his own. Terry was approximately 64 kilometres away and Crook was still in camp, happily fishing! The promised support was not forthcoming and the prospect of it was nowhere to be seen on the horizon.

Crook's failure to continue the campaign was already suspect. However, coupled with Terry's slow advance these acts are tantamount to being felonious and in the absence of any positive evidence to involve Sheridan, these two commanders must be held culpable for the events that were to follow. If Terry and Crook had been given extra instructions to delay their movements, it would explain why the overall plan (as revealed to the public,) did not result in the expected fruition. Crook was nowhere in the vicinity and Terry, accompanied by Gibbon, did not arrive in the valley of the Little Big Horn until 27th June, a full 24 hours behind schedule as we shall see. As a military commander, Terry should have made every effort to abide by the orders he had issued to Custer and support the cavalry he had deployed. Here, we are posed with yet another unanswerable question. In the light of subsequent events, how do we know for sure that the orders that Terry claims to have issued Custer are the actual orders that Custer received? In other words, Custer may have been given a different set of orders or extra instructions to the orders that Terry asserts he issued. Nothing was reportedly found on the battlefield after the fight, so it is possible. If there were differences between the sets of orders, it could explain why Custer adhered to his which were different from Terry's actions.

Unaware of the lack of support, Custer continued to follow the plan which, as far as he was aware, was still in operation. On receiving the reports from his scouts, he summoned Lieutenant Varnum to his tent. He informed Varnum of the scouts' discoveries and told him he was to accompany the Crow scouts to a vantage position where he could observe the valley of the Little Big Horn much clearer in the morning. Varnum was also instructed to send a messenger to him as soon as possible after sunrise. Custer told him to leave immediately and that he would follow a little later with the column, hopefully reaching the divide between the Rosebud and the Little Big Horn by morning. Varnum duly left as ordered, taking with him Charley Reynolds and some Arikara scouts, in addition to the Crows.

As the sun slowly sank behind the surrounding hills, Custer sent word to all his officers to report to him instantly. He solemnly informed them that the scouts had reported the existence of a very fresh trail that led over the divide towards the Little Big Horn and that he had dispatched Lieutenant Varnum with his scouts to make an observation of the valley. He also instructed his officers that the march would resume as soon as all the companies were ready, as he was anxious to reach the divide before daylight if it was at all possible. Here the column would halt as they could safely be concealed during the day, thus giving the scouts ample time to make their observations and get back to him. This would also give the exhausted soldiers and their mounts a chance to rest and prepare for an offensive against the hostiles, which would probably take place the following day, 26th June, by which time Terry and Crook should have arrived on the scene.

Although the air was warm, a strong southerly breeze began blowing and as the officers left to prepare their respective companies for departure, Custer's personal standard was blown to the ground. Lieutenant Godfrey picked it up and attempted to replace it in its original position, but once again it fell to the ground. A second attempt secured it in the soil where it fluttered furiously in the breeze. At the time Godfrey did not pay much attention to the incident, however, some time after the battle Lieutenant Wallace asked him if he remembered the event. Wallace had witnessed the incident and at the time wondered if it was an omen forecasting a disaster. It is not known whether or not Custer saw his standard fall to the ground. If he did, it was not documented.

The march resumed around 11 o'clock that evening and continued well into the night. It was at this point that Custer deviated from Terry's orders. Instead of continuing down the Rosebud, he turned his regiment west towards the divide, but it was so dark that the soldiers found it increasingly difficult to continue the march. They were tired and their horses were tired. Their stinging eyes could hardly discern the trail they were supposed to be following, even though the trail had deep ruts carved into the soil. They could only attempt to keep in line by continually riding in the dust cloud that the horses in front of them whipped up. Occasionally a breeze would sweep past them and clear the dust cloud, again stinging the eyes of both rider and mount, making them all the more sore. When this occurred, the affected companies had to stop and listen for the sound of the troopers ahead of them and then continue their march. But progress was painfully slow. Finally, after travelling a further 16 kilometres, the column came to a halt. It was now about 2 o'clock in the morning of Sunday 25th June, although the troops had lost track of time and they were too exhausted to care. The order was given for all horses to be unsaddled and the men to make camp.

The horses breathed a sigh of relief and the men settled for the night. Once they had all had something to eat, some of the men became quite talkative and began to speculate on just how close they actually were to the hostiles and how many more days in the saddle it would be before the campaign came to an end. Later, Private Peter Thompson, Company C, wrote:

> 'One old soldier said it would end just as soon as we could reach Sitting Bull. Another said, "If that is all, the campaign would soon be over, and Custer will take us with him to the Centennial." This created a roar of laughter among those who heard him. The conversation continued, each one telling his neighbour what he would take when Sitting Bull's camp was captured.'

Another man who was not able to relax that night, despite being utterly exhausted, was Mark Kellogg. A relatively young man in comparison to some of his travelling companions, he was distinctive by the fact that he was not carrying any weapons. (It would be safe to speculate that he managed to locate some weapons during the battle.) The only equipment he carried was a small black satchel in which was stored his paper and pencils, plus his tobacco and pipe. As the soldiers slept around him filling the air with a chorus of gentle melodious snoring, Kellogg was busy writing the last of his dispatches to the 'Bismarck Tribune', outlining the advance to date and ending with:

> 'We leave the Rosebud tomorrow and by the time this reaches you, we will have met and fought the red devils, with what result remains to be seen. I go with Custer and will be at the death!'

Even Kellogg had become disorientated in the darkness, for the command had already left the Rosebud and were in Davis Creek. Kellogg's oil-cloth satchel and his water stained diary were recovered after the battle and delivered to a druggist in Bismarck, a person he was known to have played chess with. The actual location of the satchel when found is not known, although it is presumed by many that he had stowed it in the pack-train before the command was divided. As this has not been substantiated, it is speculative but doubtful. He was a journalist and his satchel would have been carried with him at all times. However, it does appcar that premonitions of Custer's death were not confined to the soldiers. Even Kellogg stated that he 'will be at the death'.

Contrary to those who believe that Custer disobeyed his orders, it is clearly evident that he did not. He had followed the trail of the hostiles which took him away from the Rosebud and down Davis Creek, towards the Little Big Horn. He had also kept to the schedule and hoped to continue to do so. He had found 'sufficient reason' to change direction. Anyway, if Terry was to meet him on the Little Big Horn, Custer had no reason to stay on the Rosebud. Everything was going exactly according to plan.

Chapter 5

The First Shot is Fired

As dawn broke on Sunday 25th June, the slowly rising sun cast its long golden rays over the crest of the Wolf Mountains that lay on the divide between the Rosebud and Little Big Horn valleys. From an old Indian lookout on the edge of these heights, known as the 'Crow's Nest', three scouts diligently surveyed the river basin that sprawled before them. At first the early morning shadows that lay under a blanket of fine mist clouded their view, but as the sunlight spread along the glistening water of the river, the weary scouts realised that they were looking down on the hostile encampment they had been searching for.

It was Hairy Moccasin who had first detected the pall of grey smoke that drifted lazily over the hidden tipis. As the mist began to dissipate the smoke became clearly visible, even though it was some 24 kilometres in the distance. Goes Ahead scanned the woods, as its trees stretched out along the banks of the winding river. Beyond the dark foliage he could see some small black shapes dotting the gentle slopes of the hills. He rubbed his sore eyes and looked again. The small black shapes were Indian ponies, leisurely grazing the succulent grass glimmering in the early morning dew. There was no mistake. They had definitely found their quarry.

White-Man-Runs-Him nodded in agreement and silently slid down the rocks to where Lieutenant Varnum and the other Indian scouts were dozing. Varnum had not had much sleep in the past 36 hours, during which time he had ridden more than 96 kilometres over rough terrain and executed numerous scouting forays ahead of the column. His Crow and Arikara scouts had fared little better. Leaving 3 Crow scouts to watch the valley, he had grabbed the chance of being able to close his eyes, even if it was for only 45 minutes. At the lightest touch of White-Man-Runs-Him, Varnum's eyes opened in an instant and his long bushy moustache bristled in the hazy sunlight as the old Indian informed him of their discovery. Varnum brushed the dust from his clothes and stealthily crept up to the lookout to see for himself. His eyes were still sore and his vision was blurred, making it difficult for him to discern what his scouts were pointing out to him.

A few minutes later he was joined by Charley Reynolds, one of the civilian scouts that had been assigned to the regiment, who peered down into the valley through his field-glasses. After a short while he replaced the glasses in their case and nodded to Varnum, without uttering a word. Charley Reynolds was a man who rarely spoke, but when he did it was short and to the point. Lately, he had been quieter than usual, preferring his own company as they had marched along the trail. One of the fingers on his gun hand had become infected and at times it had been so painful that he had rested his hand in a sling. However, this morning it had eased a little, allowing him to concentrate on the job he was being paid to do. Reynolds extracted a notebook from his coat pocket, scribbled a message and then tore out the page. He handed the piece of paper to a young Arikara scout called Red Star and instructed him to deliver it to Lieutenant-Colonel Custer. Accompanied by his friend, Bull, Red Star rode off to find the soldiers.

At their bivouac along the banks of Davis Creek the troops were slowly rousing from their sleep. Coffee pots steamed in readiness over small camp fires, although very few would attempt to drink any as the water from the creek was very alkaline. Even the horses and mules were reluctant to drink the water. Red Star had no difficulty in locating Custer. He was seated by a camp fire in deep conversation with Fred Girard, a civilian interpreter. Also present were the more senior of the Arikara scouts; Bob-Tailed-Bull, Bloody Knife and Stabbed. The young Crow leapt from his horse and thrust Reynolds' note towards Custer. Trying to contain his excitement, he told Custer that they had found the hostile camp. Girard translated Red Star's hurried words for Custer, who had risen and was reading the message. Mounting his blaze faced sorrel, Vic, Custer rode bareback through the camp issuing orders to his officers. Upon his return, Bloody Knife made a remark which caught Custer's attention and in his usual brusque manner he asked Girard to translate what the Indian had said. Girard replied that Bloody Knife thought they would find enough Sioux to keep them fighting for two or three days. Custer smiled and looked across at the scout. He told Girard to inform Bloody Knife that they would deal with them in a day. Bloody Knife shook his head. He had campaigned with Custer on numerous occasions before that day and, some said, he was Custer's favourite scout. Bloody Knife did not hold much faith in 'Custer's Luck' as others did. He also knew the Sioux very well.

It is evident that Custer's Indian scouts were convinced they would eventually find very large concentrations of hostiles. The abandoned camp sites they had passed and the extremely large trail they had followed indicated that. That they conveyed their interpretations of the hostile trail is also evident, as Lieutenant Wallace confirmed in his official report:

> '..........so the scouts could determine how long before the Indians had camped there and roughly how many the Seventh might encounter. The scouts' estimates were high, much higher

> than Custer's and those of his officers. The officers, of course, still based their estimates on the numbers the agents had given on how many of their charges had jumped the reservations. There is no question that the agents' figures were too low, whether through ignorance or deceit.'

By 8 o'clock the regiment was assembled and ready to resume the march. Custer gave the order and the troops moved forward. He was dressed in a plain blue-grey flannel shirt that was open at the neck and displayed no insignia of rank, with his fringed buckskin trousers disappearing into high black leather boots. He had abandoned his familiar flamboyant attire for clothes more suitable for a campaign on the prairie. Under the broad-rimmed, light grey hat his thinning hair was short; either an attempt to disguise himself or to cheat the enemy of a trophy. He was only too aware that his flowing shoulder length hair had become synonymous with his character and would be highly prized amongst the hostiles, who had named him 'Long Hair'.

Two and a half hours later, after travelling a further 16 kilometres, the column reached a ravine just a short distance from the Crow's Nest where Varnum and his scouts were still observing the valley. Custer halted the column in the shade of a high crag and left the soldiers in the ravine while he rode forward to the lookout. Having dismounted, he followed Charley Reynolds to the edge of the rocks and scanned the valley through his field-glasses. Unfortunately, during the length of time that had elapsed before his arrival, the sun had risen further into the sky causing the valley to become obscured by a deep haze. Thus, Custer could not see anything that would indicate an Indian camp. All that was visible to him were some chalky buttes and a lone Indian tipi that was standing beside another that had fallen over. Custer was irritated. He curtly told Reynolds that he could not see any signs of an Indian camp, to which Reynolds pointed out the location of the camp again. Custer still could not see anything to indicate that the Sioux had been found, but he also knew that Charley Reynolds was not a man to make mistakes. After a moment's thought, Custer suggested that Reynolds could be right, although he could still not see any evidence to support him.

For a few minutes Custer reclined on the rocky summit. He was taking a moment to consider his next move. (Hardly a display of rashness that he has been branded with over the following years!) Although he had not been able to see any signs of an Indian camp, all the trails they had been following had led to this valley. If the hostiles were not down there where else could they be? Seeing his chance to have a word with Custer, Mitch Bouyer moved up the slope and sat next to the Colonel. He was followed by White-Man-Runs-Him. Bouyer asked Custer what he thought of the camp. The scouts were curious to know. Custer glared at him. He was in command of the column and he did not recall having agreed that the enemy was within reach. Rumours were bound to fly and that could affect his assessment of the situation. Either he had not heard Bouyer correctly or he had missed the question, but he bluntly informed Bouyer that even if there were hostiles in the valley, he was certain that they had not spotted the soldiers yet. To Custer's chagrin, White-Man-Runs-Him then told him that he had watched two young Sioux riding towards the valley and that they had been close enough to see the soldiers' camp fires earlier that morning.

Custer was furious at that remark. He must have realised that he had made a grave mistake in allowing the troops to brew coffee. If the scouts could see the smoke from the hostile camp then there was no reason to doubt that the hostile scouts could locate his column for the same reason. Although he could still not see any evidence of the hostile camp hidden in the valley, he was loath to doubt the word of his scouts whose eyes were much sharper than his. Now he had to consider the possibility that his position was known to the hostiles and that he no longer had the element of surprise. He could not allow his scouts to see his indecision or doubt. Custer snapped at the Crow scout, reiterating his claim that the soldiers had not been seen. Regaining his temper somewhat, Custer then informed all those present of his change of plan. They would wait until dark and then hit the camp from all sides, if by then he was convinced there was a camp to be hit. White-Man-Runs-Him thought the plan would not succeed and as he tried to explain why, Custer, infuriated at the apparent insolence, cut him short.

Accounts of this phase in the events are limited and hazy in content. It does appear from available documents that not only was Custer annoyed with himself, as much as his subordinates, but he was reluctant to commit the regiment into an engagement for which he did not have command of all the facts. Hardly the reckless commander we are supposed to believe he was. He knew he had made mistakes and he had to consider how much of those mistakes would affect the campaign as a whole. He had failed to see the hostile village that his scouts insisted was situated in the valley. He had not taken the correct precautions to ensure the column was not discovered, although he did suspect that his movements were probably known to the hostiles from the moment he picked up their trail along the Rosebud. And finally, it irked him that his scouts were questioning his decisions even though he was doubting their judgement. Custer was in a very unenviable position. He did not want to deviate from Terry's orders any more than he had already, yet he was being pressured into doing just that for all the indications showed that the situation had changed. He needed more information and it was not long in coming.

White-Man-Runs-Him knew that the conversation was over. He slowly rose to his feet and made his way back to the column. Custer stood and brushed the dust from his clothes. Then he followed the Indian down the slope. As he mounted his horse an officer galloped to a halt before him, sweat running down his face. Through panting breath, Captain Tom Custer excitedly informed his brother that they had definitely been spotted by the Sioux. Custer frowned and told him to calm down, but Tom Custer was having none of that. The game was now on. He continued his report by telling Custer that Captain Yates had found a loose pack on one of the mules and that a box of hard tack was missing. Custer stared at him, not in the least bit amused. It appeared that what White-Man-Runs-Him had said could be true. However, it was a well known fact that all members of the Custer family liked playing practical jokes and Custer warned his brother that if this was a joke then now was not the time to be playing one. Tom Custer assured him that it was not a joke. He continued his report by informing the Colonel that Yates had sent Sergeant Curtis and two men from F Company back up the trail to recover the box. When they found it an Indian boy was sitting on it eating some hard tack. Curtis had shot the boy thinking he was alone, however, two young bucks had seen the incident and they disappeared over the hill, riding their ponies towards the Little Big Horn valley. Curtis had ridden back to report to Yates, who had told Keogh who in turn had notified him. Tom Custer had then reported the incident to his brother. He concluded the report by adding that Herendeen had been sent back up the trail to assess the situation.

Custer did not utter a word as he wheeled his horse round to re-join the column. The Captain fell in beside him. In the ravine they could hear the jingle of harnesses as the regiment awaited further orders. Custer snapped that they were making too much noise. He seemed to become more irritable as the minutes ticked by. Of course it is probable that Custer was trying to reach the most crucial decision of his life and he was finding it increasingly difficult. If the hostiles had spotted the soldiers and he stuck to his orders, they could easily escape. On the other hand, if he attacked now he knew he would not have any support until the following day, assuming Terry stuck to the schedule. He still did not know the whereabouts of Crook and that was worrying. Then there was the doubt. Even if Indians were in the area, it did not mean that the village was. His scouts could be wrong, but what if they were right? As an experienced field commander such indecision was against his nature. Concerning the necessity of his quick decisions in battle, Custer once wrote:

> 'I am not impetuous or impulsive .... Everything that I have ever done has been the result of the study I have made of imaginary situations that might arise. When I become engaged in campaign or battle and a great emergency arose, everything that I have ever read or studied focused in my mind as if the

situation were under a magnifying glass and my decision was the instantaneous result.'

In most of his previous campaigns or battles he had had support to hand. Here, he was on his own in hostile territory with little or no information regarding the enemy. It was exactly the situation that Sheridan had foreseen. Custer was fully aware that his troops were awaiting his orders. They would obey him without question, but how could he be sure he had made the right decision? He turned to his brother and grumbled about the civilian packers. They had been the scourge of his problems since they had left the Yellowstone. He told Tom that although he had guessed that the Sioux would have scouts roaming the country, he would never have thought that they would be trailing the regiment to pick up what the packers had dropped. Tom Custer said nothing. When his brother was in a mood it was best to keep quiet.

Back on the Crow's Nest Hairy Moccasin had remained at his post, still observing the valley. Just over a kilometre away he could see about 6 Indians on horseback riding towards the trees along the river bank. They were Sioux, so he called Mitch Bouyer to take a look. Bouyer signalled for the scouts to return to the column. Things seemed to be picking up a pace. He rode down to report to Custer. Bouyer told him that the Sioux they had just seen were circling their horses, which indicated that they were signalling the camp. They had obviously seen the soldiers. Custer frowned and glanced down the creek in the direction that Bouyer had pointed. Bouyer became impatient at Custer's hesitation. He told Custer that if he didn't attack now then the Indians would scatter. Custer spun his horse round to face Bouyer. It was the second time that morning his authority had been questioned and his vexation showed. In no uncertain terms he informed Bouyer that he should stick to scouting and leave the fighting to him. Bouyer didn't answer. As he rode away to join the scouts, George Herendeen thundered to a halt accompanied by Tom Custer.

The pace was in full flow now. No sooner had Custer digested one piece of information, more was thrown at him. He was not being given much breathing space to think clearly. He snapped at Herendeen to make his report. Herendeen informed the Colonel that the fresh pony signs that had been found indicated they had been made by a war party. Custer enquired as to whether or not they had got a good look at the Indians. He needed to know whether they were Sioux or Cheyenne. Herendeen replied that he had only been able to see one and that one appeared to be a scout. He wasn't sure about the tribe.

In fact, Herendeen had found a great many fresh pony tracks way back up the trail. They had obviously been made after Sergeant Curtis had killed the Indian boy. Unknown to Herendeen these tracks had been made by Little Wolf and his small band of Cheyenne as they traversed the hills on their way to join the hostiles. They had first discovered the soldiers while they had been on the upper reaches of the Rosebud and, contrary to the wishes of his younger warriors, Little Wolf wisely decided to follow the soldiers rather than attack them. He guessed correctly what was happening and waited until the time was right to leave the soldiers and head for the camp, where he would inform the Council of the soldiers' presence.

It is obvious that Custer did not lead his troops in a reckless attack upon the hostiles. He had not moved his command while he was receiving the reports and he had carefully gauged the information before reaching any decisions. However, he was under pressure to do something. There was still no word from either Crook or Terry. Were they anywhere near his position? He didn't know. Both Herendeen and Tom Custer insisted that the Sioux were all around them preparing to attack. As they stood at present, the troops were vulnerable. Custer thought different. According to the old manner in which they fought, the hostiles could slip through and disappear again. If that happened it could take weeks, even months to track them down and engage them. He told his brother to instruct Lieutenant William Cooke, the regimental adjutant, to sound 'officer's call'. Custer then informed them that the command would undergo a weapons inspection, as he had decided to push forward and strike the Indians as soon as possible. Tom Custer turned his horse and rode down the line to find Cooke. Custer then turned to Varnum, who was waiting with his scouts, and told him to ensure his scouts were ready as they would probably see action before the sun went down.

The scouts did not need to be told. Their preparations for battle were already under way. They stripped to their breech-clouts and moccasins, then applied their war-paint as they chanted war songs. They all knew they would probably not survive this fight unless they were incredibly lucky. Custer started ahead towards the direction of the Little Big Horn valley. Where was Terry and why had he received no word from Crook? Terry's original orders had been shot to pieces and he was being pushed into making a decision he was uncertain of. He was on his own, exactly as Sheridan had planned.

The Crow and Arikara scouts had good reason to be apprehensive of the impending fight. They had read the signs and did not like what they had seen. The signs told them that the enemy was extremely large in numbers, perhaps more than they could visualise and it did not look like they were running away, which was somewhat confusing.

Stretched along the western banks of the Little Big Horn, hidden from view by the numerous trees, was one of the largest Indian encampments ever to have been assembled and the likes of which were never to be seen again. It consisted of seven huge camp circles, each camp circle being formed in accordance with the order in which the tribes had travelled. The whole area stretched some 4 to 6 kilometres from north to south and spread westward from the river. Even with the help of maps, it is almost impossible to visualise the sheer enormity of such a concentration of Indians.

To the north lay the 300 tipis of the Cheyenne. Many of the elders of this tribe could recall the attacks they had endured at Sand Creek and the Washita. Many brave men, women and children had perished at these places and the elders carried bitter memories of those horrors ever since. They had no reason to trust the army and when Sitting Bull had sent his message across the Plains, they had eagerly responded. Enclosed within this circle were some families of Gros Venure and a few Arapaho, who had strayed from their own tribe. This group of almost 1800 Indians were led by their elder chiefs, Dirty Moccasins and Old Bear. Their two other chiefs, Dull Knife and Little Wolf, had not yet arrived in the valley although Little Wolf did make an appearance later in the afternoon. (Dull Knife and Little Wolf were to make a name for themselves two years later, when they led their people on an exodus from Fort Reno on the Canadian River to their old hunting grounds on the Yellowstone.) For the present, the Cheyenne war chiefs who would lead them into battle were Crazy Head, Lame-White-Man and Last Bull. They were all seasoned warriors and had fought the soldiers many times before.

Situated south west of the Cheyenne lay the hide tipis of the Ogallala Sioux, a strong tribe of the Teton Division. The Ogallala had often fought alongside the Cheyenne when fighting the soldiers, so it was not surprising that they had camped in close proximity. In past years the Ogallala had written their epitaph across the Plains in blood, under the very chief who had signed the Treaty of 1868. Preferring to remain at the agency, Red Cloud had allowed his son, Jack Red Cloud, to represent him at Sitting Bull's Council. The leading war chiefs of the Ogallala were Big Road and He-Dog, although many warriors had opted to follow the leadership of a young warrior who had not yet attained the position of war chief, Crazy Horse. The very mention of his name struck terror in the hearts of both settlers and soldiers.

Nearer to the river, just south of the Ogallala circle, was the smaller camp circle of the Brulé Sioux, another tribe of the Teton Division. Their head chief, Spotted Tail, had also chosen to remain at the agency in Nebraska. Like Red Cloud, he did not have the stamina for war anymore and he now considered himself an elder-chief, leaving the fighting to the younger warriors. One of the minor chiefs present was Crow Dog, who would eventually murder Spotted Tail in 1881. Obviously Crow Dog was not an Indian to upset!

Encamped within one circle, just below the Brulé were two of the smaller tribes of the Teton Sioux: the Sans Arc and about 130 members of the Two Kettle tribe. The main war leaders of the Sans Arc were Fast Bear and Spotted Eagle, while the chief of the smaller group of the Two Kettle Sioux was Runs-the-Enemy. None of these warriors were to become very well-known during the Indian Wars.

To the south, just across a small tributary of the Little Big Horn, lay the camp circle of the Minniconjou Sioux. Another tribe of the powerful Teton Division, the Minniconjou had always enjoyed a very influential voice at the Council meetings. Their head chief was Lame Deer and although he was a very able leader, his name would be overshadowed by those of his war chiefs: Fast Bull, High Backbone and Hump, the latter of which was probably the most prominent Minniconjou during the battle.

A little further south of the Minniconjou camp circle, but situated a little further away from the Little Big Horn, were the Blackfoot Sioux. Their camp circle also included some small bands of Yanktonai, Yankton and Santee Sioux as well as a few Assiniboin. The main leader of the Blackfoot was Scabby Head, who again was to remain among the lesser known chiefs. However, the leader of the Santee was none other than the great Inkpaduta, who has instigated the Minnesota Massacre of 1857. Now an old warrior he was still keen to fight the soldiers. Some Indians just never stopped fighting!

At the extreme south of the encampment was the largest camp circle of them all, that of the Hunkpapa who formed the rear guard when travelling and were the last to make camp. It was the occupants of this circle, comprising of approximately 3,000 men, women and children who had formed the nucleus of the dissidents when they declared their intentions following the signing of the 1868 Peace Treaty. Their war chiefs were Gall, Crow King and Black Moon, none of whom knew the meaning of the word 'fear'. It was Gall who, perhaps, was to suffer the greatest loss of any Indian that day. When Major Reno led the first charge up the valley his soldiers' bullets struck several women and children who were running to safety, amongst them were Gall's family. On seeing nearly all of them killed Gall became incensed and his hatred of the soldiers made him uncontrollable. Some time after the battle he admitted,

"…….I killed all my enemies with the hatchet!"

The head chief and spiritual leader of the Hunkpapa was the greatest of all the Indian statesmen to emerge from the Plains, the indomitable Sitting Bull. Right from the onset of the military's enforcement of the reservation system, he had declared his intention of remaining free to live and hunt on the Plains as a Sioux should and he firmly opposed the government's proposals for the purchase of the Black Hills, stating,

> "We want no white men here. The Black Hills belong to me. If the whites try to take them, I will fight!"

Although he was no longer a warrior he was a very formidable statesman and it was this exceptional ability that he had exercised to unify all these powerful tribes. Sitting Bull was large in stature and charismatic in style. When he spoke people listened to every word. In view of the available evidence, it has been estimated that there were around 12,00 Indians assembled in the valley of the Little Big Horn, of whom there were approximately 4,000 seasoned warriors. It is worth noting here that estimates have varied considerably over the years and those quoted here are an average taken from many. Be that as it may, it was an exceptional feat on the part of Sitting Bull that should not go unnoticed.

Thus it was, secure in the safety of their large numbers that the Indians found themselves on the morning of Sunday 25th June. To them it was life as usual with the young boys tending the pony herds or swimming in the river. The women were busy either fleshing fresh antelope skins or digging for wild turnips in the hillside and the men were either fishing or talking amongst themselves about the defeat of the blue-coats on the Rosebud. No one had any problems and the morning was warm, sunny and peaceful, but the hostiles were by no means complacent.

Around mid-morning a 25-year old Ogallala by the name of Eagle Elk returned to the encampment with his scouting party. They had been away for the past eight days keeping a watchful eye on Crook's soldiers as they made their retreat from the Rosebud. On their return journey they had looked for some game to hunt but they couldn't find any. Eagle Elk felt sure that the game had been frightened away by soldiers in the area but, like the game, he had not seen any. Sitting Bull was concerned. Indians lived in harmony with nature, sharing the same dangers, so he knew they had not scared the game away. As he listened to the others idly chatting around the fire, he had a growing conviction that something was wrong. But there had been no reported sightings of soldiers.

Other Indians felt an uneasiness in the air as well. A 17-year old Minniconjou called Iron Hail had slept late and his younger brother was already tending their ponies on a small creek. As Iron Hail quickly ate his morning meal his uncle became increasingly agitated. Eventually he turned to Iron Hail and said,

> "When you finish eating go help your brother with the horses. Something might happen today. I feel it in the air."

Iron Hail did as he was told and headed for the creek. Black Elk, a young Ogallala, was already tending his family's pony herd, his uncle's words were still ringing in his ears,

> "...........If anything happens today, bring back all the horses as fast as you can. Keep your eyes on the camp at all times."

When the fighting began, Black Elk did exactly as he had been told. These accounts have been repeatedly recorded and lead us to believe that some Indians may have had a sixth-sense. In any event, they have been vividly remembered through the years.

Up on the hills to the east of the Little Big Horn, where the small creeks created gullies that broke up the landscape, two young Hunkpapa boys, Deeds and his brother, Brown Back, were rounding up ponies that belonged to Deeds grandfather. They were assisted by their young Ogalalla friend, Drags-the-Rope. The ponies had strayed during the night and the boys had been sent out to bring them back. As the other boys rounded up the ponies, 10-year old Deeds had found a box lying in the grass. Prising the lid free, Deeds knelt to taste the hard tack inside. As he did so a shot rang out and Deeds fell to the ground, the bullet searing through his chest and shattering his lungs. Sergeant Curtis, of Company F, had fired the first shot of the day. But he had not just killed another Indian boy, for Deeds was the nephew of Sitting Bull and it would not just be his death lamentations that would fill the air by nightfall.

PART THREE

'Far up the lonely mountain – side,
My wandering footsteps led;
The moss lay thick beneath my feet,
The pine sighed overhead.

The trace of a dismantled fort
Lay in the forest nave,
And in the shadows near my path
I saw a soldier's grave.'

Mary Ashley Townsend

Chapter 1

The Thunder of Hooves

By midday the sun had risen high overhead and it was burning hot, with very little breeze to moderate the temperature. Taking advantage of the scorching heat, the flies appeared to have multiplied in their thousands and they swarmed all over the soldiers and their mounts, relentlessly biting the warm flesh at every opportunity.

At 'Officer's Call' Custer briefed all those present on the current situation as he saw it. He told them that he had been reliably informed by his scouts that their presence had been discovered by the Sioux and that as they no longer had the element of surprise, they had no option but to attack now and drive the hostiles to where Terry and Gibbon would contain them. There was no mention of Crook marching up from the south to support them. As Custer had received no word from Crook to the contrary he assumed the campaign orders were still effective. He then instructed all officers to complete a weapons inspection and ensure that their companies were prepared for action. They would resume the march when he was satisfied the command was ready.

Custer then took a little time to prepare himself for the final march. Beside him his horse, Vic, waited patiently for his master to mount. Custer slipped into his fringed buckskin campaign jacket and tied his red cravat under the collar. All his earlier doubts and fears seemed to have vanished and his old self-confidence had gained the upper hand once more. Every nerve in his body must have tingled with excitement as they had prior to previous clashes with hostiles. He had been successful then and he had no doubt he would be so today. All preparations completed, Custer mounted his horse and gave the command to advance in columns of two's.

With White-Man-Runs-Him guiding the path across the divide, Custer followed with his regiment at a fast trot. Beside him, riding his familiar grey mule was Mark Kellogg. His mule was so small that Kellogg's feet almost touched the ground, but this plucky little animal was sure footed and had no difficulty in keeping up with the much larger cavalry mounts. Within minutes they had crossed the divide and reached the head-waters of the small creeks that flowed into the Little Big Horn. The valley yawned before them and yet there was still no visible sign of any habitation in the area. Custer called a halt and through his adjutant, Cooke, he divided his regiment into four battalions.

The advance battalion was assigned to Major Marcus Reno, a 41-year old officer who, although he had encountered Indians in Washington Territory, had never fought the Sioux. His penchant for liquor frequently drove him to clash with Custer who was abstemious. However, he was a soldier who would obey orders to the last letter and as the regiment's senior ranking officer, Custer had no option but to trust his judgement under fire. Reno's adjutant was Second Lieutenant Benjamin Hodgson and at 28-years of age was already a seasoned campaigner of the Seventh. The battalion comprised of Company A, commanded by Captain Myles Moylan; Company G, under First Lieutenant Donald McIntosh; and Company M, led by Captain Thomas French. With the addition of the two surgeons, Henry R. Porter and James M. DeWolf; Second Lieutenant Charles Varnum and his Indian scouts; plus various attached civilians, the battalion numbered some 222 officers and men in strength.

The second battalion under the command of the regiment's senior Captain, Frederick Benteen, consisted of Benteen's own Company H; together with Company D led by Captain Thomas Weir and Company K under the command of First Lieutenant Edward S. Godfrey. In comparison to Reno's battalion, Benteen had a total of 143 officers and men under his command, with no civilians or scouts.

The pack-train with its civilian packers was under the command of First Lieutenant Edward Mathey, who had a few military personnel from various companies that were also under his direction. Company B, under the command of Captain Thomas McDougall, was detailed as escort to the pack-train, although who would assume overall command should it prove necessary is not clear. This third battalion numbered 128 officers and men in strength.

The remainder of the regiment rode with Custer. Under the command of Custer's able adjutant, First Lieutenant William Cooke, the headquarters detachment consisted of 10 men, including Custer, and 4 civilians. The battalion was comprised as follows: Captain Thomas Custer with Company C; First Lieutenant Algernon Smith and Company E; Captain George Yates with Company F; Captain Myles Keogh and Company I; and First Lieutenant James Calhoun with Company L. The total military strength of Custer's battalion was 210 officers and men.

With the addition of some Crow scouts from Varnum's command, Custer's battalion was comparable in strength to Reno's battalion, although Custer had more companies and, therefore, more officers. Official records are very misleading concerning the strength of the regiment at the Little Big Horn. The Seventh was seriously under strength at that time, a fact that few historians bother to mention. In actual fact the Seventh was under strength to the tune of

217 officers and men due to a number of very nefarious reasons. This amounted to another battalion! These absences included Colonel Samuel Sturgis, the Commanding Officer of the Seventh, and the regiment's senior Major, Joseph Tilford. One officer was exceptionally conspicuous by his absence and that was Captain Michael Sheridan, who had been conveniently assigned to his brother in Chicago, General Philip Sheridan. It must also be mentioned that one officer and three men were en-route to join the regiment, although they did not manage to do so before the battle. Of course, the majority of those absent also includes those on sick leave or in confinement, but it does not detract from the fact that the Seventh was seriously under-manned, which Custer must have been aware of. It is evident then that Sheridan had ensured that the Colonel commanding the Seventh and his brother were not only out of the line of fire but also out of the way to give Custer a free rein.

Custer's choice of officers in his battalions has also caused much speculation over the years. Under his own command Custer had gathered his family and friends, those who obviously loved and respected him. Major Reno, as second in command and of field rank, had been detailed a comparable battalion but with officers of temperate loyalty. Reno had no respect for Custer. He was an uninspiring officer, whereas Custer was charismatic and flamboyant, and Reno commanded his troops strictly according to the military manuals of the day. Custer was far more flexible in all areas. Benteen's battalion appears to be comprised of officers all of whom had displayed discontent with the Colonel, including the Captain himself. Was this selection a deliberate ploy on Custer's part or did he make a huge mistake? Then there was the pack-train with its escort. By the time Custer split the column into the assigned battalions, the park-train and escort were more than several kilometres behind the regiment and no-one was making any effort to reduce the distance. Both McDougall and Mathey stated later that the mules were giving them problems, but that had been the case since the start of the campaign and they should have got themselves in order by this time. Of course the burning question is, that aside from his own battalion, how many of the remaining officers could Custer rely upon to go to his aid should the need arise? The answer is very few, if any at all.

Through his adjutant, Custer ordered Benteen to swing his battalion to the left and down behind some bluffs to scout for any hostiles in that vicinity. Three years later, at the Reno Court of Inquiry, Benteen stated,

> "My orders were to proceed out into a line of bluffs...........: to pitch into anything I came across and to send word back to General Custer at once if I came across anything.
>
> I had gone about a mile [1.6 kilometres] when I received instructions through the Chief Trumpeter that if I found nothing

> before reaching the first line of bluffs to go on to the second line of bluffs with the same instructions.
>
> ....I received orders, through the Sergeant Major that if I saw nothing from the second line of bluffs then to go into the valley, and if there was nothing in that valley to go on to the next valley.
>
> The angle of my march to the route rout of the regiment was about 45 degrees, a left oblique."

Benteen duly swung his battalion south west towards the bluffs. He had not been assigned any scouts to guide him and, as such, had to rely on his own judgement in leading his command in the right direction, even though he was unfamiliar with the terrain.

Custer then turned his attention to Reno, directing the Major to cross to the left bank of Ash Creek (now known as Reno Creek), while he remained on the right and it was in this formation that the two battalions continued to march. The pack-train continued to trail behind, although it does appear at this point that for most of the time the battalions were in sight of each other should support be needed. (With the exception of Benteen's battalion of course.) Custer was obviously being more cautious than he has been given credit for.

Around 2 o'clock the Crow scouts found an abandoned tipi situated on the northern side of the creek. This was the tipi that Custer had previously observed from the Crow's Nest. A few minutes later the Crows were joined by some Arikara scouts, who rode around the tipi striking it with their short whips. One Arikara slashed at the hide with his knife and peered inside, quickly withdrawing making the sign of the dead. As the scout re-mounted his pony, Custer's column slowed to a halt. On the opposite side of the creek Reno brought his command to a halt and watched.

The burial lodge belonged to a Sans Arc Sioux by the name of Old-She-Bear. He had been shot through both hips during the fight against Crook on the Rosebud and he had suffered in excruciating agony while his tribe had been camped on Ash Creek. When all the hostiles had moved on to the Little Big Horn, his family had stayed with him until he had eventually succumbed to his wounds earlier that morning, only hours before Custer's arrival. When they had completed the preparation of his body for the spirit world, his family had also moved on to re-join the hostiles, leaving Old-She-Bear to make his departure to another world.

Leaving his column by the edge of the creek, Custer rode over to have a word with his scouts. He was accompanied by Fred Girard and Mark Kellogg. Through his interpreter, Custer told his Arikara scouts that he wanted them to charge the Sioux and capture their ponies. This was a hugely important manoeuvre which would put the hostiles at a distinct disadvantage against his mounted troops. Custer also informed the scouts that they would not have an easy time of it and if they had the will to win, they must display absolute courage. Finally, he ordered the scouts to attach themselves to Reno's command across the creek.

As the scouts crossed the creek and Custer returned to his column, Girard called to him,

> "Here are your Indians General, running like the devils!"

Custer looked in the direction that Girard was pointing and a few kilometres ahead he could see some Indians riding into the valley. They were actually a few Cheyenne who had been hurriedly traversing across the Plains to join the hostiles in their stand. So far they had managed to avoid contact with any soldiers and now the village was within their grasp. Unfortunately, they were too far away for Girard to identify them as Cheyenne and not Sioux. Custer was still concerned that he could not see any indication that there was a hostile village in the valley. Nevertheless, he gave the order to advance and attack when they made contact. Saddle girths were tightened and all excess equipment discarded, littering the ground around the burial tipi with military equipment and personal rubbish. On the other side of the creek, Reno's troops also lightened their load. When both battalions were ready, the comparative stillness of the ravine was broken by the sound of a bugle call and the battle flags were unfurled. Custer's personal guidon, red over blue with white crossed sabres in the centre, was carried by Sergeant Robert Hughes of Company K. He would not survive the ensuing fight.

Custer ordered the scouts to pursue the galloping hostiles, but they refused to move. They would not start an offensive without the close support of the soldiers. The scouts were convinced that a large camp lay ahead and, therefore, too many Sioux for them to handle alone. Furious at their deliberate disobedience Custer spurred his horse past them and signalled for his column to move on. He then sent adjutant Cooke across the creek with his orders for Major Reno.

The orders that Cooke relayed to Reno were overheard by Reno's subordinate officers, some of whom later testified at the Reno Court of Inquiry. It is worth noting a few of the testimonies as they show different recollections of the words Cooke actually used, even though they all basically say the same thing. The interpretation is significant as different people can interpret the same words to mean something different. Thus what Cooke understood to be the orders may not have been seen as the same as Reno or his officers. According to Major Reno:

> 'Lieutenant Cooke came to me and said, General Custer directs you to take as rapid a gait as you think prudent and charge the village afterwards and you will be supported by the whole outfit.

Lieutenant Wallace testified:

> 'General Custer's order to charge was, I think, promulgated to Major Reno's command by the Adjutant..........
>
> The Indians are about two miles and a half [just over 4 kilometres] ahead, they are on the jump. Go forward as fast as you think proper and charge them wherever you find them and we will support you.'

Fred Girard also stated the Lieutenant Cooke relayed Custer's orders to Reno:

> 'You will take your battalion and try and overtake and bring them to battle and I will support you. And take the scouts along.'

It is interesting to note the different phrasing of the order, although it must be said that the Reno Court of Inquiry was not convened until two and a half years after the battle and, as I said before, it is normal to say that no two people would remember the exact same thing. Having said that, both Reno and Wallace recalled that the rapidity of the gait was left to the Major but only Girard mentions taking the scouts. All were agreed that Reno was told to engage the Indians, albeit differently phrased, and they all stated that Reno's command would be supported. However, only Reno mentions the village. If Custer was still uncertain as to the probability of a village in the valley, it is doubtful that he would have referred to it in an order. We can only speculate, but it does appear that verbal orders given in the field were very much liable to varying interpretations by those directed to relay them, not to mention those receiving them Alternatively, Reno may have been testifying in retrospect as a village was discovered to have been in the valley after his attack on the hostiles. In any event, there is no doubt that Reno and his command firmly believed they would have the support of Custer and his troops once the fighting began. It is also obvious that Reno and his command trusted Custer's word as an officer, for the order was instantly obeyed. However, the lack of solid communication between Custer and his battalion officers was to prove a decisive factor in the next few hours.

Reno acknowledged the order and as Cooke returned to Custer's column, he led his troops forward at the trot. Hodgson rode to the right of Reno and Wallace rode to his left. After crossing the creek, Reno formed his battalion with two companies in line and one company in reserve at the rear. Varnum and his Arikara scouts joined Reno as ordered, but their position in the march is not clear. Custer watched Reno's troops disappear from view and after ordering his men to set the burial tipi alight, he led his battalion forward swerving to the right over the bluffs that had so far sheltered them. With the Crows riding in advance, the troops followed along the high ridge. Nerves mingled with anticipation. They were going to see some action at last.

At this point in the chain of events, neither Custer nor Reno had any idea of the exact whereabouts of Benteen and his command. At the Reno Court of Inquiry when Reno was asked as to whether or not he knew where Benteen was, he replied,

> "Not the most remote. There was no plan communicated to us if one existed. The subordinate commanders did not know of it."

Reno also testified that he had no idea where the pack-train was either. No one knew where Terry or Crook was and now the regiment had been effectively divided, no one knew where Custer was for sure. It was common belief that Reno's troops believed they would be supported, if not by Terry or Crook, then by Custer. If Custer believed he would be supported then so did they.

Benteen was completely out on a limb. He had no visual contact of any of the other battalions and if he were to be attacked by hostile warriors he did not have any confidence in receiving support to cope with that. He led his column across the bluffs to the left as ordered, but to his horror he discovered that the terrain was totally unsuitable for cavalry to traverse it, being nothing but small rolling hills and gullies. For a while he kept going even though he knew it was a futile mission. To relieve the monotony on the men and their mounts, Benteen sent First Lieutenant Frank Gibson with six troops from Company H ahead of his command to reconnoitre the terrain. Gibson found no sign of an enemy camp or any hostiles, who were supposed to be in the area and he reported that fact to Benteen. The ground became increasingly difficult to ride over, with jagged hills to their left that were gradually pushing the soldiers across to their right. Benteen later stated:

> 'I went to the second line of bluffs and saw no valley and I knew the Indians had too much sense to go to any place over such rugged country………… that if they had to go in that direction they had a much better way to go.'

Eventually Benteen decided to continue the march to the right and pick up the trails of Custer and Reno, although he had no idea where they had gone. The route back was the same angle as before, only bearing to the right. Benteen continues:

> '………… And as there were no Indians there and no valleys I thought my duty was to go back to the trail and join the command.'

He found the trail approximately one and a half kilometres ahead of the pack-train, which was still slowly advancing behind the troops. Benteen turned his command to follow the trails and came upon a morass, where the creek was joined by a few small tributaries. The ground was treacherous and soggy, with deep imprints of many horses passing through. As their horses were thirsty, Benteen allowed the column to halt and water their mounts. Just as he was about to move on, two mules from the pack-train rushed into the morass and became stuck in the mud. This was not Benteen's problem and as the pack-train was approaching the marsh he decided not to interfere and he advanced his column along the trail towards the Little Big Horn. As the battalion reached the burning tipi, Benteen was met by Sergeant Kanipe of Company C, who had instructions for the officer of the pack-train to bring the packs forward. Benteen gestured to the trail behind him and told Kanipe the pack-train was not his responsibility, but it was back along the trail somewhere. Sergeant Kanipe rode off down the trail to find Captain McDougall shouting to Benteen's troops as he passed,

"We've got them boys!"

From his own accounts it is obvious that Benteen expressed no urgency in carrying out his orders or in attempting to join either Custer or Reno. He had conducted his survey to the south at a leisurely pace and he continued his advance towards the valley at a walk, stopping periodically to water the horses. He made no attempt to link up with the pack-train even though he knew hostile Indians were in close proximity. In fact, after the brief encounter with Sergeant Kanipe, Benteen appears to have shown no concern for the safety of his own men, much less those of Custer or Reno.

A few kilometres further on Benteen was stopped by Trumpeter John Martin (also known as Giovanni Martini,) of Company H. His horse was bleeding profusely from a bullet wound and he was excited. He informed Benteen that the Indians were fleeing and he carried a written message for him from Lieutenant Cooke:

> 'Benteen come on. Big village. Be quick. Bring packs. P.S. Bring packs.'

Trumpeter Martin was the last soldier from Custer's column to have seen the Colonel alive, although no one was aware of that fact at this point.

The message from Cooke had been clear. 'Bring packs.' But Benteen decided not to send for them or wait any longer for them to appear. He later stated:

> 'I asked Martin, after reading the note, about the village. He said the Indians were all "skedaddling"; therefore there was less

> necessity for me to go back for the packs. I could hear no firing at that time.'

However, Benteen did show the message to Captain Weir, however Benteen did not ask Weir any questions and Weir did not volunteer any advice. Once again this shows a serious lack of communication between the officers, which was to prove a fatal flaw in the chain of command. It is also blatantly evident that in not responding to the written message from Cooke, even though Benteen knows it is probably a verbal order from Custer, he is deliberately disobeying an order, something he has never adequately justified. Benteen had friends and acquaintances in high places. Had they tipped him off about Sheridan's plan? It is highly possible but not provable.

Leading his column forward Benteen passed some of Reno's Arikara scouts who had returned from the valley with a number of captured Sioux ponies. They informed Benteen that there were a great many hostile Sioux in the valley and pointed westwards. At last the Captain and his men could hear gunfire from ahead. Some serious action was certainly taking place but who was in the thick of it ? He spurred his men forward and rode towards the sound of the guns. It was almost 4 o'clock in the afternoon.

Reno had not been so fortunate. By around two-thirty that afternoon he had reached a ford where he could cross the Little Big Horn. During the ride down Ash Creek he had become more and more apprehensive concerning the situation he was riding into. His conviction that he was surrounded by hostile Indians in overwhelming numbers grew in intensity as his troopers drew nearer to the village. He felt as though he was being drawn into a wild hornet's nest and there was nothing he could do to stop it. Twice he had sent word to Custer, informing him of his convictions and requesting further instructions. Reno later stated:

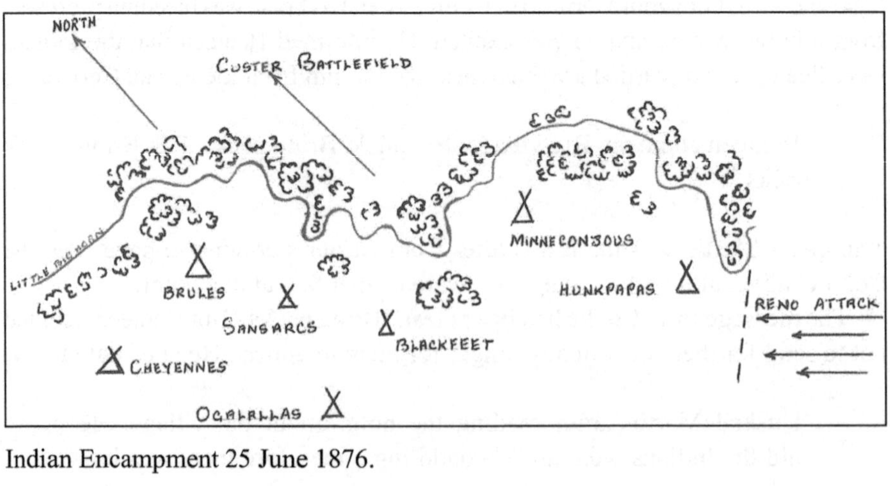

Indian Encampment 25 June 1876.

> ‘First I sent a man who was known in Army parlance as my ‘striker’ named McIlhargey to General Custer with my compliments and to say that the Indians were in front of me and in strong force. Receiving no instructions in reference to that, I sent a second time – a man named Mitchell who was about me in the capacity of cook. They were the nearest men I could get hold of quick. That was some minutes after I was convinced that my opinion was correct. I still heard nothing to guide my movements and I went on down the valley to carry out my orders.’

Private Archibald McIlhargey and Private John Mitchell, both of Company I, were never seen alive again. It is presumed they were killed with Custer’s battalion, assuming of course, that they did manage to reach it.

On reaching the ford at the Little Big Horn, Reno allowed his troops to water their mounts in the clear, icy water with the result that the actual crossing became a very haphazard affair lasting some 10 to 15 minutes. William Taylor, a Private in Company A, later wrote:

> ‘Into it our horses plunged without any urging, their thirst was great and also their riders. While waiting for them to drink I took off my hat and, shaping the brim into a scoop, leaned over, filled it and drank the last drop of water I was to have for over twenty-four long hours. The horses having been watered, we rode out of the river............’

Having crossed the ford, Reno’s command rode through the thick underbrush and onto the lush grassy flat land, where they dismounted and tightened their saddle girths. Yet again there appears no urgency for the soldiers to take the offensive. They are in a prospective battle zone where there are probably more hostile Indians than they have ever seen, yet the officers make no attempt to secure the lines.

Forming his men abreast in columns of fours, Reno grouped his command ready for the attack. With himself a little off-centre, Lieutenant Varnum rode on his left accompanied by his Arikara scouts; to his immediate right he placed Captain Moylan with Company A; and further on his right rode Captain French with Company M. Lieutenant McIntosh was ordered to bring up the rear with Company G. It was a text-book formation, leaving no surprises. After ensuring that all the preparations were complete, Reno led his men at a trot into the valley. As the minutes passed the trot became a gallop and Reno was in a full charge heading towards the southern end of the hostile village. Lieutenant Varnum could be seen swinging his hat in the air and he was heard to shout,

> "Thirty days furlough to the man who gets the first scalp!"

First Sergeant John Ryan of Company M, later recalled,

> "We were very anxious for the furlough, but not so particular about the scalp."

Across the river, high on the ridge, Custer was rapidly moving his troops north, using the steep bluffs to conceal his presence. As they traversed the uneven ground, Lieutenant Cooke rode up to the Colonel with a message from Fred Girard, informing him that rather than fleeing the soldiers the hostiles were actually attacking Reno's battalion. Riding with Cooke and a small escort, Custer found a high bluff from which he could observe the valley. He could now view the huge encampment in its entirety and see the masses of hostiles below, extremely agitated and stirring up the dust with their ponies. On seeing Reno's command at full gallop towards the hostiles, Custer waved his hat as a gesture of support, but very few of Reno's troops had the time or the inclination to either notice this or acknowledge it. They had their hands full, literally, with screaming angry hostiles. Custer could see that Girard was right, the hostiles were vehemently attacking the hapless Major with all the aggression they could muster. However, having committed Reno and his troops to the offensive in the valley there was nothing Custer could do, even in the way of the promised support from where he was at present. He could not recall them for that would have resulted in the annihilation of the soldiers as the hostiles overran them. The only thing he could do was to swing his force northwards in the hope he could find a suitable ford in the river so he could attack the furthest end of the village and relieve the pressure from Reno. Returning to his waiting column Custer gave the order for Benteen to bring up the pack-train. Being an immigrant from Italy, Trumpeter Martin did not have a very good understanding of the English language, so Cooke scribbled the message and handed the paper to Martin, who duly galloped off to find Benteen.

At the southern end of the camp, Sitting Bull was in the Hunkpapa Council Lodge engaged in deep conversation with Crow King, Rain-In-the-Face, Black Moon and Kill Eagle. For some time Kill Eagle had expressed his desire to return to the Standing Rock Agency with his followers and for most of the morning the discussion had been quite heated. Persistence won the day. The Council members had been quite persuasive with the result that Kill Eagle had decided to stay. As he neared the end of his lengthy speech, the door flap flew open and a Hunkpapa warrior burst into the lodge, casting a bright ray of sunlight across the earthen floor. Fat Bear informed the Council members of the death of Deeds up in the hills and that the soldiers who had killed him were now riding to attack the camp.

Outside, the Council members found the camp in an uproar of confusion. Women rushed past clutching their young children and taking them to the relative safety of the hills, west of the camp circles. The elderly hobbled after them trying desperately to avoid the excited warriors as they dashed in all directions to prepare for the ensuing fight. Dust flew thick in the air, being kicked up by the ponies of the mounted warriors who spun their ponies round in circles, frantically calling to their friends and families to hurry. The approach of the soldiers had caused panic that rippled through the tribal circles. But through the turmoil, the excited warriors were preparing for the offensive.

Sitting Bull headed straight for his tipi. His earlier premonition of a disaster appeared to be coming to fruition, although he was still not exactly sure whose fate it related to. Inside his tipi, he buckled on his cartridge belt and grabbed his weapons; a .45 calibre revolver and a Winchester carbine. He would fight to his last breath if necessary. In the sun his pony pawed at the ground, impatient to be a part of the excitement. Sitting Bull mounted the blaze faced black stallion and rode bareback through the camp circles, rallying the warriors into a rough assemblage of organisation. Through the swirling dust cloud, his voice could be heard loud and clear above the howling and whooping warriors,

> "Brave up! We have everything to fight for. If we are defeated, we will have nothing to live for. It will be a hard time, but fight like brave men. Brave up!"

Although he had been aware that the soldiers were moving against them, the sight of Reno's command charging up the valley towards the camp circles was the first indication that Sitting Bull had that the troops were in such close proximity. Without actually realising it, Custer had indeed caught the hostiles by surprise but he did not have the forces to capitalise on it.

Crow King was the first Hunkpapa warrior to react to the attack from the valley. He swiftly mounted a counter offensive against Reno and during the bitter fighting two of his brothers, White Bull and Swift Bear, were killed. Crow King was quickly followed by another Hunkpapa warrior chief, Black Moon. The fighting was fierce and frantic. They had to stop the soldiers from actually entering the village at all costs. Once Reno's attack had been repulsed, Crow King joined Crazy Horse in the fighting against Custer's soldiers. In any event it was this spontaneous action by Crow King that tipped the balance of the fight firmly in favour of the hostiles.

The most controversial battle in the history of the American West had begun.

Chapter 2

Baptism of Fire

A full cavalry charge is an awesome sight to behold and having begun, it gathers momentum until the inevitable clash with the enemy which then halts all further progress. Adrenaline courses through the veins of both rider and mount, mixing with the natural resources of excitement and fear as the trooper leans forward in the saddle allowing his horse to stretch into a full gallop. So it was with Reno's command. Having initiated the charge as ordered, Reno had no alternative but to see it through. As hooves thundered through the grass with tipis looming nearer and nearer, he realised that the hostiles were not running away. In fact it was the opposite. The Indians were amassing to meet his attack, so he ordered Lieutenant McIntosh to bring Company G into line. The village was vaguely visible through the swirling dust stirred up by the Indian ponies and on seeing the tipis through the dust, many of Varnum's Arikara scouts broke with formation and veered off to the left to attack the Sioux pony herds. Capturing the ponies not only prevented the warriors from using them, it also provided the scouts with valuable battle prizes. Unfortunately for Reno, those scouts who managed to secure some of the ponies, rode off down the valley with them and did not participate in the fight any further. Reno later stated:

> 'The Indian scouts had run away except three or four and we did not see them again until we got to the river.'

As the soldiers drew nearer to the village, Crow King and his Hunkpapa warriors swarmed out of the dusty mist to meet them. Every small ravine seemed to conceal more hostiles, who did not hesitate to attack. Bullets and arrows filled the air from all directions, although only a few found their mark. For the present the Indians seemed hesitant to counter attack the soldiers. They hung back, screaming insults at the troopers but keeping their ponies between the enemy and the village. Reno suspected a trap. Already the Arikara attack on the pony herd had not been a veritable success. It had not been a complete failure, but only a few ponies were taken before making their escape. Those who were not successful re-joined Reno's left flank, amongst whom were Bloody Knife and Young Hawk.

By now the Sioux had begun to move to the left and on seeing this Reno knew he could no longer maintain the offensive. It was obvious even to a rookie private that the hostiles vastly outnumbered the soldiers. His attack on the village had failed and he was in a very precarious position. Glancing towards his rear, Reno could see no sign of the promised support. There were no soldiers on the bluffs either and as the minutes ticked by, the Sioux were growing in numbers and seemed to be all around him. Some time later Reno recalled:

> '....... I could not see Custer or any other support, and at the same time the very earth seemed to grow Indians, and they were running towards me in swarms, and from all directions.'

Small groups of Sioux were gradually making their way towards the rear of the column and if they were allowed to achieve this, all hope for Reno and his men was lost. Dust, smoke, bullets and arrows filled the air and mingled with the wild howls and war-whoops of the hostiles. They were mean and angry and out for blood. This was Reno's first experience of a fight with the Sioux and, like many of the young troopers who rode with him, it must have seemed as though he had ridden straight into the jaws of Hell! Private William Taylor, of Company A, recorded his experience of that charge some time later:

> 'A glance along the line showed a lot of set, determined faces, some of them a little pale perhaps, but not altogether with fear:
>
> .... there was no flinching on the part of anyone. To most of us it was our first real battle at close range. Our baptism of fire, a new and strange experience, to sit up as a human target, to be shot at and not return the fire, was a little trying, but our turn was at hand.'

Private William Slaper, of Company M, also recorded the event when he wrote:

> 'Soon commenced the rattle of rifle fire, and bullets began to whistle about us. I remember that I ducked my head and tried to dodge bullets which I could hear whizzing through the air. This was my first experience under fire. I know that for a time I was frightened and far more so when I got my first glimpse of the Indians riding about us in all directions, firing at us and yelling and whooping like incarnate fiends, all seemingly naked as the day they were born, and painted from head to foot in the most hideous manner imaginable.'

Frantically throwing his hand up in the air, Reno called a halt and gave the order to dismount and prepare to fight on foot. With every fourth man withdrawn to hold the horses, Reno only had about 140 men hurriedly forming a skirmish line. It was a very risky manoeuvre considering the vast numbers of hostiles they were facing. However, his officers were of no doubt that the Major had done the right thing, even though the situation was increasingly perilous. Lieutenant Hare, second in command of the scouts under Varnum, later remembered:

> 'If Reno had continued to advance mounted, I don't think he would have got a man through; the column would not have lasted fifteen minutes. His dismounting and deploying was the only thing that saved us.'

Already Reno's battalion had suffered the first of its casualties. During the final phase of the charge, Sergeant William Heyn, of Company A, had received a bullet in his chest, but he managed to remain with his Company and continued to fight. Private George Smith, of Company M, had not been so fortunate. When the order had been given for the column to halt, his horse bolted carrying him head-long into the oncoming Sioux, who dragged him from his saddle and clubbed him to death.

The firing from both sides was considerably heavy and Reno's left flank was under increasing pressure. He had been on the skirmish line for 15 to 20 minutes, alongside Captain Moylan, when he received word that the Indians were gradually turning the right flank of his line. Reno moved towards the river to see for himself and, sure enough, he could see the hostiles filtering through the trees to attack from there. He rode back to the skirmish line where Lieutenant Hodgson informed him that the Indians had been moving to their left and rear. If he wasn't careful his command would be surrounded and slaughtered. Reno told Hodgson to bring the skirmish line into the timber around the horses. Hodgson reacted immediately and Reno turned his attention to the river, which now lay to his rear. As the troops retreated into the timber, Private (Henry) James Turley, of Company M, could not control his horse. The roar of the fight had totally unnerved the animal and it bolted straight towards the Hunkpapa camp circle with its rider. Turley was never seen alive again.

The riverbank formed a natural defence for Reno's troops, but the position was untenable. The firefight was intense and the Indians had increased in number threatening to crush the command. There was no sign of Custer, or anyone else for that matter and Reno was under no illusion concerning the situation. He felt he had been abandoned to his fate. The battalion had been effectively scattered by the hostiles, reducing the soldiers to fight in small pockets and unless Reno could regroup his men, they were all going to die. Across the river he could see some bluffs and if he could get his command up there, he was sure the rest of the regiment would see their plight and go to his aid. But first, his men would have to reach those bluffs.

The fighting in the timber had become chaotic. The hostiles were tightening their hold and as they closed in they were making as much use of the trees for cover as the soldiers were, if not more. This was their kind of fighting and they were extremely good at it. Ammunition was now critically low and it was imperative that the soldiers had replenishments. Several horses had been hit as bullets whizzed through the air, leaving some troopers without their mounts and casualties amongst the men were also increasing. Reno found Bloody Knife in a clearing amongst the trees and using sign language, he asked the scout what he thought about their position. Bloody Knife replied that they were surrounded by the Indians and their chances of remaining alive were pretty slim. That was all the Major needed to know. Reno instructed Captain Moylan and Lieutenant McIntosh to mount the men and take them to the edge of the timber, where they would be formed in columns of fours. He then ordered Lieutenant Hodgson to inform Captain French to do the same. As the officers raced off, Reno shouted to the troops near him to stand to horse and then ordered them to mount.

His words died away, swallowed up in the mounting turmoil. As he wheeled his horse round a large number of Indians crashed through the trees, firing on the startled troops at point-blank range. One of the first to be cut down in the hail of bullets was Private George Lorenz, of Company M, who fell from his horse screaming and clutching his stomach. Another casualty at this instance was Bloody Knife, who toppled from his mount shot between his eyes. As the bullet shattered his skull, brains and blood erupted in the air covering Reno's face and splattering his tunic. This sudden outburst from the hostiles had taken Reno completely by surprise. He had lost his hat and for those precious minutes he had also lost his sense of command. Wiping the bloody mess from his face with his neckerchief, he then tied it around his head to keep his hair from obscuring his vision. By his side Captain Moylan oversaw the formation of the battalion. There was no doubt that Reno was visibly shaken by the death of Bloody Knife and through the haze of dust, smoke and blood, he began to shout bizarre orders at his troops, adding to the confusion.

Having been told to dismount and then mount, the soldiers were at a loss as to what they were supposed to be doing. The rapid fire from the hostiles was now intense and many soldiers fell as they struggled to obey orders that did not make any sense. Others misunderstood the orders and quite simply started to ride out of the timber, while other soldiers were totally oblivious of any commands being issued. One thing is certain is that no one recalled having any bugle calls and it is certain that any commands shouted at this point would have been drowned out by the sheer noise of the fight.

Reno shouted further orders for his men to follow as he wheeled his horse round and crashed through the trees, heading back towards the river. Those who had heard his order followed at a gallop, but there were those who had not heard it and they struggled after him in a confusion of fear and panic. These bloodthirsty hostiles were not taking any prisoners! Private William Taylor, of Company A, later wrote:

> 'The situation was most serious, it was so sudden and incomprehensible.................. Each man ahead of me had his right arm extended firing his revolver at a parallel line of yelling Indians and I at once followed suit.'

The retreat from the timber became a disorganised rout and it was during this flight that Reno consequently suffered the heaviest casualties. Having been ordered to gather his men at the edge of the timber, to be formed into columns of fours, it is interesting to note that Lieutenant Donald McIntosh, of Company G, had not done so. Thus when the remainder of the battalion had escaped the trees and were galloping towards the river, McIntosh and his Company were left behind. Of course, it is possible that the increase in the number of hostiles had opposed him carrying out the order, ensuring that the soldiers stayed to fight. No one will ever know for sure. However, on seeing the battalion leaving the vicinity at a great speed, McIntosh tried desperately to rally his men to make a run for it. At the edge of the timber his horse was shot from under him and, on seeing him fall, his men hesitated and then fell back. Reno was, by now, way ahead lost in a blur of dust and McIntosh knew that the Indians would not hesitate to make good use of their advantage. Mounting a stray horse, he decided to try to break though again. However, the Indians had seriously increased in numbers upon seeing the soldiers run towards the river and amidst high pitched victory whoops, they were surging forward to give chase. McIntosh now found his line of retreat effectively cut off. Fighting furiously for their lives, the men of Company G were gradually forced towards the river where McIntosh was eventually dragged from his horse and killed. Roughly a dozen men died with him with the remaining terrified soldiers only just managing to join Reno's retreat after a fierce hand to hand fight.

McIntosh was not the only officer to find himself left behind in the timber. Doctor Henry Porter, Acting Assistant Surgeon, had been administering aid to a dying soldier in a small clump of bushes and he had not heard the orders given to retreat due to the din of the battle. Charley Reynolds had just been killed, having warned the doctor that the Indians were shooting at him. Porter's orderly had vanished and he was totally unarmed. He had been left alone, with no means to defend himself and, for all appearances, cut off from any escape. As the dying soldier breathed his last breath, bullets slammed into the bush and all around him. The surgeon knew had had to get out or die. Unbelievably, Porter managed to lead his horse to the river bank unharmed, with hostiles running past him only a few metres away. Walking slowly through the swirling dust the Indians may not have spotted him or they could have been too intent on catching up with the fleeing soldiers to worry about one man. No one will ever know for sure, but Doctor Porter made a very successful escape down to the river.

The surgeon's horse was a powerful black charger, but it had become terrified by the continuous rapid gunfire and the yells of the Indians. It resisted Porter's efforts to mount it. The animal plunged and reared, frantically trying to free itself but Porter gripped the reins with grim determination. He knew that if his horse bolted he was as good as dead. He repeatedly tried to mount the horse, but with the animal pulling and lurching from side to side, it was almost impossible. Finally, worried that he might be attracting some unwanted attention, Porter made a supreme effort to mount the horse and away it flew with him grimly hanging on, straight through the mass of Indians who were chasing and harassing Reno. As mount and rider ran the gauntlet a hail of bullets showered the air around him, but as Porter had no control over his horse he just stayed low and prayed that he was heading in the right direction. Fortunately the horse dashed into the river, splashed through the water as fast as it could and climbed the bluffs in a pure panic until it reached the safety of Reno's new position.

The enraged hostiles took full advantage of Reno's panic-stricken retreat. They charged after the stampeding soldiers and using their sheer weight of numbers, they managed to swing Reno's battalion back towards the river and away from the ford the soldiers had been heading for. Reno reached the banks of the Little Big Horn and plunged down the 2 metre drop into the water, with his men pouring down after him. Here the swift running water was approximately 1.5 metres deep, making the crossing slow and precarious but not impossible. With men already in the water and more pushing in after them, the column became a confused bunch providing an easy target for the Indians to shoot at. And shoot they did! There had been no rear-guard deployed to keep the enemy at a distance. It was every man for himself and this provided the hostiles with an easy 'turkey shoot'! Captain Moylan and Lieutenant Varnum had tried to stem the soldiers' mad dash to safety, but panic had set in and there was no controlling them. Captain Moylan later testified,

> "The command moved forward at the trot and then at the gallop ……… the Indians closed in on both flanks and fired into the columns. There were many Indians in the woods. The firing to the rear was severe. A good many men were wounded and some were

> killed. When I reached the river I found it full of horses and men. I stopped at the head of my people and tried to get them together."

Lieutenant Varnum also stated later,

> "When I came out of the timber there were a great many Indians riding along the column with Winchester rifles across saddles, firing into the column. A great many were in the bend next to the river ....
>
> As the command rode out and across, the men were using revolvers.......................
>
> they had to jump the horses into the river............
>
> But my horse nearly threw me as he jumped on the other side..........
>
> the command started its retreat in column of fours at a fast gallop. The crossing was not covered."

Reno's battalion was now in a mad scramble to cross the river and reach the comparative safety of the bluffs. Halfway across, Lieutenant Hodgson was hit by a bullet in his thigh. The missile passed through his leg and into his horse, killing it instantly in the swirling water. As the unfortunate animal sank beneath him, Hodgson struggled to remain afloat. His leg was bleeding profusely and hampered his movements considerably. It was at this moment that Trumpeter Charles Fischer, of M Company, dashed into the water and as he neared the stricken Hodgson, he called to the Lieutenant to grab his stirrup. Hodgson grabbed the stirrup and Fischer towed him across the river. The opposite bank was now under a most galling fire from the Indians who were now actually riding into the water and shooting at the terrified troopers as they tried to escape. Many soldiers were actually pulled from their horses while still crossing the river. As Fischer's horse climbed the bank, dragging Hodgson with it, more shots rang out and Hodgson fell to the ground, Sioux bullets having finally found their mark. Reno had not only lost his battalion adjutant, he had also lost a friend.

The officers and men of Reno's battalion were completely stunned. They had begun their charge against the Indian encampment full of hope and excitement, confidence and panache, with an air of bravado. However, the hostiles had not run from them as they had been told they would. They had actually faced the soldiers and stopped a cavalry charge, moreover they had completely routed the hated soldiers and now they were amassing for the kill. The battalion's miraculous escape from the timber had been a chaotic stampede, although not many of the soldiers would actually admit that that had been the case. Private William Slaper, of M Company, later commented,

> "I cannot say that the retreat from the river bottom – and further on – had a very military experience, but I can say that I saw nothing disorderly about it, although so many had gone on ahead of me and were so far in advance that what they did, or in what order they retreated, I cannot say with positive certainty."

Others were not so hesitant in praising Reno for regarding the safety of his men as paramount. Lieutenant George Wallace, of Company G, stated,

> "I think Reno did the only thing possible under the circumstances. If we had remained in the timber all would have been killed. It was his duty to take care of his command and to use his best judgement and discretion. I think his conduct as to courage was good. I saw no evidence of fear then or at any time."

Captain Myles Moylan, of Company A, endorsed Wallace's statement when he later testified at the Reno Court of Inquiry,

> "If we had stayed thirty minutes longer in the timber, unsupported, I doubt whether we would have gotten out with as many as we did. If we reached the other bank there was the possibility of aid coming up. We could not have successfully resisted the force of Indians if they had followed to the river; we had not sufficient ammunition. The command was not, however, actually driven from the timber. It was virtually so, however, and would have been actually in a very short time."

As for Reno, he condoned his actions even though it had cost the lives of many of his command, when he stated,

> "I thought it was my duty to give those men the best chance I could to save themselves and it was impossible to have a victory over the Indians..........
>
> That the rest might possibly save their lives from the desperate position we were placed in."

He also justified his decision to make for the bluffs and hold that position,

> "I thought my duty was there, to see about the direction of the column and have facilities for observing the ford and the hill on the other side and I would be on top of the hill to rally and reform the men."

In view of the evidence available, there is no doubt that Major Reno executed his orders to the best of his ability and when faced with overwhelming odds he pulled his command from the fight in an effort to save their lives, which he ultimately did for many. However, from various witness statements, it is also evident that Reno did briefly lose command of his battalion and that the ensuing flight from the timber was not conducted in accordance with army regulations. It must be taken into account that Reno's first baptism of fire with hostile Plains Indians had been fast, furious and extremely traumatic. He had not received the support he had been promised and, as such, Reno's actions were what would have been expected of any army officer under the same precarious circumstances he had found himself dealing with.

By now the Indians had become intoxicated with victory and their confidence overflowed. They had set the brush alight to flush out any remaining soldiers from the timber and they had not only out-flanked Reno's command, they had chased the fleeing soldiers back across the Little Big Horn. Many soldiers had been killed and many riderless horses were galloping freely all over the place trying to escape the slaughter, their reins flaying wildly as young Indians ran around trying to capture them as prizes. Reno had lost approximately one third of his command either killed, wounded or missing. Indian casualties, on the other hand, had been considerably less. The fight in the valley had resulted in the deaths of seven Sioux and one Cheyenne, with a further two Sioux having received mortal wounds.

Sitting Bull was prepared to end the fighting now that these soldiers had been severely beaten and there were many warriors who were inclined to agree with him. Of course, at this point he had no idea that there were more soldiers to deal with. He hoped that this was the last of the fighting and that these soldiers would return home to tell their officers and wives that the Indians had won a great victory. Other warriors did not feel the same way, however, and having chased Reno's troops up onto the bluffs the hostiles took up concealed positions from which they could sustain intermittent fire to keep the soldiers pinned down. If they were lucky a bullet or an arrow might find its mark.

At first glance it appears utterly amazing that so few Indians had been killed in the fight as opposed to the much larger number of soldiers. The answer is quite simple, although by no means complete. During the early investigations into the battle, it was strongly contested that the Indians had repeating weapons, such as Winchester or Henry rifles, at their disposal. This conclusion had been erroneously reached in 1877 when the surrendering Indians were disarmed. (Obviously the hostiles were too wily to hand over their good firearms and many were carefully concealed from the soldiers.) The weapons that were given up consisted mainly of old rifles whose real purpose should have been in a museum, even then. Very few repeating rifles were collected at all. However, recent excavations of the battle area have revealed that the Indians did, indeed, possess repeating rifles and, what is more interesting, they also used the soldiers' own carbines against them. Split cases have been found indicating that the Indians were adeptly picking up army ammunition to use in their much larger rifles. They had little concept of the calibres of guns. It must also be remembered that Indians are trained to hunt from an early age and therefore pick their targets carefully, whereas the soldiers were firing their weapons wildly in all directions. It must be conclusively apparent that the soldiers did not really have a chance against the more proficient and highly confident Sioux and Cheyenne. An important fact that Crook knew from his recent engagement, but did not pass on.

Having managed to cross the river and escape the lethal hostile fusillade at point-blank range, the exhausted soldiers and their equally tired mounts then had to ascend the steep bluffs that loomed up before them. With bullets whizzing through the air it was a monumental objective to achieve. Private William Taylor, of Company A, later recalled his experience:

> 'After a hard struggle I climbed the steep bank, the rapid pace and exertion over the river had completely exhausted my horse and he stood trembling with fatigue and refused to go any further..............
>
> I dismounted and amid whistling of bullets stood there for a few moments waiting for him to get his breath. Then I tried to lead him along but he would not budge..............
>
> Things looked serious indeed, for to be dismounted in the face of hundreds of Sioux warriors but a short distance away, was like looking into your grave.........'

Private William Slaper, of Company M, had a no less harrowing experience:

> 'After getting across the river, I had the steep bluffs to climb.
>
> .... all the time being under a murderous fire from the Indians hidden in the brush along the river.
>
> On the way up I passed the body of Doctor De Wolfe, one of our surgeons, who had been shot and killed while trying to gain the top.'

It appears that Private Slaper had, like many others, climbed the wrong bluffs. These were already occupied by the hostiles who killed all those who came their way. Slaper was lucky, Acting Assistant Surgeon James Madison De Wolfe was not. He was shot and scalped in plain view of the terrified troopers. Private Edward Davern, of Company F, witnessed the final moments of De Wolfe as he scrambled up the wrong bluff:

> 'I saw Lieutenant Wallace shoot at some Indians who were killing a man three or four ridges from us...............
> I afterwards learned it was De Wolf they were killing.'

Three other Privates are also known to have fallen on these bluffs; Elihu Clear (or Clair) of Company K, along with Henry Gordon and William Myer, both of Company M. If nothing else it does display how disorganised the companies were during the retreat.

On reaching the summit of the bluffs Reno organised the remnant of his command into a skirmish line, to cover those who were still crossing the river and attempting to scale the bluffs. Totally exhausted, his men fell into line and began a covering fire. Gradually, most of what remained of his battalion reached the top of the bluffs and fell on their knees gasping for breath. Reno quickly assessed his position. It was not the best of places to entrench his men, but the scattered sage bush did offer a little cover and, as luck would have it, the Indians had relaxed the pressure a little. In fact their firing had been reduced to a few scattered shots now and then. They had ridden through Hell itself and now the soldiers still faced a living nightmare.

Taking advantage of the lull in the fight, Reno surveyed his situation. From this position he could look down into the valley where a huge number of Indians were still congregating and he observed them stripping the bodies of his fallen troopers, then scalping and horribly mutilating them. It was a dreadful sight and if he could see it then so could his men beside him on the bluff. The bush was aflame and the smoke obscured his vision beyond that point. Reno turned back to his command and made a note of the casualties. His adjutant, Hodgson had been killed; one of his surgeons, De Wolfe had also been killed; he had lost two of his civilian interpreters, Charley Reynolds and Isaiah Dorman, both of whom had been killed in the valley fight; he had seen nothing of Lieutenants McIntosh or De Rudio so he presumed they had also been killed. He had been reliably informed that he had lost almost a third of his battalion and sixteen other men were also still missing. Reno had no idea where the rest of the regiment had got to and he knew that his position on the bluff was tenuous to say the least. Silently he prayed for some relief.

Reno later stated that ten wounded soldiers were able to reach the top of the bluff with their horses. He placed the wounded in the care of Dr Porter and, as many were from Company A, he instructed Captain Moylan to ensure they were well cared for. Reno then located Lieutenant Hare and enquired as to whether or not he would act as adjutant as Hodgson had been killed. Hare dutifully obliged and set about resuming some sense of order amongst the enlisted men. Reno then sent a messenger to locate the pack-train. Ammunition was now extremely low and its replenishment was a priority. After the arrival of Benteen, the Major also sent Lieutenant Hare to hurry the pack-train.

Indian fire had become sporadic, almost non-existent, putting the soldiers' nerves on edge. Some of them began to dig in using knives, spoons and mess kits to break up the sun-baked soil. Others lay on their backs clutching their carbines to their chests, taking a break before the fresh onslaught began. Now, they all had a few minutes to reflect on their horrendous experiences. They had escaped and were lucky to be alive. Private William Taylor, of Company A, later wrote:

> '......... I have wondered how a man felt, when he believed that almost inevitable sudden death was upon him. I knew it now, for our escape was little less than miraculous when one considers the overwhelming number of Indians ...... the pitifully disorganised condition in which we made our death-encircled ride......... pursued by a howling mass of red warriors, naked to the waist, who, maddened and desperate by the terrified cries of their wives and children......... rushed from their camps and caring nothing for their own lives, were determined to save their families or die.
>
> They seemed to us, in all their hideousness of paint and feather, and wild fierce cries, like fiends incarnate, but were they?'

In those few minutes of respite what was uppermost on the minds of officers and men alike were the whereabouts of Benteen with his column, as yet unscathed, and McDougall with the pack-train carrying their desperately need supplies. Where were they. Then there was regiment's commanding officer. Where was Custer and his promised support?

Chapter 3

Bravery is Not Enough

The horrific circumstances in which George Armstrong Custer and the men of his battalion met their deaths beside the banks of the Little Big Horn is not a mystery. They were not only overwhelmed by the sheer weight of numbers of the hostile warriors, they were cleverly out-flanked as well. What has remained controversial over the subsequent years is not only the tactical movements that Custer employed, but the reasons that he had been placed in such a precarious position in the first place. Military experts and historians have repeatedly speculated on the sequence of events concerning Custer's command following the division of the regiment, each proffering their theories and desperately trying to claim that they have found the answers to the enigma, when most have not. However, it is the devout archaeologists who have unravelled much of the mystery that has continued to shroud the battlefield long after all the participants have died.

For many years, the Indians who had been engaged in the fight with Custer refused to discuss it. They were only too aware of the inimical attitude the white people displayed towards them and they were inherently afraid that a chance remark would hold them or their heirs solely responsible for so many soldiers' deaths, not to mention Custer. Even when the survivors did finally relate their experiences, their testimonies were treated with suspicion, many were accused of blatant exaggeration or even lying, which ultimately questioned their credibility. It is, therefore, not surprising that such a rich source of valuable information from eye-witness accounts has been lost over the years, a shameful misconduct that has left modern historians bereft of priceless evidence. All is not completely lost though. Recent excavations of the battlefield have yielded many well-kept secrets of the dead and revealed that the Indian testimonies were, in fact, correct thus proving the so-called 'experts' wrong in their assumptions.

Having watched the departure of Reno and his men as they followed the course of Ash Creek towards the Little Big Horn, Custer took a few minutes to reflect on the events so far and the hasty decision he had been forced to make. He had split his command to attack the hostile village. This was a text-book procedure that had been used successfully many times in the past. The question is, was it the correct tactical manoeuvre for this campaign ? Whilst allowing the soldiers freedom to attack the enemy from more than one direction, it was also risky as it left the battalions short of manpower should the Indians stand their ground or counter-attack. (A prime example of this was Reno's fight in the valley.) Custer's divided forces should have been able to deal with anything they may encounter and the battalions should always remain at a distance where they could support each other. (Reno had no such support.) This was text-book strategy, if Custer's information concerning the hostile numbers or their old methods of fighting was still in force. Neither was. Custer had not been given a more realistic number of hostiles he would likely encounter and their information of their methods of fighting was shamefully incorrect. (Crook could and should have corrected this misnomer, but he didn't.) Custer could only assume that Crook was in position to the south, as their orders directed. That being so, why did Custer send Benteen and his troops in that direction? Was he hoping that Benteen would locate Crook and guide him to the river? He had received no communication from either Terry or Crook, thus he had no idea whether he could count on their support or not. He knew that the deployment of his troops was the correct move, but was it in accordance with the limited intelligence he had at his disposal? He had no idea of the whereabouts of Terry or Crook and he did not have enough information concerning the enemy he was about to engage. All he knew, and that was not a certainty, was that he had probably found the hostile village and that the Indians had discovered his presence, thus removing the element of surprise. This was not a perfect scenario and Custer knew it.

There was no sound in the valley except for the intermittent jingle of the iron bits in the horses' mouths and the spasmodic creak of saddle leather. Both horses and men were eager to get going. If Custer did have any reservations concerning his actions he didn't show it. Up on the high ground towards his right, he and his Crow scouts had observed some mounted warriors looking in their direction. He decided to move his battalion towards the warriors to see if they were strong enough to engage him or just a scouting party.

Leaving the quiet waters of Ash Creek, Custer swung his column to the right and climbed onto the high bluffs that stretched to the north. The mounted warriors had now disappeared. Slipping down behind a knoll, his troops found themselves in thick brush and cottonwood trees, shielding their view of the valley. Halting the column, Custer detailed a few men from Company F to reconnoitre the bluffs ahead. He also sent some Crow scouts to the edge of the bluffs to scan the valley below. These are not the actions of a reckless or impulsive commander. Custer was probing the area and gathering information in order to proceed. However, it also shows that he was being exceptionally cautious and probably doubting his own decisions or his information.

Upon their return the Crow scouts informed Custer that they had not seen any large bands of Indians in the valley and they could not discern whether or not there were a great number of tipis down there. Given their acute eye-sight we have to wonder if the Crows were looking in the right area of the valley. Small groups of trees would obscure part of the southern end of the hostile encampment, but the sheer size of the remaining camp circles should certainly have been visible from this point. In any event, as the warriors on the bluffs had now disappeared, Custer deduced that the village had been warned of his presence and that the hostiles could be on the run. He surveyed the vicinity ahead for any signs of a gully or ravine that would enable him to reach the river. He needed to get across. Not seeing any indication of a ravine, Custer gave the order to advance in columns of four.

Custer had no idea of the exact locations of Benteen or McDougall should he need support. However, if his calculations were correct, Reno should be on the verge of engaging the hostiles although he could not hear any gunfire. Before the battalion moved off, Custer dropped to one knee in silent prayer and then he rose and addressed each of his scouts individually. He thanked them for their valued service and unimpeachable faithfulness. As he finished Captain Keogh rode up to inform him that Reno had crossed the river without incurring any resistance and he was now galloping up the valley. Custer was jubilant. All his doubts were now cast to the wind and he was his old self once more, confident and zealous. Everything seemed to be progressing according to his plan and he was sjure they would be victorious.

The battalion moved on with Custer setting the pace. The small ponies of the Crow scouts were hard pressed in maintaining their lead against the larger cavalry mounts. On reaching a small creek Custer allowed the men to water their horses as they crossed but directed them not to allow the horses to drink too much.

The march continued with the soldiers traversing the broken terrain towards the high point on the bluffs. The Crow scouts were becoming increasingly worried at the apparent absence of any Indian activity in the valley. There was no sign of Reno's battalion, although a huge dust cloud was obscuring their view of the area. What was more worrying was that there were no signs that the hostiles were evacuating the village. The Crow scouts had, of course, informed Custer that he would encounter a great many hostile warriors and yet, only a handful had been seen and those had become elusive. Where were they? Just below the high point on the bluff Custer ordered another halt and, accompanied by Trumpeter Martin, he ascended the knoll to take stock of his position. Although he had a clearer perspective of the valley, much of the hostile encampment was still hidden from view by the undulating landscape of the bluffs and the numerous clumps of trees along the riverbank. It was obviously far larger than Custer had imagined and he appeared both surprised and pleased. There was little sign of any activity which led him to remark,

> "We've got them. We've caught them napping!"

Custer turned in his saddle, removed his hat and waved it at his column waiting at the base of the knoll.

> "Custer's luck boys! We've got them. We'll finish them off, then go home to our station!"

Trumpeter Martin remembered the incident just a little differently:

> 'After he saw the village, he pulled off his hat and gave a cheer and said "Courage boys, we will get them, and as soon as we get through, we will go back to our station."'

Whatever the exact wording, it is clear that Custer was more than just jubilant. With the village so peaceful he really believed that he had the element of surprise. He could not have been more wrong.

By now Reno had halted the charge, formed a skirmish line and was heavily engaged with hoards of screaming hostiles. During the fight, Lieutenant De Rudio saw Custer wave his hat from the ridge. He later testified at the Reno Court of Inquiry:

> '.......... While I was in the woods General Custer, Lieutenant Cooke and another man I could not recognise came to the highest point of the bluff and waved their hats and made motions like they were cheering. I judged that his column was behind the bluff............
>
> I supposed Custer's command was coming down some of those coulees to join us but they did not; and as pretty soon after, firing began on the other side of the village, I argued that he wants us to attack the rear of the village...........
>
> I recognised General Custer and Lieutenant Cooke by their drcss. They had on blue shirts and buckskin pants. They were the only ones who wore blue shirts and no jackets; and Lieutenant Cooke besides had an immense beard. The third man I did not recognise and he many have been an orderly.'

De Rudio appears to have sown amazing coolness whilst under fire, for his description of the scene is extremely detailed. Although Cooke did not ascend the hill with Custer, it is possible he may have joined him a few minutes later. Nevertheless, given that Custer and De Rudio were in different locations at that time, it is evident that De Rudio did observe Custer waving his hat on the bluffs.

De Rudio was not the only person to notice Custer's movements on the bluff. As he returned from the Reno fight One Bull, the hereditary chief of the Hunkpapa Sioux, also saw Custer on the bluff with his soldiers. He approached Sitting Bull and told him they must fight new soldiers. Sitting Bull was adamant that they should protect the women and children, adding,

> "This is the second party of soldiers to march against us today. More may come. It may be some sort of trap for us, so be wary."

He pointed to the warriors who were engaged with Reno and told One Bull that there were plenty of warriors there to take care of those on the bluffs. Other Indians had seen Custer's column as well and many broke off from fighting Reno's troops to rush down the valley to meet the new threat.

On the bluff Custer watched as his column began the descent through Cedar Creek into Medicine Tail Coulee. His brother had joined him on the knoll and after conferring for a few minutes, Tom Custer returned to his Company and ordered Sergeant Daniel Kanipe to go back down the trail and locate Captain McDougall,

> "Tell him to bring the pack-train straight across the high ground. If any packs come loose, don't stop to fix them; cut them off and come quick. There's a big Indian camp. If you see Captain Benteen, tell him to come quick."

Kanipe galloped off, back the way they had come. He would not see his Company Officer alive again.

The high bluffs from where Custer observed his column and the valley, gradually sloped to merge with a series of ravines. This was Cedar Coulee and it ended abruptly to reveal a cutting through which a small tributary ran to merge with the Little Big Horn. The Indians knew this opening as Medicine Tail Coulee and where it broadened out to join with the Little Big Horn there was a natural ford enabling mounted men to make an easy crossing of the river. On emerging from Cedar Coulee, Custer halted his column for the last time. Here equipment was checked and girths tightened yet again. Custer instructed Trumpeter Martin to ride back along the trail and bring Captain Benteen up with McDougall and the pack-train to support his attack. He was obviously unaware that his brother had already called for support. Custer's instructions, like his brother's, pose an enigma for neither of them knew the whereabouts of either Benteen or McDougall and they did not know whether the two battalions were in sight of each other to carry out the commands. For all Custer knew, Benteen was in the southern vicinity and McDougall was back up the trail as ordered. Communication between the officers was non-existent. He could only hope that Martin could find them in this rough terrain and avoid any contact with the hostiles in doing so.

As Martin turned to leave, Lieutenant Cooke rode over to him asking him to wait a moment. Cooke scribbled a message in his notebook, tore out the page and handed it to the Trumpeter:

> 'Benteen. Come on. Big village. Be quick. Bring packs.
> W.W.Cooke
>
> P.S. Bring packs.'

The adjutant then instructed Martin to ride as fast as he could to find Captain Benteen. He also told him that if it was safe, to return to the regiment. If it was not, he was to remain with Benteen. This last order from Cooke is also puzzling. He is instructing Martin to remain with Benteen if it is not safe to return to the battalion, yet Benteen has been called upon twice to go and support Custer. Martin knew his chance of survival in this hostile country was slim. He also knew that Custer urgently needed Benteen and his men, along with McDougall and the pack-train. He saluted, turned and kicked his horse to ride back up Cedar Coulee towards the bluffs. Most accounts agree that Trumpeter John Martin was the last white man to see Custer and his battalion alive.

As Martin disappeared from view, Custer's Crow scouts flushed out a few Sioux warriors who had been concealed at the entrance of Medicine Tail Coulee, silently watching the movements of the soldiers. On being discovered they attempted to stall the column by waving buffalo robes at the horses to scare them, which they followed by firing their rifles in the air. (The latter was obviously a signal to the nearby camp.) When this failed, they ran down the coulee shouting the alarm. Lieutenant Smith gave chase with part of Company E, followed by Lieutenant Sturgis with another platoon from that Company. It is not known if Custer had ordered these officers to chase the Indians. Company E had formed the vanguard for the battalion, so any initial clash with the hostiles would have fallen to them. As the coulee broadened the Indians stopped, daring the soldiers to follow. Smith and Sturgis halted their soldiers. They were not going to be lured into a trap. Smith ordered his men to open fire, which only succeeded in driving the Sioux across the ridge. Unfortunately, these few Indians appeared to be growing in numbers. From just a few there were suddenly a great many. On seeing very little opposition, Custer brought his headquarters detachment, along with Captain Yates and F Company, in line with the remainder of the column. Yates would remain in the rear when the column moved forward. There is no doubt that all things said and done, Custer had caught the hostiles by surprise but he had no idea that they would stand and fight.

Watching Smith and Sturgis chase the Sioux warriors up onto the opposite ridge, Custer called his troops to a halt and instructed Mitch Bouyer to release the scouts so they could return home. Why? Knowing as he did that a brutal fight was about to erupt, why would he release vital manpower that he might be in desperate need of? He had already sent for Benteen and McDougall so he must have had some inclination that the opposing forces were going to be stronger than he had been led to believe. The Crows had been the ancient enemies of the Sioux for many generations and they must have had quite a few old scores to settle. Why was Custer denying them the chance to fight and possibly get some trophies? Custer's actions were weird and alien to his character. In any event, Bouyer turned to a young Crow scout by the name of Curly and said,

> "Curley, you are young yet. You do not know much about fighting. I think you should leave us. The Sioux have thousands more warriors than we do. We have no chance at all."

Handing Curley his field glasses, Bouyer continued,

> "Ride back over the bluffs and head east. Watch for a while and if it looks like the Sioux are beating us then go to General Terry and tell him we are all killed. Now go!"

Bouyer turned his bay horse and rode across to Custer.

After watching the actions of Smith and Sturgis a little while longer, Custer led the headquarters detachment towards the base of the east ridge. Captain Keogh, who had been left in command of the remainder of the column, moved his troops forward to follow Custer. The Crow scouts, including Curley, had begun moving to the bluffs. Just as Sturgis called a halt, around 15 Cheyenne warriors charged up the coulee and on seeing Custer with the main column, turned towards the east ridge and swept past Sturgis with his troops galloping up onto the high ground where they turned and waited. Sturgis did not follow. He was too astute for that. He could see Smith riding down towards him with his platoon and Custer had also emerged into view with his troops.

Across the river from Medicine Tail Coulee the Cheyenne camp circle was almost deserted. Apart from just four warriors, those that remained were either too old to fight or infirm. White Elk, a Cheyenne warrior, lay in his tipi unable to take part in any fighting. During the fight at the Rosebud he had accidentally shot himself through his left thigh and he was furious with himself. Bobtail Horse, a Cheyenne Elk warrior, had not finished making his battle charm when the alarm had been raised of Reno's attack. He did not go with the other warriors as they rushed to defend the Hunkpapa camp circle. It would have been too dangerous to fight without his charm. Now it was ready, he would fight. He grabbed his old muzzle-loading rifle and leapt astride his pony. From his tipi he had a clear view of Medicine Tail Coulee and he stared at the dust as it advanced towards the river. Soldiers were coming down the coulee to ford the river. Bobtail Horse raised the alarm and the three other warriors ran with him to the riverbank. One of the warriors who immediately opened fire across the river was White Cow Bull. He was older than Bobtail Horse and a full Ogallala warrior, but he had never fought soldiers before. Through the haze he could see the bearded soldiers, their blue jackets covered in so much dust they merged with their horses. As the warning reverberated through the camp circles, warriors detached themselves from the Reno fight and rushed to meet the new threat. No fighting hostiles were running away!

Some of the Crow scouts had stayed with the column. Their smaller ponies found the piles of shale slippery under foot. The battalion was now advancing at a fast trot and the Crows had to push their ponies hard to catch up with Custer. On seeing them galloping abreast of him he called out to them to leave the fight and go back. Either the Crows could not hear him or they failed to understand him, for they just kept going. If they were going to die then they would die fighting as warriors should. Of course there is the possibility that the Crows would not abandon their oath to serve the army. Whatever the reason, these Crow scouts did not survive the battle and they never received any recognition for their bravery.

Medicine Tail Coulee broadened as it reached the bank of the river. Although it was a natural ford it wasn't much of one to speak of. The bank by the coulee was a gradual slope covered with gravel. The river itself, was quite shallow allowing horses to cross with ease, but the opposite bank where the hostiles were, was quite steep rising sharply to over half a metre from the gravelly shore. The fresh Indian ponies had no difficulty in ascending the bank, but it was not so easy for the tired cavalry mounts that were much larger.

The first troopers to reach the water's edge were those of E Company under Lieutenant Sturgis. Then the incredible happened............. Instead of crossing the river the troops stopped. Sturgis surveyed the hostile camp ahead. The son of the Regimental Colonel, Sturgis had only graduated from the Military Academy a year before and had never fought Indians before now. It would not be unnatural for him to view the huge village with mounting trepidation. First Sergeant Frederick Hohemeyer sat astride his charger beside him. Hohemeyer was considerably more experienced than Sturgis and would no doubt have given good counselling to the 22-year old about to experience his first encounter with hostiles. However, even Hohemeyer must have viewed the huge array of lodges with awe. For a few minutes a deathly silence hung over the ford. The soldiers stood quietly absorbing the scene ahead, with the Indian defenders watching them in complete disbelief. It was eerie and surreal. Sturgis appeared mesmerised by the sudden serenity that had enveloped him. He gingerly led his platoon forward, stopping at the cool water's edge. Still the hostiles held their fire. They could not believe the weird actions displayed by the soldiers. Sturgis was concerned his men were heading for a trap. Where were all the hostiles? Without warning some mounted Ogallala warriors splashed through the water from the west and began to fire on the motionless troops. The defenders snapped out of their hypnosis and joined in the deadly fusillade. The tranquillity of the moment was gone.

Sturgis was clearly startled and shouting orders to his troops to follow, he plunged his horse into the water. Arrows and bullets whistled through the air as the Indians increased their determination to stop the hated soldiers from crossing the river. Midway, First Sergeant Hohemeyer was killed. His body would be found later in Deep Ravine, identifiable only by the name tag on his sock. Sturgis was the next to fall and although some blood-stained clothing of his was later found in the abandoned camp-circles, his body was never located or at least, never positively identified. Sturgis was quickly followed by the Company guidon bearer and the first attempted charge across the river ground to a halt. This opening phase of the Custer fight has been extremely misleading in the past, with Sturgis being confused with Custer or his death being omitted from some accounts entirely. However, overwhelming evidence does support the conclusion that it was Second Lieutenant James Sturgis who was killed during that first attempt to cross the ford.

By all accounts the charge had been stopped and the Indians watched as troopers jumped from their horses to recover the guidon and the bodies of those who had fallen. Custer emerged from the confines of the coulee but he could not quite see what was happening. The frantic scene before him was obscured from his view by the horses splashing and rearing in the water, adding to the haze that swirled around it all from the gun smoke. The troopers of Company E had now succeeded in dragging the bodies from the water and as they redeployed on the riverbank, Custer assessed the situation. He knew that if he did not cross the river now all would be lost. Unfortunately his hesitation gave the hostiles the vital time they needed to deploy their warriors to meet the attack. For a brief second the soldiers were relieved to be given a short respite as the men and mounts were physically exhausted. Sitting Bull recounted later,

> "When the soldiers attacked they were clearly exhausted, but they began to fight at once; but by then our camps were roused, and there were plenty of warriors to meet them."

The reasons why Custer halted the column at this point are not clear, as are many of the subsequent decisions he made that day. Having seen that Sturgis was dead, he may have considered that the ford here was too risky. He had no idea of the number of hostiles on the other bank; he may have suspected an ambush (a favourite tactic of Indian warfare); or he may simply have stopped to allow the troopers of Company E to regroup, as Lieutenant Smith had now joined with Sturgis's platoon. What is certain is that Custer's indecision, yet again, allowed many more incensed hostiles to defect from the Reno fight to attack his column.

Gall, War Chief of the Hunkpapa Sioux, was one of the first to arrive with his warriors. He had been instrumental in stopping Reno's charge in the valley and he had tried to cut off Reno's retreat to the bluffs. As the Sioux ponies splashed through the water, Smith dismounted his troops and set up a skirmish line along the bank. Two Moon, Chief of the Cheyenne had also arrived to counter the soldiers' attack. Very soon the exchange of gunfire made the air heavy with smoke, clouding the view of all the participants. Perhaps it was this sudden eruption that jolted Custer into action, for he turned in his saddle, shouted an order and the column moved forward at a fast trot. He had to cross the ford.

Custer reached the water's edge with Mitch Bouyer riding on one side and First Sergeant Robert Hughes, carrying Custer's personal battle flag, on the other. Not far behind rode Mark Kellogg, trying desperately to keep up with the pace Custer was setting. As the vanguard splashed into the water, frenzied whoops pierced the air as Gall charged through the cottonwood trees to meet them. This sudden attack by Gall, together with the murderous fire from the opposite bank, startled Custer. He must have realised by now that the Indians were fighting with renewed tenacity. They were not running away! Smith's E Company was returning fire to cover the column, but very few bullets were finding their mark. The Cheyenne were too well concealed. For the second time the soldiers had been stopped from crossing the Little Big Horn.

Custer reined in his horse and turned to stop the column. As he did so, First Sergeant Hughes fell from his horse having been caught by a hail of Cheyenne bullets. A nearby trooper grabbed the flag before it hit the water. Excited by the smell of gunfire, many of the soldiers' horses became unmanageable. One such horse dashed across the river straight towards Two Moon and his Cheyenne, who brought the rider down riddled with bullets. Another casualty during this frantic clash was Mark Kellogg, who fell on the river bank, a victim of the Cheyenne fusillade. As Gall pressed home his attack, troops from Tom Custer's C Company had swung to the right of Smith and were returning fire at a rapid rate. Chief Ice, a Cheyenne, fell trying to chase after the retreating soldiers. Myles Keogh had also reached the ford with I Company and stationing his men to take the left of Smith, he also covered Custer's retreat. There has been much controversy surrounding Custer's attempt to cross the ford. Many accounts categorically state that he made no attempt to do so, but Indian survivors claim that although he did not go into the water, he did in fact reach the water's edge. Either way the soldiers' situation was hopeless. One of the Crow scouts who was on the bluff with Curley, was White-Man-Runs-Him, who stated in a later interview,

> "I know for sure that Custer went right to the river bank. I saw him go that far."

To the rear of the battalion, Captain George Yates had been left on the east ridge with F Company. The lower point of the east ridge formed a divide between Deep Ravine and Medicine Tail Coulee. Yates had been shadowed by Wolftooth, a Cheyenne sub-chief, with his 130 warriors. Yates had made no effort to engage them, neither did he attempt to stop them from manoeuvring into position. Wolftooth split his warriors into two groups. The first group followed behind Companies C,I and L as they advanced down Medicine Tail Coulee. Then they re-joined Wolftooth, on the upland ridge to the northern side of the coulee. The Indians made no attempt to conceal their movements which Yates must have observed and yet he made no move to engage them at all. This poses yet another anomaly, why did Yates not engage Wolftooth and his warriors, for in not doing so he allowed Wolftooth to occupy a key position on the ridge, which would subsequently have a fatal effect on the battalion?

Custer had been effectively thwarted in his attempt to cross the ford but he had not given up. As the exchange of fire across the river intensified, the Indians had been halted but it was only for a brief moment as others joined the foray, eager for a fight. He called his officers for a very brief conference. Only a few minutes earlier he had been joined by 25-year old Boston Custer, his younger brother. Sickly in health, Boston Custer had joined the campaign hoping to benefit from the fresh western air. He had been engaged as a civilian forage master, travelling with the pack-train. However, wanting to be with his brothers, he had left the safety of the pack-train and followed Custer's route across the bluffs. His arrival had encouraged Custer to believe that this route was still open and that Benteen would arrive soon with McDougall and the pack-train. Boston Custer was also able to inform his brother of the last known whereabouts of McDougall. Although Boston's information was correct it was also misleading and there is little doubt that it had a profound influence on the critical decisions his brother would make. Captain Yates would also have informed Custer about Wolftooth and his small band of Cheyenne warriors.

Custer had less than a few minutes to assess the situation and re deploy his troops. Wolftooth could present a problem, so he decided to send Yates with F Company across Deep Ravine towards the upland ridge to flush the Cheyenne from their positions. Leaving his brother-in-law, Lieutenant James Calhoun in reserve with Company L, he resolved to make yet another attempt to cross the ford with his headquarters detachment and Companies C and I.

The troops of Companies C and I had already dismounted along the bank and, together with Company E, were returning fire across the river whilst holding their horses. It was difficult for the troopers to steady their aim and stop their frightened mounts from bolting, which some succeeded in doing. Orders shouted by their officers could not be heard above the tumultuous uproar of the engagement. Through the thickening gun smoke, bullets and arrows continued to cut through the air, whilst the terrifying whoops and yells of the hostiles rose above the thunderous cracks of carbines and rifles. Two Moon had been joined by the Hunkpapa Chief Crow King and, together with Gall, they pressed home their attack. As more Indians joined the melee and splashed into the river, Custer must have realised that any further attempt to cross the ford would be futile. He must also have realised that he was no longer on the offensive. He was on the defensive and if his battalion was going to have any chance of survival, he had to get his troops up onto the high ground where Benteen and McDougall could reach him more easily.

Custer's withdrawal from the river signalled a victory to the hostiles. Gall splashed across the river followed by his sanguinary warriors. Crow King also joined in the charge, leading hoards of Hunkpapa and Blackfoot Sioux eager for the kill. To their left, Comes-In-Sight and Brave Wolf led their Cheyenne through the swirling water in support. Through the smoke the soldiers could see a mass of painted warriors and waving war-bonnets bearing down on them, all yelling fierce battle cries that must have sent a shock wave of icy terror to their very souls. Everywhere they looked they could see hideously daubed hostiles riding straight at them. As they drew nearer and nearer they seemed to multiply. There was just no end to them. The soldiers' staunch resistance rapidly drained giving way to panic and they began to fall back towards the mouth of the coulee, firing at the advancing Indians as they retreated.

Custer had already turned his headquarters detachment and was heading up Deep Ravine to where Yates and F Company awaited him. He had, in all probability, issued orders for the other companies to follow him, but the noise of the fight had prevented them from being carried out. The battalion was now fragmenting, a situation that was definitely not favourable to the soldiers. Tom Custer pulled his men back from the riverbank and followed his brother up Deep Ravine. Keogh retreated back towards Calhoun and together they ascended the bluffs through Cedar Coulee. Why they did not follow Custer's route is unknown. They would have known that the battalion had to regroup, although it does appear that they may have chosen this route in the hope of finding Benteen and or McDougall somewhere near. Having been the first to engage the hostiles, Smith and E Company were the last to leave the river, following behind Tom Custer's company as they scrambled up Deep Ravine. It has been estimated that 28 troopers from E Company were killed trying to climb through Deep Ravine, although many of their remains have never been found or identified. Terror-crazed, the soldiers were in full flight from the ford and the Indians were not slow in taking advantage of it.

Until now, Crazy Horse had not participated in the Custer fight. Having successfully repulsed Reno's attack, the wily Ogallala had retreated to his tipi where he conducted a spiritual ritual in order to prepare himself for battle. Reno had taken the Indians by surprise and Crazy Horse had ridden into the fight completely unprepared. It has been stated that Crazy Horse was held with such high esteem within Indian circles, that wherever he rode warriors would flock to follow him. He had been responsible for the Fetterman Massacre in 1866 and for the Indian victory on the Rosebud. His warriors grew impatient waiting for him. Now he was ready to fight. He leapt astride his pony and raced through the Cheyenne lodge circle, heading north. His warriors followed in disbelief. Crazy Horse was heading away from the fighting. As he rode, a cry went up through the village,

> "He is charging! He is charging!"

and more warriors attached themselves to his band. It must have been electrifying for the hostiles. Crazy Horse was on the move! He will crush the hated soldiers! On reaching the end of the Cheyenne lodge circle, Crazy Horse charged across the Little Big Horn and up on to the bluffs, north of where Custer was now headed for.

During their mad scramble up and out of Cedar Coulee, Keogh's I Company had overtaken Calhoun's L Company, leaving Calhoun and his men stretched out behind. Contrary to army training, there was no proper withdrawal. It was every man for himself. There was no regrouping of the companies, much less the battalion. Confusion and fear ousted logic and it was to be the soldiers' downfall. Gall spurred his warriors forward, keeping a relentless pressure on the straggling troopers. Riderless horses galloped across the ridges in an attempt to escape the mayhem, many streaked with the blood of their dead rider. Other horses had been brought down to form breastworks.

The first of the companies to be overrun was L Company, with Calhoun and Lieutenant Crittenden killed as they tried desperately to reach Keogh. Having been effectively cut off from the rest of the battalion, they had grouped together and fought to the last man. As Company L left the coulee, Sergeant James Butler was wounded and had fallen from his horse. He was a man of exceptional courage and no stranger to conflict, however harsh and cruel. Having begun his military career in the British Army, Butler had served with distinction in the American Civil War and had seen active service with the Seventh since its formation in 1866. With blood pouring from numerous wounds, Butler slowly struggled to his feet and stood his ground, continuously firing his carbine at the yelling hostiles as they raced around him. After holding them at bay for some minutes he suddenly fell back, his arms and legs spread-eagled. An astute Indian sniper had found his mark and Butler was silenced from a bullet in his chest. Beneath the broken body a large number of cartridge cases were later discovered, indicating that he had sold his life dearly.

It should be noted here that recent excavations of the area have revealed that locations of spent cartridge cases do not always correspond to the finding of the bodies of the fallen troopers, such as Sergeant Butler, although Butler was an exception. Most of the time it indicates that the soldiers were firing their weapons whilst running from the hostiles. Bodies were also moved when the Indian women stripped and mutilated them.

Caught in a slight hollow, a few metres north of Calhoun, Captain Keogh and his I Company were the next to fall in the wave of frenzied warriors. Keogh made numerous attempts to regroup his company in a brave but futile attempt to reach Custer. He had already witnessed the deaths of Calhoun and Crittenden, and had watched helplessly as the Indians overran L Company and headed for him. These same hideously painted fiends drove straight into his command, some mounted shrieking wildly, others concealed in the numerous gullies raking his men with a steady fire. Keogh constantly exposed himself to the enemy by riding back and forth along the ridge, encouraging his men to stand their ground and fight. As the numbers of Indians gradually increased, Keogh must have seen that his position was now untenable and that Benteen was not going to arrive in time to save them. His horse had been shot through his right shoulder with the bullet passing through his mount and shattering his right knee. He charged at some Sioux who were attempting to stop Company F from joining Custer, although it was only a valiant gesture for he finally fell from his horse from loss of blood. The Sioux and Cheyenne charged forward and completely enveloped the two companies leaving the dead and dying scattered around as they rode on to the high ridge. Keogh raised himself up on one elbow and surveyed the scene of the bloody slaughter. He glanced back towards the ridge behind him where he could just see the remnants of Custer's command firing continuously from a breastwork of dead horses. Within seconds, a Sioux warrior had seen the Captain's movements and had shot him. Keogh was found with three bullet wounds in addition to the shattered knee. In 1881, the Sioux Chief of the Great Council Lodge, Red Horse stated,

> "The Sioux for a long time fought many brave men of different people, but the Sioux say that this officer was the bravest man they ever fought. This officer saved the lives of many soldiers by turning his horse and covering their retreat. Sioux say that this officer was the bravest man they ever fought."

The fight on the high ground, above the Little Big Horn must have been the most horrific and terrifying experience ever encountered by the men of Custer's battalion. Stumbling over terrain that was totally unsuitable for their mounts and devoid of any comprehensible command, the soldiers were quickly fragmented and decimated by the ever increasing, overwhelming numbers of the Sioux and Cheyenne, who swarmed over them with nothing to stop them. The battalion had been split into two parts allowing the hostiles to divide and conquer. This is evident from the positions where the bodies were found later. However, the Indians had also sustained their share of casualties as well.

An Ogallala Sioux by the name of Long Elk was seen riding around with blood gushing from his mouth, before he eventually toppled from his pony. One Sioux lurched away from the ridge and fell into a nearby gulch with his lower jaw completely shot away. Another Sioux, who had been firing at the soldiers whilst concealed behind some sagebrush, suddenly fell back with a bullet between his eyes. Black-White-Man, another Ogallala Sioux, had been shot through the shoulder whilst hanging from the neck of his pony, firing arrows at the soldiers. The bullet travelled through his body and lodged in his hip. He died within hours of the Custer fight, content in the knowledge of their crushing victory. The Indians were also recipients of 'friendly fire'. Interpreting for Crazy Horse a little while after the fight, Horned Horse stated,

> "………the smoke and dust was so great that foe could not be distinguished from friend. The horses were wild with fright and uncontrollable. The Indians were knocking each other from their steeds, and it is an absolute fact that the young bucks in the excitement and fury killed each other, several dead Indians being found killed by arrows."

A few women also accompanied the warriors into battle. A pretty Ogallala by the name of Walking Blanket Woman, rode dressed in the full regalia of a warrior. Her brother had been killed during the Rosebud fight and as she was the only surviving member of her family that was able to fight, she determined to avenge her brother's death. On seeing her amidst the warriors, Rain-In-The-Face called out,

> "Behold, a brave young woman rides with us! Let no warrior ride behind us!"

Another account mentions a Hunkpapa woman by the name of Moving Robe Woman, who also rode with the warriors during the Custer fight. Moving Robe Woman was implicated in the death of Isaiah Dorman, an interpreter attached to the Reno battalion. However, no evidence can be found to support her complicity, although she did admit at a later date to delivering the 'coup de grace' to two wounded soldiers on the Custer battlefield. There is also the account of Antelope Woman, a Cheyenne who had survived Custer's attack on Black Kettle's village in 1868. Having no children of her own, she was extremely fond of her nephew, Noisy Walking, and she rode onto the high ridge looking for him. It was not until many hours later, when the fight was over, that Antelope Woman found her nephew. He was laying in a gully having been shot and stabbed.

On reaching the high ridge (now known as Last Stand Hill), Custer turned his command north, away from the direction he was expecting Benteen and McDougall to arrive from. This decision does not make any sense at all. He had spotted another coulee that led down to the river, further north of the village, so it could be argued that he was attempting yet another crossing of the river to resume the offensive. That being the case, Custer must have felt assured that his battalion was still firmly intact and that Benteen, with McDougall, was at least in sight. He does not seem to have realised that his battalion had been split in two and almost slaughtered. We have to wonder what state of mind Custer was in. He should have tried to consolidate his forces into a more effective group. Of course, he must also have reached the dreadful conclusion that Benteen and McDougall were not coming to his aid and that his fate had been sealed.

Riding across the ridge, Custer was suddenly confronted by the hoards of Ogallala and Cheyenne warriors who swarmed up from the gullies ahead of him. Crazy Horse had effectively blocked his advance leaving Gall, Lame White Man, Crow King and Two Moon to cut off any hope of retreat. Hurriedly forming a breastworks from the horses, Custer and the remnants of his command prepared to make their final stand. Just below him, Tom Custer's company and the survivors of Company F were stretched out along the high ground leading to Deep Ravine. E Company had been completely wiped out, save for Lieutenant Smith who had ridden as fast as he could to inform Custer that the rear-guard had fallen. Custer was now hemmed in with no chance of recue or survival. Steadily, the Indians grew in number and gradually advanced nearer and nearer. Most of them were now dismounted and maintaining a steady fire at the soldiers, with only a few still riding across the field.

Having stopped Custer from advancing and having now forced him into a defensive position, Crazy Horse swung his warriors to the right to attack the straggling vanguard of Companies C and F. With over 1000 screaming Ogallala and Brulé Sioux bearing down on them, some of the terrified troopers tried to run to safety, only to be cut down as they did so. So many futile mistakes were being made by this command. Many soldiers were shot in the back or side as they desperately tried to defend themselves against the hostiles' mounted charges. There were so many against so few, it was a complete slaughter. Many soldiers had inadvertently exposed themselves to long range fun fire, a totally unexpected style of hostile combat. Other troopers were ridden down and killed as they ran towards Custer's position, firing and re-loading their carbines as they did so. Suddenly, the surviving soldiers appeared to go completely crazy. Instead of shooting the enemy, they began to shoot at each other. Before the Indians could charge again, all but four were now dead. These four mounted their horses and attempted to escape the carnage, resulting in three of them being killed immediately. The fourth, presumed to be Lieutenant Henry Harrington of Company C, broke away and galloped up the river. He was hotly pursued by some hostiles who kept up a constant fire and watched in amazement as he put his revolver to his head and shot himself.

The whole area was complete bedlam now. Cavalry horses bolted in all directions with blood pouring from several wounds. Soldiers lay dead everywhere, mingled with those who were severely wounded. Here and there, small pockets of troopers tried in vain to make a stand, only to be flushed out by the Indians and killed. Even though the afternoon sun was bright, the whole terrain appeared darkened by the heavy pall of gun smoke and dust. Companies C, E, F, I and L had all been annihilated, save for a few stragglers who had managed to reach Custer's position, many of whom had been fatally wounded. Exposed soldiers were shot by the hostiles concealed in the gullies, while mounted warriors stampeded the horses away from the ridge. This was a crucial factor of the battle, as extra ammunition was carried in the saddle-bags and the loss of the horses meant that the command could not maintain their fire for very long. Ammunition was critically low by now, with no hope of replenishing it other than taking it from fallen comrades. The Indians on the other hand, had picked up plenty of ammunition and extra weapons from the slain troopers, which they used to good advantage.

Tom Custer and Yates had also managed to escape to the ridge and, together with Custer's remaining troops, they returned fire on the screaming enemy. Altogether there were around 50 survivors, but their numbers soon dwindled as Indian bullets found their mark. Custer and his officers must have realised that their end was near. A small group of soldiers attempted to escape towards Deep Ravine, but they were quickly ridden down and killed. The enraged Indians were giving no quarter. This was their day! Finally, the Sioux and Cheyenne closed in for the kill. Those that were wounded or had not attempted to run, were overrun and slaughtered where they lay. It is more than possible that Custer was either dead or dying by this time. He was found shot in the left chest, with another bullet wound in his temple. Nearby lay his brother Tom, his younger brother Boston and his nephew, Henry Armstrong Reed. Their swift end was almost an anti-climax to the adrenaline rush of the bitter fight.

It is not known who actually killed Custer, although many warriors have laid claim to the act, including White Bull, Chief of the Minniconjou Sioux. However, many have also claimed to have 'counted coup' on the dead commander, including Two Moon, the War Chief of the Northern Cheyenne. Other claims to fame are more gruesome, like that of the Hunkpapa War Chief, Rain-The-Face, who boasted that he cut the heart from Tom Custer's body and ate it! Most claims can be dismissed as elaborations on the facts as it has been recorded that the majority of Indians who participated in the fight did not know it was Custer who had attacked them. At a later interview, Low Boy a chief of the Ogallala stated,

> "Everything was in confusion all the time of the fight. I did not see General Custer. I do not know who killed him. We did not know till the fight was over that he was the white chief............. No white man or Indian ever fought as bravely as Custer and his men."

As the thick pall of gun smoke and dust drifted aimlessly across the high ground, the sanguine stench of blood wafted up from the lifeless bodies of men and horses. An eerie silence engulfed the small gullies and knolls, broken only by the intermittent pistol shots as a few Indians meandered among the fallen soldiers, using the army revolvers to administer the final 'coup de grace'. Slowly the victorious Indians withdrew from the scene. They had their own dead and wounded to take care of. Red Horse stated later that the Sioux had many casualties during the fight with Custer, adding,

> "Now the Sioux had many killed. The soldiers killed 136 and wounded 160 Sioux." (Unfortunately, this cannot be verified.)

Red Horse had played a prominent role in the Custer fight and in 1881 he was persuaded by an army surgeon, Dr Charles McChesney, to record the events by drawing pictographs of the battle. When he had finished, Red Horse had completed 41-pages that constitute a valuable historical account of the battle and an invaluable source for historians. However, considering the huge number of Sioux that actually participated in the Custer fight, their casualties appear to be extremely light.

It has been widely documented that Keogh's claybank gelding, 'Comanche,' was the only living thing found on the battlefield. In actual fact there were several severely wounded horses on the field after the battle. Too badly wounded they were quickly dispatched, but why was 'Comanche' not afforded the same fate, after all he was just as badly wounded. Although no evidence exists concerning the ownership of the other horses, it is more than possible that 'Comanche' was saved because he was an officer's mount and it would make good publicity out of a terrible disaster to do so. It would show those in the east that the military treated their horses humanely. No one will ever know the real truth. The point is, 'Comanche' was saved, he did perform all the duties required of him and he became the Nation's 'darling' for many years afterwards.

Custer's final moments have been depicted in numerous paintings and illustrations, a few of which do provide military enthusiasts with snippets of tantalising information. It all depends on the date they were painted, although sadly, none of them can claim to be historically correct. Most portray Custer standing proud firing his pistols into swarms of Indians, which is against all the evidence that is known. As has already been stated, by the time the Indians decided to end it all, Custer was more than probably mortally wounded (if not already dead,) and it is doubtful he would have been able to stand. Edgar Paxson's painting, completed in 1899, has been dubbed the most accurate reconstruction of Custer's final moments. It shows Trumpeter Voss tenaciously blowing his bugle, calling for help that would never arrive. If correct, the chances are that Captain Thomas Weir, of Benteen's battalion, would have heard the bugle, even through the roar of the battle, when he attempted to go to Custer's aid. Weir later confirmed that he could hear a bugle call. There are other small mistakes too, but they do not do the work any injustice. It is a magnificent work of art and probably the best portrayal to date.

One final note of interest concerning that fateful Sunday afternoon, that has been widely documented as being genuine is that Captain Anson Mills, of the 3rd Cavalry, had grown restless waiting around in General Crook's camp on Goose Creek, Wyoming. In an effort to relieve the boredom, Mills undertook a scouting foray into the hills. Far to the northwest the Captain observed a huge column of smoke or dust rising into the sky. He called it to the attention of his fellow officers, who all agreed that it had either been caused by a forest fire in the mountains or, perhaps, by some Indians setting fire to the grass. Unbeknown to Mills or his associates, they were technically correct but not quite. It was smoke and dust rising into the sky, but it was the residue of battle above Custer's command as they fought for their lives beside the Little Big Horn.

Chapter 4

Defend or Die

The bluffs where Reno and the survivors of his command had so desperately sought refuge were just over 6.5 kilometres south of where George Armstrong Custer had made his final stand. They were a myriad of small gullies and ravines, each of which afforded the pursuing Indians ample protection as they infiltrated the broken landscape. Although Reno's position did offer a little protection from the Indian assaults as they attempted to scale the bluffs in the west, his entrenchment was precariously exposed to the bluffs that rose above them. Thus, having dealt with Custer, many hostiles rode to these higher bluffs and settled down to inflict a fusillade of rifle fire into the exhausted and terrified soldiers below.

Considering the nightmare they had just experienced, Reno's officers had remained completely calm throughout. Private William Slaper later wrote:

> 'Captain French was as "cool as a cucumber" throughout the entire battle and although I searched his face carefully for any signs of fear, it was not there. He had such perfect self-control that I had to admire his courage and bravery...............'

Captain Thomas Henry French was 33 years old at the time of the battle. He had enlisted as a private in the 10th U.S. Infantry in 1864, rising through the ranks to become a First Lieutenant by the end of the Civil War. Promoted to Captain in 1868, French was assigned to the Seventh Cavalry in 1871. A veteran of numerous battles, he knew the value of keeping a level head when under fire and could therefore command his troops competently and efficiently.

Reno, on the other hand, appears to be suffering from some form of battle fatigue, if not in a state of shell-shock. There is little doubt that the ferocity with which the hostiles had repelled his attack had unnerved him and the death of Bloody Knife, whose brains had splattered him, would not have helped his condition. However, in view of the circumstances in which he and his battalion had found themselves confronted with, Reno had acted responsibly in extricating his men from the valley to the relative safety of the bluffs, even if it did not conform to army regulations. His only downfall during the retreat was the fact that it had not been conducted in an orderly manner thus probably contributing to the deaths of many of his command. (But then Custer was also guilty of this in his flight from the river.) It must still be said, that many men now entrenched on the bluffs owed their lives to his snap decision in the timber. Once on the bluffs, reality seems to have set in and whilst Reno did what he though was best for the disposition of his men, it was his officers who actually deployed them and undertook the entrenchment of the command. There are numerous conflicting accounts concerning Reno's conduct during the early stages of the defence on the bluffs. It is doubtful that the troopers had any time to give any thought to it until a much later date, being relieved at the fact they were still alive.

Reno's orderly, Sergeant Edward Davern, does not appear to have given Reno's conduct any thought until he was asked to do, two and a half years later at the Reno Court of Inquiry. He stated that Reno showed concern for his welfare,

> "When I got to the top I saw Major Reno. He asked me if I had any water. I said no and he gave me some."

It should be noted here that Davern's horse had been killed during the flight from the valley, thus leaving him to ascend the bluffs without his canteen or carbine. However, other accounts are not so complimentary. Private William Taylor's memories of the flight, obviously on reflection, describe Reno's demeanour somewhat differently:

> 'Major Reno was walking around in an excited manner. He had lost his hat during the 'charge' and had bound a red handkerchief about his head, which gave him a rather peculiar and unmilitary appearance.'

The skirmish lines formed and the wounded having been placed in a depression at the southern end of the bluff, Reno took a few minutes to survey his position. His forces were spread very thinly around the edges of the bluff, with Companies A and G forming a line between them. Company G had lost McIntosh, their commanding officer, and most of the men during the retreat, leaving the remaining soldiers to the command of 27-year old Second Lieutenant George Wallace. (Wallace would survive the Little Big Horn only to be killed at Wounded Knee 24 years later.) Company A had sustained a large number of wounded during the retreat, many of whom were now in the care of Dr. Porter. Their commanding officer, Captain Myles Moylan, had also survived although First Lieutenant Charles De Rudio was missing. Company M had also suffered casualties, although the numbers were not as devastating. Reno had still received no word from either Benteen or McDougall. He urgently needed re-enforcements to fill the gaps in the skirmish lines and ammunition was getting seriously low.

Glancing to the south, Reno could see a dust-cloud rising over the bluffs. Squinting his eyes against the bright sunlight, he could just discern through the haze the blue uniforms of Benteen's column. Reno could not contain his relief or excitement at the sight of fresh troops and he rode across the bluff to meet them. Although it was but a short distance and he did, in fact return, Reno was technically AWOL at this moment. He has deserted his command. It is not clear whether or not Reno had informed his officers of his intention, although the evidence available indicated that he did not! Talking rapidly and obviously in an excited state, Reno informed Benteen of their narrow escape and explained the situation as it then stood. Benteen appeared to be much calmer but then he had not experienced the trauma of facing frenzied hostiles. As the column moved towards Reno's defences on the bluff, the Indians began to direct their fire to these fresh mounted soldiers. However, Benteen later admitted that he was somewhat perplexed when he encountered Reno. He had last seen the Major when he was with Custer, prior to his little sojourn to the Badlands in the south, and he had assumed they were still together. Benteen showed Reno the note Trumpeter Martin had given him. Reno read the note, then passed it back without a comment. Having escaped the fury of the hostiles himself, Reno must have realised that Custer was in serious trouble. Benteen must have thought the same, yet Custer's situation was not discussed other than Benteen enquiring of Custer's location. Reno stressed the precariousness of his own situation and urged the Captain to join forces to defend the bluffs. This poses yet another question. Why did Reno not order Benteen to deploy his troops? He was of senior rank to Benteen. Uncertain of Custer's location, Benteen decided to remain with Reno and await the arrival of McDougall and the pack-train.

Reno appeared to be completely demoralised by the whole affair, which did not inspire confidence amongst the men. Periodically he had displayed competent leadership but at other times his behaviour was totally irrational. Whilst awaiting the arrival of McDougall, Reno took advantage of the lull in the fighting and attempted to retrieve Lieutenant Hodgson's body from the base of the bluff. Benjamin Hodgson was a popular officer with all ranks of the Seventh and a close friend of Reno. Thus, hoping Hodgson was just wounded and not dead, Reno wanted to bring his friend to safety. Leaving Benteen in command, he took Sergeant Culbertson and a couple of troopers down to the riverbank where they found Hodgson's body. Indian sharpshooters soon spotted the little detail and heavy fire began to pour across the river.

Stunned at Hodgson's death, Reno had to be urged by Culbertson to return to the bluff before they too were killed. Reno removed the Lieutenant's ring and keys before scrambling back to the defences. Hodgson's watch and chain were already missing from his pocket, his body was later recovered, under heavy fire, by Sergeant Benjamin Criswell of Company B.

Benteen was furious at Reno's futile attempt to recover Hodgson's body. There were obviously more urgent matters to be attended to, such as the location of Custer's battalion. Gunfire could now be heard far off to the north. Lieutenant Charles Varnum, who was in bad shape himself, heard the firing:

> '………… a few minutes after Benteen came up, I heard firing away downstream and I spoke to Lieutenant Wallace. I don't recollect any except that one time. I had borrowed a rifle and fired a couple of long range shots when I heard it. I said "Jesus Christ, Wallace, hear that – and that!" It was not like volley firing but a heavy fire – a sort of crash-crash – I heard it only for a few minutes. It must have pertained to Custer's command at the other end of the village. I thought he was having a warm time down there.'

Lieutenant Winfield Edgerly, of Company D, also heard gunfire in the distance:

> 'Shortly after I got on the hill, almost immediately, I heard firing and remarked it – heavy firing, by volleys down the creek. Captain Weir came to me and said General Custer was engaged and we ought to go down. I said I thought so too …….. I heard the fire plainly.'

Throughout much of the evidence available, numerous testimonies conflict with each other as to the actual time scale of events. However, from the testimonies it can be concluded that Benteen joined Reno on the bluff while the Custer fight was well under way. It is therefore obvious that if Benteen had acted on Custer's message when he received it, he would have had plenty of time in which to take his column to support Custer's forces, although it is debatable whether or not he would have had any influence on the outcome. In all probability, Benteen's battalion would have been annihilated as well, leaving the remnants of Reno's command to suffer the same fate a little later. McDougall, of course, had the extra ammunition but not the men to defend it and in dealing with him, the hostiles would have captured the valuable supplies.

It was obvious to all ranks by now that Reno's authority was slipping away from him. Upon his return to the bluff he had a lengthy conversation with

Benteen, which was noticed by all. Unfortunately there does not appear to be any record of what was actually discussed It is evident though, that Benteen had assumed command of the combined forces. Reno did instruct his adjutant, Lieutenant Hare, to locate McDougall and hurry the pack-train, as Hare later stated,

> "......... Reno ordered me to go and find out where the packs were and get them up as soon as possible. I went back one and a half miles [approximately 2.4 kilometres] met them, and told them to hurry; and to cut out the ammunition as soon as possible and send it ahead."

Captain Weir wanted to ask Reno for permission to take Company D to the sound of the guns. He was an experienced officer but he could also be impetuous. Weir was extremely loyal to Custer and he distrusted his battalion commander, Benteen. It is also clear that he regarded Reno with contempt, being utterly disgusted at Reno's lack of authority. Available evidence does not indicate whether or not Weir actually asked Reno for permission to take his Company D to the aid of Custer. What is irrefutable is that Weir returned to his men, mounted his horse and, together with an orderly, rode north across the bluffs to reconnoitre the area. Assuming that Weir had obtained permission Edgerly mounted D Company and followed him. Edgerly later stated,

> "I mounted the men and started out without orders supposing he had got permission to go. We went down about one and a half miles [2.4 kilometres]; he keeping on the ridge and I in a sort of valley. When we got on the ridge we saw a great many Indians riding around and firing at objects on the ground."

Weir and Edgerly had witnessed the final moments of the Custer fight, whereby the Indians rode through the fallen soldiers administering the 'coup-de-grace'. The Indians saw the troopers about the same time as Weir and Edgerly were observing them, and in less than no time were redeploying to meet the new threat.

Hare returned to the bluff shortly after Weir and Edgerly had departed. He reported to Reno who ordered him to take a message to Weir:

> '........... he told me to go to Captain Weir, who had advanced while I was gone for the packs, and tell him to open communication with Custer and he would follow as soon as the pack-train was up.'

Hare duly chased after Weir to deliver Reno's message.

This whole incident regarding Weir's unauthorised advance actually put the entire command at risk. Not only did he ride into an area theoretically swarming with angry hostiles, but he also brought the command to the attention of the frenzied Indians, which could have initiated another fierce engagement. It appears that some of the officers were not or could not think clearly and as such, acted on impulse. Unfortunately, Weir never explained his actions as he died less than six months after the battle, in New York. Officially his death was recorded as the result of pneumonia, but close friends maintained that he died of severe depression and confusion. He could not forget the images he had witnessed of Custer's final moments.

Reno's reluctance to move his forces in support of Custer is another anomaly that will never be successfully answered. Some accounts have argued that Reno's refusal was due to the fact that Custer had failed to support him. That is a petty argument and can easily be dismissed. Reno would obey his orders to the last letter, but he was not an officer to use his own initiative. In other words, he had to be ordered or told to do anything. He did not have the gumption to think for himself, especially in difficult situations. This could explain why Benteen assumed command. Other accounts state that Reno was reluctant to move out on account of the wounded. If the wounded were unable to travel and had to be left behind, it was almost certain death at the hands of the hostiles. Of course, Reno was also awaiting the arrival of McDougall with the pack-train. It was an awkward situation and rank certainly played its part as well. Benteen may have assumed command but it seems it was Reno that the men looked to for confirmation of orders. Such a conflict of authority could have been terminal for the command, were it not for the other officers who guided their men through the fight with confident expertise.

It was not until late afternoon that Captain McDougall finally arrived on the scene with the much-needed pack-train. A box containing 1000 rounds of ammunition was opened and distributed amongst the troops, while McDougall conferred with Reno and Benteen. The decision was made for the command to follow Weir in the direction they assumed Custer to be. On a wider scale the regiment was even more fragmented than Custer's battalion and the officers knew it was sound military practice for the regiment to reform. It is not clear who actually made the decision and issued the orders, for it was not recorded, but once again Benteen seems to have taken the lead. Captain Koylan was detailed to escort the wounded with Company A and carry those who were unable to walk or ride. Thus, with Benteen's battalion leading the advance and Reno's command bringing up the rear, the troops moved out following the trail that Weir had taken.

Ahead of the column being led by Benteen, Thomas Weir had reached a high knoll that overlooked the valley of the Little Big Horn, giving him a panoramic view of the Plains to the north. (This knoll has since become known as 'Weir Point'.) In the distance he could discern groups of horsemen riding over the Plains and through the ravines, creating large dust clouds that impaired a clearer vision. Lieutenant Hare had delivered Reno's message, but Weir could see no definite sign of Custer. Hare, on the other hand, was observing huge numbers of screaming hostiles rapidly advancing towards them, and taking advantage of his adjutancy, ordered Weir to return to Reno. He then returned along the ridge where he met the column and reported to Major Reno, who later testified:

> 'Lieutenant Hare came back and said that he had taken the responsibility of using my name and ordered the return of the command on account of the number of Indians he saw. The orders were communicated to the other officers.'

Weir had now reached Benteen and between them they decided to make a stand on the ridge. Reno, on the other hand, had already decided to return to the bluff:

> 'I had been impressed with the position I first reached on the hill; it was nearer water and if the Companies in the rear could hold the Indians in check, we could get there.'

It appeared that Reno's seniority won again, although it was Benteen who actually directed the retreat in the face of increasing enemy fire, as he later stated:

> 'We had not been there but two or three minutes before the gorge was filled with Indians rushing towards us .... then we fell back to where we were corralled............. I had thrown Captain French's troop in line at a right angle with the river, to hold that point, dismounted, till Weir's troop got through, and then retreated slowly .... This didn't finish as well as I hoped and expected it would.'

The Indians swarmed over the hills, attacking the retreating soldiers at every opportunity, making French's position intolerable. Fighting every inch of the way, the troops gradually fell back to entrench themselves back on the bluffs. (It has since become known as 'Reno Hill'.) In view of the large numbers of Indians now amassing around them, the soldiers' casualties were extremely light. Edgerly reported only one man wounded, who had to be abandoned on the ridge.

Benteen recorded that during the retreat the Indians had not made the most of the opportunities afforded them. However, by the time the soldiers had returned to the bluff the Indians had taken advantage of the numerous gullies and brush to rake the bluff with a murderous fire. Private William Taylor later recalled:

> '……we returned to the place we had left but a short time before. By this time the Indians had us completely surrounded and opened a furious fire.'

Private William Slaper also recorded the encounter:

> '…….. we were compelled to turn about and retreat to our first position on the hill. Even here, we were not in a protected position. There were higher ridges than the one we were on, which were immediately occupied by Indian sharpshooters, who poured heavy volleys down upon us.'

The wounded were hurriedly placed in the depression, with the horses staked around them to offer a little protection and the soldiers flattened themselves on the ground, whilst attempting to throw up some kind of breastworks. First Sergeant Ryan later stated:

> 'We also formed breastworks from boxes of hard bread, sacks of bacon, sacks of corn and oats, blankets, in fact anything that we could get hold of.'

Despite these attempts, there were some soldiers whose positions were still exposed to both a frontal fusillade and a sweeping fire from the rear. Bullets scattered the dry soil, struck the horses, killed troopers and wounded others. Private Slaper recalled these desperate moments:

> 'We were ordered to lie flat on our stomachs and stay down, and not to expose ourselves, for the least sight of any position of the body was the signal for a volley from the Indians. It was not long before we were carrying more wounded men to the hospital.
>
> We were not very well entrenched, as I recall that I used my butcher knife to cut the earth loose and throw a mound of it in front of me upon which to rest my carbine.
>
> That same afternoon, while lying face down on the ground, a bullet tore off the heel of my left boot as effectively as though it had been sawn off!'

Others were not so lucky. Private James Tanner, of Company M, was mortally wounded whilst scattering some Indians who had crept too close to the breastworks. Frank Mann, a civilian packer, was shot in the head during a long-range engagement with hostiles on the ridge. Another unlucky trooper was killed as he sheltered behind a cracker box. The bullet passed straight through the box. Benteen described the heavy fire the Indians inflicted all afternoon:

> 'After our line was formed, it was about as lively a fire as you would like to stand up under. You only had to show a hat or a head, or anything to get a volley. The Indians close to us did not expose themselves. The only thing you could see would be the flash of a gun. We got volleys, but could not return them.'

Considering the haste in which their retreat and subsequent entrenchment had been conducted, the defence positions had miraculously formed lines in Company formation. To the north of the bluffs stood Captain French with Company M; to his right, along the eastern ridge were Companies K, D and G respectively; to his left along the western ridge that overlooked the valley, was Company B. To the south-east, Captain Moylan and Company A formed a line of defence next to the remnants of Company G and at the extreme southern end of the bluff, Benteen was deployed with Company H. In view of the fact that these defence lines had to be implemented whilst under extremely heavy fire from the hostiles, the respective Company officers had exacted their organisation superbly, a fact that seems to have been overlooked. Captain Godfrey's Company K had sustained the first onslaught of the Indians following the retreat and he was alarmed at the inadequate protection he and his men had:

> 'Everybody now lay down and spread himself out as thin as possible. After lying there for a few minutes I was horrified to find myself wondering if a small sagebrush, about as thick as my finger, would turn a bullet, so I got up and walked along the line to caution the men not to waste their ammunition.'

Godfrey also ordered the men who were good marksmen to do all the return firing and the remainder to keep them supplied with loaded weapons.

As the soldiers crouched behind their meagre defences, the Sioux and Cheyenne maintained a steady heavy fire from their concealments in the surrounding gullies and the ridges above. They had taken many of their weapons from the dead soldiers throughout the day, but it is doubtful if they had the ammunition to use them in a sustained fusillade. In some instances, what army ammunition they had managed to find, they used in their own larger calibre rifles. Recent excavations have revealed that using the army issue ammunition in the larger calibre weapons, caused the brass shell to split. Most of the Indian volleys came from the north and east, which was only about 457 metres distant. Those to the south and west of the defence position, appear to have preferred closer combat where it could be achieved. Some even got close enough to throw arrows and soil over the soldiers, while others actually 'counted-coup' on dead soldiers slumped over the breastworks!

It was through these huge numbers of internecine warriors that George Herendeen made his appearance. The 32-year old civilian scout had been left in the timber during the retreat from the valley and, together with eleven troopers (three of whom were wounded,) he had made his harrowing escape towards the defences on the bluff. As he neared the breastworks, Varnum scrambled down the bluff with some troopers to help them reach safety.`

Throughout the afternoon and early evening the Custer battlefield was a hive of activity. Many Indian women and young boys had climbed up to the ridges and were looting the bodies of the fallen soldiers. Scavenging was part of the Indian way of life, although recycling would be a better term today, for anything that could be of use was taken rather than items of value. (This is in contrast to the soldiers who would loot abandoned Indian villages or burial tipis for souvenirs or valuable items.) A few Indian women took their revenge out on some soldiers by mutilating them, but this was not a common factor on the field of death. Sitting Bull expressed his concern over this activity as he had asked that no mutilation should be carried out or any looting to take place. Some of the women, obviously emotionally disturbed by the loss of a relative, ignored his request and set about the vanquished foe with relish. With the warriors racing off to renew the fight with Reno and Benteen, Indian casualties slowly made their way back to their respective camp circles. Sitting Bull was among those who helped to take care of the wounded, including his nephew White Bull, who had returned with an injured ankle. The Sioux leader knew they had exacted a brilliant victory over the soldiers, his dream had foretold that it would happen, but he was also aware that other soldiers would soon come to hunt them down and many reprisals now lay ahead. But at the moment, the Sioux and Cheyenne could celebrate their victory and mourn their dead. Many brave warriors, red and white, had fallen that day.

As the sun slowly dropped behind the Big Horn Mountains in the west, the Indian fire that had been so intense gradually ground to a halt, with just a few sporadic shots echoing across the hills. The besieged troops on the bluff settled in for a very uneasy night. All the officers and men were exhausted, hungry and very thirsty, especially the wounded who were in dire need of water. Reno had ordered the breastworks to be re-enforced and shallow rifle pits dug out. Ammunition was distributed, along with a handful of rations, but the mood remained sombre. Through the darkness the men could see the flames of huge fires among the tipis in the valley. They could hear the Indian drums pounding ceaselessly, the constant beat gnawing at their nerves and the sounds of the hostiles shouting and whooping drifted up to the bluffs. The soldiers had been detailed shifts, taking it in turns to have two hours sleep with two hours on duty. In taking up his position as sentinel, Private Taylor later wrote of this harrowing time:

> 'It had been a day of intense excitement, of desperate struggle and final triumph, such a day they had never known before. The sudden appearance of the soldiers at the very edge of their camp, the rally of the warriors in defence of their homes, the defeat of the white men, of whom over two hundred lay cold in death on the plains and hills nearby, a tribute to the prowess of the Indian. And what a booty had fallen into their hands, everything that horsemen needed. Horses, saddles, blankets, and the arms, over 200 carbines, as many revolvers and ammunition to fit, money and all kinds of clothing. There was indeed much cause for rejoicing...........
>
> But it was not all exultation. In many lodges lay a cold red form ....the lifeless form of a husband and father who had rode out so bravely but a few hours before to defend all that he had in life.............
>
> In other tepees, stretched out on a form suffering serious wounds, some even fast approaching the ghost land of their fathers.......For those who were dead there were loud lamentations, wailing deep and sincere...........'

For a soldier who had fought these people for his very survival, Taylor shows a remarkable empathy for his enemy. However, it must be remembered that Taylor wrote these words after the battle when he had time to reflect upon the events as a whole.

As the soldiers laboured under the cover of darkness, Reno toured the defences constantly making sure the men were well protected and that they had sufficient supplies of ammunition. On the western side of the bluff he noted that Captain McDougall's B Company was sparsely stretched along the ridge and as M Company had more men in their ranks, he changed their positions over so that B Company could effectively hold the northern approaches with Company K and M Company could defend the western slope.

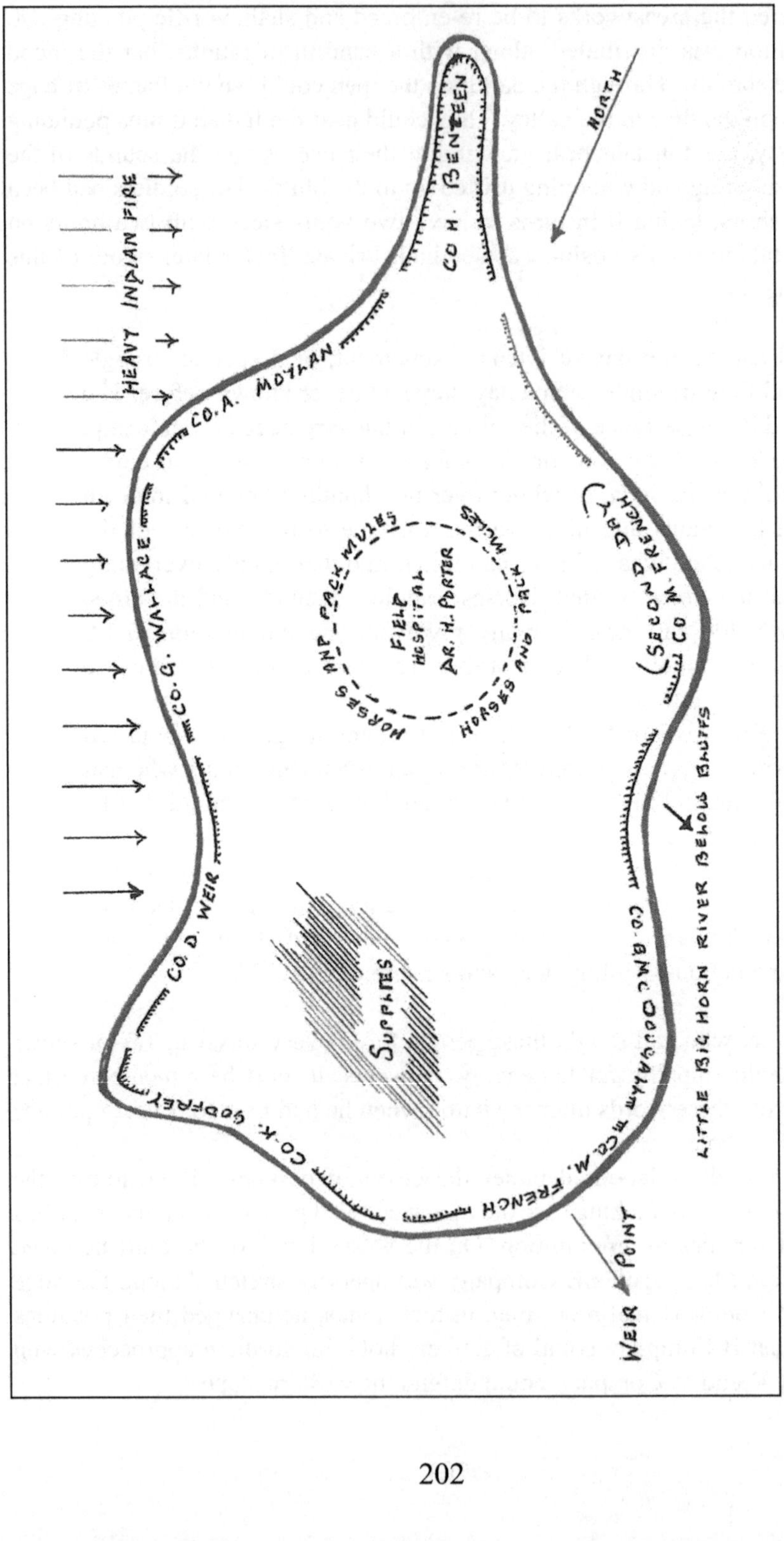

Reno-Benteen Defence Positions 25/26 June 1876.

Some accounts have referred to a drunken argument that supposedly occurred between Reno and some of the civilian packers. There is no positive evidence to support this. At the Reno Court of Inquiry, two civilian packers, B.F. Churchill and John Frett, categorically stated that Reno was drunk and that he was abusive towards them. This may have been deliberately concocted as many civilian packers had to be driven out to the lines by officers and some were accused by all ranks of stealing from the mules once the fighting had ended. Other officers firmly stated that Reno was not drunk on the night of the 25th June or at any other time, including Benteen who testified:

> 'I was with Major Reno all the time the night of the 25th.......... He was as sober as he is now. He is entirely sober now and was then. There was no time, during the 25th or 26th when there was any indication of drunkenness on the part of major Reno. I know nothing about any altercation with a packer except by hearsay. I know they robbed the packs, and robbed me.'

It is evident that the civilian packers were not held in esteem by the officers of the Seventh. However, Reno admitted that he did have an argument with a civilian packer during the night, stating:

> 'On the 25th I went round the line and came to the packs, and found a great many skulkers and drove them out .... I asked one of the men what he was doing there. I was annoyed. I cannot recall his reply, but I know it angered me and I hit him.'

Reno also admitted that he had had one drink, but it is evident from his actions regarding the defences that he was not drunk. He also admits that he hit one of the men, which neither Churchill nor Frett acknowledged in their testimony.

Thus, having assured himself that the defences were well deployed, Reno took a well earned break. Sitting with Benteen, he discussed the whereabouts of Custer and his forces, although neither officer had the slightest notion that Custer was dead. It was just unthinkable. As Reno later stated:

> 'It was supposed that he could take care of himself, as well as we could. He had nearly as many men as I did; more than when I opened the fight.'

It was then agreed that they should attempt to send a message to Custer in the hope he could come to their aid. In any event, Reno wrote four messages and, through Lieutenant Varnum, managed to persuade some Crow scouts to deliver them. Here, the accounts are conflicting. Varnum stated that the Crows didn't even want to attempt to get through to Custer. Mathey states that the scouts tried to get through, but on encountering huge numbers of Sioux and Cheyenne still roaming the vicinity, they returned, refusing to try again. (Mathey has also commented that he didn't really know one way or another.) McDougall was certain that the whole issue was hearsay, but then considering that neither Mathey nor McDougall were privy to Reno's discussions with Benteen, their statements are inconsequential. Reno confirmed his action when he said:

> 'My effort to communicate with Custer the night of the 25th was as much for my benefit as for his. I had no concern, nor as much, about his position as for my own.'

Just before dawn in the early hours of the morning, the Indians amassed around the bluff and renewed their fire with such intensity that it shook the exhausted soldiers. The stamina of these people was amazing. Only 12 hours had passed since their ferocious fighting; first with Reno, then Custer and finally, Reno and Benteen. They had then danced and sang throughout the night and yet, they were still ready to renew the fight. On the other hand, the soldiers were mentally and physically shattered and they had been without water for over 24 hours. With the rising of the sun the heat began to take effect and the wounded began to deteriorate rapidly. Dr Porter became so concerned that he advised Reno and Benteen of the seriousness of the situation. He told them that if the wounded did not receive any water soon some of them would most certainly die. The two officers were sympathetic, but there was little they could do at that point.

The slowly rising sun offered better visibility for the Indians, with some becoming more adventurous by trying to draw the soldiers' fire in an attempt to get them to waste their ammunition. A few even exposed themselves by standing erect and then dropping out of sight as the soldiers opened fire. It is not surprising that this practice was soon abandoned when some of the Indians were shot as they stood up. The soldiers had good marksmen too. Heavy fire was resumed from the higher ridge on the east, with bullets whizzing through the air and hitting the dry earth. It was not long before the Indian marksmen had found their range and the soldiers fell from the impact. The hardest hit were those on Benteen's line of defence, Companies D and K. Benteen found Reno and informed him of the problem. Reno enquired as to where the Indians were, could Benteen actually see them? Benteen replied that he could and they ought to drive them out. Reno gave his permission, but it is clear from the available evidence that he was reluctant to do so.

Reno instructed Captain French to reinforce Benteen's lines with men from Company M, as the lines would be thinly stretched while Benteen made his charge. Benteen returned to the southern end of his lines to organise his counter attack. Under the cover of darkness a few Indians had crept very close to the soldiers and their steady fire was taking its toll on the weary troopers, which they could ill afford. Edgerly later recalled that Benteen told his troops,

> "Alright, ready boys; now charge and give them Hell!"

With Benteen leading the charge and his soldiers yelling wildly, they swung round the southern point and took the hostiles completely by surprise. The troops charged into the small ravine for about 40 or more metres, pushing the Indians back almost to the river, before returning to their lines. Fortunately Benteen only lost one trooper killed in the foray, Private James Tanner, and when a young Sioux ran up to his body to 'count coup', he was shot several times as he ran back for cover. Nevertheless, considering Benteen's charge had been made on foot, it had been extremely successful and the pressure on the lines had been relieved.

Hostile fire still remained deadly accurate from the high ridge to the east, as Sergeant John Ryan later stated:

> 'There was a high ridge on the right to the northeast and one Indian in particular I must give credit for being a good shot. While we were lying in the line he fired a shot and killed the fourth man on my right. Soon afterwards he fired again and shot the third man. His third shot wounded the man on my right. I thought my turn was coming next. I jumped up, with Captain French and some half a dozen members of my Company, and, instead of firing straight to the front, as we had been doing, we wheeled to our right and put in a deadly volley. I think we put an end to that Indian as there were no more men killed at that particular spot.'

The Indians remained persistent though, altenating their fire between heavy volleys and intermittent shots. Fortunately for the soldiers they did not make any serious assaults as they had the previous day. Around midday, a few Sans Arc Sioux made a charge up the face of the bluff, but it was vehemently repelled and the warriors did not attempt it again. By now, Indian fire had begun to wither with just a few sporadic shots ringing out to keep the soldiers pinned down.

Obtaining water for the wounded was now a priority. All the troops were acutely thirsty and, probably in desperation, there was no shortage of volunteers to attempt the descent into the small ravine at the southern end of the bluff. The hostiles, of course, were quick to spot the volunteers as they scrambled down the slope laden with canteens and kettles, and they opened up with a murderous volley of fire to impede the soldiers. Private Slaper wrote:

> 'Volunteers were called for to venture to the river. This was extremely hazardous, as the Indians were occupying the brush along the opposite bank of the stream and commanded every approach to the water.'

The first dash for the water took well over an hour to complete and upon the return of the volunteers, the water was distributed amongst the wounded. For the men along the lines the thirst was fast becoming unbearable, as Captain Godfrey recalls:

> 'The excitement and the heat made our thirst almost maddening. The men were forbidden to use tobacco. They put pebbles in their mouths to excite the glands and ate some grass roots, but they did not find relief.'

One soldier actually urinated in his cup and after he had drunk it, seemed to go crazy. He climbed out of his rifle pit and ran down the slope, where he was immediately shot down by the waiting hostiles. Private James Adams of Company H, also recalled the terrible thirst:

> '.......... The sun beat down on us and we became so thirsty that it was almost impossible to swallow.'

Captain Benteen called for more volunteers to go down to the river for water. Four men from Company H and sixteen troopers from other Companies immediately responded to the request, many of whom were subsequently awarded the Congressional Medal of Honor for their bravery. The four men from Company H; Sergeant Roy Geiger, Blacksmith Henry Mechlin, Saddler Otto Voit and Private Charles Windolph, stood high on the southern ridge and fired a steady volley at the trees that overshadowed the small ravine, while the other volunteers scrambled down to the clear cool water. The hostiles returned this fire and on the way down Private Michael Madden, a Saddler of Company K, was shot in the leg and had to be hauled to safety by one of the Crow scouts. His lower right leg had been shattered by a bullet and had to be amputated a few days later, but he survived the fight and lived to tell his thrilling story right into old age. The other volunteers managed to reach the stream and filled all the containers they had. The Indians tried desperately to stop the small group, showering them with arrows and bullets during the whole exercise, as Private Slaper recalled:

> '.......... An Indian managed to put a hole through the camp kettle I carried, so that I lost a good amount of water.'

It took a further several attempts before they had managed to obtain enough water for the present, although it was not until darkness fell that the soldiers were able to obtain the much needed water for the men and horses.

As the sun traversed across the sky and morning became afternoon, the heat became intolerable and the stench from the rotting carcasses of the dead horses added to the soldiers' misery. Flies buzzed around in their thousands drawn to the decaying flesh. The hostile fire had, by now, almost ceased save for the odd few shots here and there as the Indians withdrew to their camp circles in the valley. To the north, Captain French and Sergeant Ryan stood up and continued to fire at the enemy while they were still in range and, according to official military records, those were the last shots fired in the Battle of the Little Big Horn.

In the valley, the Sioux and Cheyenne women struck the lodges and loaded their possessions on the travois and ponies. Word had been received that there were more soldiers approaching the valley from the north and, although they did not know how many, it was decided that they had had enough fighting for a while. They had wounded to take care of and they must have feared dreadful reprisals for the momentous victory they had won. It is a strange fact that although they had more than enough warriors to completely slaughter Reno and Benteen's forces, they did not do so. In any event, the Indians were leaving. From the bluffs the soldiers watched the activity with interest. During the late afternoon a few warriors rode to the base of the bluff and looked up at the exhausted troopers. Then they wheeled their ponies round, set fire to the grass and rode back to the camp circles. Within a few hours the immense procession of mounted Indians, women, children, old people, dogs and ponies pulling travois, slowly emerged through the dense cloud of smoke and began their trek towards the Big Horn Mountains. The long column, wide at the vanguard, gradually became thinner towards the rear and was protected by mounted warriors who rode along the flanks. Private Windolph remembered the scene:

> '...... It was like some Biblical Exodus .... A mighty tribe on the march.'

De Porter also witnessed the departure:

> 'The village moved away. There was a large body of Indians and ponies. It seemed a mile or two [1 to 3 kilometres] and a quarter of a mile [approximately 400 metres] wide. I judge there were from 2 to 3 thousand Indians, men women and children.'

As the winding column crossed the plateau in the distance, it formed a striking silhouette against the reddened sky of the setting sun. Below the bluffs, the valley appeared deserted except for the scattered debris, which was the only indication that the huge village of camp circles had ever been there.

Although the soldiers reviewed the departure with relief, grave doubts about the reasons of the mass exodus soon set in. Some thought it was only a ruse to flush the soldiers out only to be ambushed and killed to the last man. Others presumed that the hostile Indians had become short of ammunition and were moving their families out of the firing line before attempting a final assault on the bluffs. (It must be remembered that these troops still had no idea of the fate that had befallen Custer and his forces. Therefore, they would not know that the Sioux and Cheyenne had captured over 200 army weapons and the ammunition to use with them.) There were, of course, those who hoped that Custer had found General Terry and were leading Terry's forces back to rescue them. Whatever their thoughts were, they all shared the fear that the Indians would return in the morning to finish them off. No one gave any thought that Custer might be dead. That was unthinkable.

Darkness fell and with no sign of the hostiles the shattered troops breathed a sigh of relief. The nauseating stench from the dead troopers and horses, as the flesh decomposed, was overwhelming so Reno decided to move to move the command a little closer to the river. Captain Godfrey later wrote:

> 'The stench of the dead men and horses was now exceedingly offensive, and it was decided to take up a new position nearer the river. The Companies were assigned to positions, and the men were put to work digging pits with the expectation of a renewal of the attack.'

It is evident that all the troops were convinced that the morning would bring fresh hostilities and if they were not prepared, this would be their last fight. Rations were then distributed and the men settled down to await the dawn. Private Taylor wrote:

> 'With relaxed nerves and tired bodies we stretched ourselves out on the bare ground for the first good, whole night's rest since the 23rd.'

During the early hours of the morning, just before the break of dawn, First Lieutenant Charles De Rudio surprised Reno and Benteen by climbing the bluffs and reaching the lines. He was accompanied by Private Thomas O'Neill of Company G and both men had been presumed killed. They had been left behind in the timber when Reno's command had retreated in the valley, along with Fred Girard, a civilian interpreter, and Billy Jackson, a civilian scout. Throughout the 25th and 26th they had carefully dodged being discovered by the hostiles that swarmed around them, during which time they had become separated from Girard and Jackson. They had been concealed along the bank of the river during the afternoon of the 26th and they watched as the Indians had moved out of the valley. By nightfall they had finally located Reno's position and decided to make for it. De Rudio later testified:

> 'As soon as it was dark I dropped into the river. The water was up to our armpits. We got across and on the bluffs. It was moonlight but cloudy. When the moon was out of the clouds it was very bright and we were still afraid there were still Indians there. When we got nearly to the top I said we'd better not rise suddenly, because if there were still some Indians there, they would fire; so we laid flat and rolled over.'

Private O'Neill described the final moments of reaching Reno's position:

> 'At last we came near enough to hear the sound of voices, but could not distinguish whether they were our men or not........... We crawled along the ground on our stomachs .... expecting every moment to be detected and shot at. At last we heard someone exclaim in a loud voice, "Bring that horse here". I recognised the voice of Sergeant McVaey of A Troop, whereupon I called out to him.
>
> "Mac, don't shoot on us. It is O'Neill and Lieutenant De Rudio! Several voices thereupon shouted "Come on in!" which we did in double-quick time. We were in the hands of our comrades at last!"

Neither man had had any food or drink for over 40 hours and although they had not managed to snatch any sleep either, they had to relate their adventures before they could get any sleep that night. During their conversations they discovered that Girard and Jackson had only appeared minutes before they had.

For the soldiers, the Battle of the little Big Horn was finally over. However, for the Sioux and Cheyenne, with their Arapaho and other allies, a new battle for survival was about to begin.

Chapter 5

Their Duty Done

Of all the military commanders who saw active service on the frontier the name of Brigadier General Alfred Terry does not seem particularly impressive. In comparison to such incendiary personalities as George Crook or Nelson Miles, the former lawyer was of a different calibre altogether. In reviewing the Indian Wars he appears to have been sorely neglected by historians who seem content just to credit him with being George Custer's commanding officer during the 1876 campaign. The truth is rather different, however. Having distinguished himself throughout the Civil War, Terry was given command of the Department of the Dakotas in 1866. Two years later he was a member of the commission that negotiated the Treaty of Fort Laramie with Red Cloud and in 1875 he became a member of the Allison Committee that was formed to attempt the outrageous purchase of the Black Hills, following Custer's immensely successful expedition of the area. Thus, Terry was the Departmental Commander who oversaw the troop engagements during the war with the Sioux and Cheyenne, answerable only to his superior officer, Philip Sheridan.

However, it does appear that Terry was more suited to working on committees than to actually campaigning in the field. As an able leader he preferred to rate the welfare of his soldiers above any unplanned forays with the hostiles, thus maintaining a harmonious respect from both his officers and enlisted men. Being an able leader of men does not always constitute a meritorious commander and, unfortunately for Terry, his leadership abilities were offset by the fact that he was an unimaginative soldier and certainly no military genius, an almost suicidal feature during such times on the Plains. He could follow orders and this is exactly what he was doing in June 1876.

Terry's personal handicap, coupled with the slow laborious movements of Colonel Gibbon's infantry column was certainly not conducive of a victorious outcome of the campaign, unless of course, it had already been predisposed by a higher authority. Previous clashes with hostile Indians had revealed that the use of infantry was a prominent handicap when fighting mounted warriors, who could easily out-manoeuvre the foot soldiers. If this was already a well- known fact, why were infantry employed on the current campaign? Official documents concerning the disposition of troops and initial orders are hard to locate and the few examples that are available do not shed any light on the question. (It appears that Sheridan had been very thorough in covering their tracks.) Moreover, it is evident that Terry, having been assigned infantry, had to make the best of what he had. In a dispatch of the 2nd July 1876, he wrote to Sheridan:

> 'The plan adopted was the only one that promised to bring the Infantry into action and I desired to make sure of things by getting every available man. I ought to have a larger mounted force than I now have but I fear cannot be obtained.'

As this dispatch was written after the event it could be construed as Terry making excuses for the disaster. He was clearly up against a much faster enemy which had surprised him. What has been noted is that the Terry & Gibbon column did proceed at an alarmingly slow pace, much slower than necessary and very much below the actual capabilities of foot soldiers. If Terry had been ordered to proceed at a leisurely march, he certainly covered up the fact by stating in the same dispatch:

> 'The movements proposed for General Gibbon's column were carried out to the letter............'

In contrast to Terry, Colonel John Gibbon was a career soldier from the outset, who repeatedly found himself a participant in numerous Indian encounters that have shaped American history, although he was never more than a supporting player. Prior to the Civil War he had seen active service in Mexico, followed by the bitter struggle to subdue the Seminole Indians in Florida. The Civil War brought more laurels and the war's end saw him appointed Colonel of the 36th Infantry, moving to command the 7th Infantry in 1869. It is interesting to note that this latter service saw him employed against hostile Indians, with one of his duties being to guard Union Pacific railroad workers from Indian attacks. Therefore, in retrospect, it may have been Gibbon's knowledgeable experience of Indian warfare that found him a participant in the present campaign, even though his infantry were of little use.

Documentation concerning the movements of Terry and Gibbon following Custer's departure is virtually non-existent. There are the official reports, of course, but they tend to concentrate on the disaster and subsequent events. A few memoirs exist however, but they tend to contradict each other and it is difficult to piece the puzzle together. Captain Grant Marsh, skipper of the 'Far West', says that it was a couple of days before Terry and Gibbon began their move to the Big Horn River. Gibbon, however, states that his command was ferried across the Yellowstone on 24th June and they immediately began their march along the Big Horn, moving towards its junction with the Little Big Horn. Writing an account of the campaign a year later, Gibbon also states:

> 'I had been attacked with a very severe illness the night before, had remained in bed all day and was unable to move. General Terry accompanied the command in person, leaving me on board to meet the columns at the mouth of the Little Big Horn.'

The illness Gibbon refers to has been attributed to an attack of colic and it was his medical officer, First Lieutenant Holmes O. Paulding, who had insisted that he remain on the supply steamer. Paulding had only recently been appointed to the Army Medical Department and had been the post Medical Officer at Fort Ellis, where Gibbon's 2nd Cavalry had been stationed. At 24 years of age, he was not in the best of health to accompany a campaign such as this for he was already experiencing early signs of a heart condition that would eventually be the cause of his demise seven years later. Nevertheless, Paulding performed his duties admirably even to the point of joining a patrol that was sent to scout some bluffs on 26th June. Paulding's counterpart in Terry's column was Captain John W. Williams, who bore the awesome responsibility of maintaining the health of almost a thousand officers and men, including the supervision of five other medical officers within his team. Considering the arduous conditions these medical officers had to endure to execute their duties, including an acute shortage of supplies and the constant fear of a hostile attack, they received poor renumeration for their efforts. It is surprising that they remained within the department to administer their skills.

By midday on 26th June, Captain Marsh had deftly manoeuvred his steamer along the waters of the Big Horn and entered the mouth of the Little Big Horn. Even though the Big Horn was high from the summer flood, he still experienced some difficulty in steering the steamer through the obstacles it presented. The 'Far West' was a stern wheeler supply steamer that had been chartered by the Army at $360 a day. Of shallow draught, she would draw only 76 centimetres of water when laden, but her Captain was finding it increasingly difficult to maintain an acceptable progress. Finally, Marsh gave up and tied the streamer to an island in mid-stream. He was approximately 18 kilometres from Custer's battlefield.

Gibbon remained on board, leaving Terry to assume direct command over both columns and forge ahead. Terry had expressed no doubt that the 'Far West' would reach the mouth of the Little Big Horn, even though no steamer had entered these waters before. Marsh had been extremely cautious, but he had achieved his objective. Gibbon, feeling none the worse for his illness, observed two horsemen approaching from the bluffs. They were one of his staff officers and an orderly, who informed Gibbon that his infantry column was but a short distance up the river and that Terry had ridden ahead with the cavalry and Gatling guns. Gibbon decided he would re-join his column and meet up with Terry. There had obviously been enough delay, in fact their slow progress would put the columns a full 24 hours behind schedule!

After a short ride of roughly 6 to 8 kilometres Gibbon soon caught up with his infantry column, still laboriously marching across a plateau and it was not long before he reached Terry with the cavalry, who had just resumed the march after a brief rest. Terry informed Gibbon that their scouts had reported Indians in the vicinity of the Little Big Horn, although it was not as yet clear who they were. It was not long before First Lieutenant James H. Bradley, the officer commanding the Crow scouts, reported that several Indians had been sighted up ahead and that they had fled across the Little Big Horn when his scouts gave chase. In their urgency to gallop away the Indians had inadvertently dropped various articles which gave the impression that they were Crow warriors and not Sioux or Cheyenne. Bradley was directed to send his scouts to communicate with these Indians and, if possible, to bring them back. Both Terry and Gibbon assumed that if they were Crow Indians they must have been sent by Custer to find them. Terry's best interpreter had been left on the 'Far West' being too unwell to continue, so he had to rely on another interpreter to translate, mostly through sign language.

As the information was slowly revealed, the credulity seemed beyond comprehension. The interpreter duly announced that Custer's command had been entirely cut to pieces by the Sioux who were now,

> ".............chasing our soldiers all over the hills and killing them like buffalo."

In his report to the Secretary of war, written later that year, Terry wrote of the incident:

> 'Their story was not credited. It was supposed that some fighting, perhaps severe fighting had taken place; but it was not believed that disaster could have overtaken so large a force as twelve companies of cavalry.'

Of course, Terry is reflecting the view of all his forces with this statement, and it must be remembered that he was not privy to the orders for the campaign as a whole. Therefore it is quite understandable that they would have been shocked at such news.

Their thoughts having been thus intimidated, the demoralised long blue column slowly meandered its way towards the Sioux and Cheyenne abandoned camp circles. As they drew nearer, so the number of hostiles in the hills increased, but they did not engage the soldiers. Not too far ahead, huge columns of smoke could be plainly seen, rising out of the valley. Gibbon wrote later:

> 'We had to remain for some time on the high bluffs overlooking the valley of the Little Big Horn, up which the smoke of fires continued constantly to increase in volume.........'

A little further on, the columns finally found a trail that led from the bluffs into the valley and having crossed the river through a deep ford, they halted. Gibbon clearly stated at the Reno Court of Inquiry, three years later, that they proceeded to march up the valley on the left bank. Later, in an article for 'The American Catholic Quarterly Review', he detailed the terrain:

> 'On our left ran the stream bordered with timber and brushwood and some distance on our right the valley was bounded by low rolling hills. In our front the stream after cutting into the bluffs crossed the valley from right to left, the timber shutting out all view beyond, save above its top appeared a sharp mountain peak, on the edges of which could now and then be indistinctly made out a few moving figures, and just beyond the peak the smoke appeared to have its origin.'

Incredibly, Terry allows the column to rest for an hour and a half, during which time the horses were allowed to graze and the troops permitted to make coffee. If, as he has been led to suspect, Custer is in urgent need of his assistance then why does he not proceed with all haste? While the troops rested, Terry sent couriers ahead to contact Custer's command. Two of his guides, Bostwick and Taylor, volunteered for the mission and shortly after their departure, Terry resumed the march. Indians were now to be seen in large quantities within the surrounding hills although they showed no sign of being hostile, preferring to watch the progress of Terry's forces. As the sun began to fade, Bostwick and Taylor returned and duly informed Terry that they were unable to make contact with Custer or his command as they had run into large numbers of Indians and they were unable to get past them. With the darkness of the night now enveloping them he had no wish to encounter an enemy he could not see in the daytime, much less at night. Terry had chosen a site well out of range from both the river and the sloping bluffs, instructing his soldiers to lay on their rifles in readiness for an attack. It is painfully clear that Terry was not at ease with his situation.

At the break of dawn, 27th June, the column breakfasted on hard tack, bacon and coffee before resuming their march along the valley. Neither Terry nor Gibbon had managed to incur much sleep, each officer reflecting on the campaign for their own reasons. As the column prepared to move on, Gibbon sent Lieutenant Bradley on ahead with a detail of Crow scouts to reconnoitre the east side of the Little Big Horn, while the troops continued their march along the west bank. Bradley was well versed in Indian warfare. Deploying his scouts in a skirmish line, he cautiously advanced along the valley. No Indians were to be seen now. Gibbon later described the advance:

> 'The trail, forced into the hills on the right by the encroachment of the river, led through rough ground around a bend in the stream, and as the view opened into the valley beyond, we caught [site], through the scattered timber of a couple of Indian tipis standing in the open valley. The advance guard with flankers out on the hills to the right moved rapidly to the front, whilst a party of mounted infantry, which had crossed the river, scouted the hills on that side. As soon as the Gatling guns were passed over the rough portion of the trail, the whole command, well closed up, moved in compact order up through the open valley beyond..............'

Around 9 o'clock, one of Bradley's scouts reported seeing an object not that far in the distance, which appeared to be a dead horse. Closer inspection revealed that the object was, indeed, a dead horse. In fact it was a cavalry mount. Bradley halted his scouts and rode to the brow of a hill to survey the terrain. Below lay the scattered bodies of Custer's command and their horses. Waving for his scouts to follow, Bradley galloped down the hill and on to the field of death. Within minutes he had counted over 206 slain cavalrymen including George Custer and his accompanying family. According to the 'Helena Weekly Herald', dated 27th July 1876, Bradley gave an account of his discovery, which was strange in the extreme considering the newspaper appeared the very day that Terry's march was resumed and Bradley actually found the bodies:

> 'Of the 206 bodies buried on the field, there were very few that I did not see, and beyond scalping, in possibly a majority of cases, there was little mutilation. Many of the bodies were not even scalped and in the comparatively few cases of disfiguration it appeared to me rather the result of a blow than of a knife............'

Either Bradley was not familiar with Indian practices or he chose to ignore it, for this account is in complete contradiction to the many witnessed who reported or testified at a later date.

While Bradley viewed the grisly scene, Terry and Gibbon had reached the remains of the Indian encampment. What had once been a bustling, thriving community was now a place of desolation, with only a few tipis still standing. The first tipis they encountered were occupied by dead Indians, all laid out as befitted their warrior status and according to their rituals. To the soldiers it appeared as if the camp had been abandoned in great haste, for the whole area was strewn with lodge-poles, various skins, pots, pans and other daily objects. However, it is evident that the hostiles had not left the encampment in a hurry, for Reno and his survivors watched the Indians depart at a fairly leisurely pace. The debris Terry's men saw was quite simply that; the debris of an abandoned camp. Gibbon later described other finds amongst the discarded items:

> '……….amongst the rubbish, someone had picked up a pair of bloody, drawers, upon which was plainly written the words, "Sturgis's, 7th Cavalry", whilst a buckskin shirt, recognised as belonging to Lieutenant Porter, was discovered with a bullet hole passing through it.'

The column passed though the deserted encampment in complete silence. The soldiers were obviously stunned at the sights they were seeing and at the enormity of the area that the Indians had occupied with camp circles. On the sagebrush flats, just south of the village, Terry ordered the column to halt and form a camp. This was the very ground that Reno and his forces had charged and been severely repulsed. A few minutes later Bradley returned with his scouts and duly reported his gruesome discovery to Gibbon.

A few kilometres further south, still maintaining their defensive position on the bluff, Reno and the remnants of his forces watched the approaching dust cloud with trepidation. Captain Godfrey later described the scene:

> '…………. A cloud of dust was observed ……………..
> The assembly was sounded, the horses placed in a protected situation, and camp kettles and canteens were filled with water.
> An hour of suspense followed …………………..'

Reno obviously suspected that the Indians were trying to lure him out into a trap. He was not going to let that happen. His forces were to stay where they were, although he did put the soldiers in readiness for another attack. As the dust cloud edged closer, the men on the bluff could just determine the dark blue coats of the soldiers as the column steadily made its way down the valley. Speculation as to who it might be ran at fever pitch through the ranks, mixed with the excitement of finally being rescued. Some thought it was Custer returning to relieve them, others suggested it might be Terry as he was supposed to rendezvous with them, while others thought it could be Crook as he should have been in the vicinity by now. In actual fact, the survivors on the bluff did not really care who was in the valley so long as it not the Sioux or Cheyenne. If those approaching were wearing blue, it meant that their dreadful ordeal was over. It did not take Reno long to ascertain that the blue column was definitely lines of soldiers and that General Terry was leading them. Directing Lieutenants Hare and Wallace to ride down and report their position, Reno also gave them a letter to hand to Terry:

> 'I have had the most terrific engagement with the hostile Indians. They left their camp last evening at sundown moving due south in the direction of the Big Horn Mountains. I am very much crippled and cannot possibly pursue, Lieutenants McIntosh and Hodgson and Dr De Wolf are among the killed. I have many wounded and many horses and mules shot. I have lost both my own horses. I have not seen or heard from Custer since he ordered me to charge with my battalion (3 companies) promising to support me. I charged about 2 pm, but meeting no support was forced back to the hills. At this point I was joined by Benteen with 3 companies and the pack-train rear guard (one Co.). I have fought thousands and can still hold my own, but I cannot leave here on account of the wounded. Send me medical aid and rations. As near as I can say now I have over 100 men killed and wounded.'

The two Lieutenants mounted their horses and rode down into the valley. On reaching the point where Reno had formed his skirmish line, they met with Terry and Gibbon. Lieutenant Wallace later gave an account of the meeting:

> 'In compliance with the orders of Major Reno, I mounted my horse and rode down across the ford where we had retreated from and met General Terry beyond that point where our skirmish line had fallen back. I reported to him that I had been sent out by Major Reno to show him the approaches to his position. He then asked me who was there. I told him: Major Reno with seven companies and he went on to ask me in detail what had occurred: how the fight had commenced and the result. When I got time I then asked him where Colonel Custer was and received the reply that gave me to understand that they had all been killed.'

On listening to the verbal reports of Wallace and Hare, Gibbon realised that no-one of Custer's command had been seen by the survivors on the bluff since the regiment had been split two days ago. (Gibbon's deduction was not strictly correct. Two members of Custer's force had been sent to Benteen requesting re-enforcements and the pack-train. They were now with Reno's command on the bluff; Sergeant Daniel Kanipe of Company C and Trumpeter John Martin of Company H.) It was not difficult to reach the obvious conclusion that the bodies Bradley and his scouts had found were those of George Custer and his battalion. Having read Reno's letter, Terry accompanied Wallace and Hare to Reno's position, leaving Gibbon to establish the camp.

Terry's arrival on the bluff was greeted by tumultuous cheers from the survivors. Private Edward Pigford, of M Company, sums up the relief they all felt when he later wrote:

> 'I never saw anything in all my life that looked as good to me as Terry's men!'

Terry appears to have shown no emotion. After exchanging greetings with Reno and his officers, he informed them of the reports he had received concerning Colonel Custer. As Terry spoke an eerie silence enveloped the bluff: Custer and all his men had been killed. Kanipe and Martin must have been stunned by the news and the lucky escape that had befallen them. For Reno's men, what had been a joyful relief now turned into stunned grief, as the realisation struck home that many of their friends had not survived to see this day. Captain Godfrey recalled:

> 'There was scarcely a dry eye; hardly a word was spoken, but quivering lips and hearty grasping of hands gave token of thankfulness for the relief and grief for the dead.'

Following a brief conference, it was decided to transfer the remnants of Reno's forces down into the valley to camp with Gibbon's columns.

Gibbon had eventually selected a site for the camp, but it had not been easy. The valley was black from the effect of the bush fire and smoke hung in the air, clinging to their uniforms and scorching their throats. The grass that was available for the animals was nearer the river where it had been too green and damp to burn. In making a cursory survey of the area, Gibbon found evidence that a conflict had, indeed, taken place as he later wrote:

> '..........I came upon the body of a soldier lying on his face near a dead horse. He was stripped, his scalp gone, his head beaten in,

> and his body filled with bullet holes and arrows. Close by was another body, also close to a dead horse, lying like the other, on its face, but partially clothed, and this was recognised by one of our officers as the body of Captain McIntosh. More bodies of both men and horses were found close by ....'

The odour of the dead bodies, both men and horses, was becoming increasingly offensive. After all, they had lain where they fell for over two days now and they were not only bloated, but blackened by the sun as they slowly decayed. Gibbon set details to haul away the horses and bury the soldiers, then he rode to the bluff to determine the condition of Reno and his men. On the way he passed more bodies of men and horses, lying scattered in the burnt sage brush at intervals. On reaching the ford, several more dead horses were found. It is strange to note that although Gibbon had detailed soldiers to bury the remains and clear the area of the dead horses, there is no reference to suggest that he made any attempt to identify these fallen men, except for McIntosh. Thus, he had no idea of what Company they had belonged to, much less their names or ranks.

On reaching the summit of the bluff, Gibbon noted the lines of rifle pits and numerous dead animals, horses and mules, lying about in every direction, some of which had obviously been used for breastworks. Turning towards the river he had a panoramic view of the valley and beyond. He could determine where Reno had charged the hostiles and where the huge village of camp circles had been. In the distance he viewed the Big Horn Mountains, whose summits were still partially covered with snow where they rose into the sky. Glancing down the river he could now see the high ridges that obscured the rolling hills, where it was believed Custer and his men now lay. Gibbon harboured no doubt that an immense struggle for survival had taken place and he listened intently to the stories detailing the experiences of the officers and men who had endured sheer Hell for the past two days, each one pointing out specific positions in the valley or across the bluffs.

The wounded were still lying under the shelter of tents, being tended to by Dr Porter and his attendants. Having extricated himself from the deadly clutches of the hostile Indians in the valley, he found that he was the only surgeon on the bluff, De Wolf having been killed. For over 48 hours this 26-year old physician dodged arrows and bullets as he administered aid to the wounded and yet his heroism was never recognised by the higher authorities. There does not appear to be any reference to suggest that Terry's Medical Officer, Captain Williams, actually scaled the bluffs to assist Porter, although one of Gibbon's officers, Charles Austin Coolidge, a First Lieutenant of Company A, 7th Infantry, was sent up to assist as he was found to have some medical experience. Thus it appears that Williams supervised the preparation for the wounded when they were transferred down to the valley later that day.

Moving the wounded was a slow and painful process and, here again, accounts vary as to how it was executed. Gibbon states that the majority of the 52 wounded men had to be carried from the bluff and as there were no stretchers or litters in the command, they had to be improvised:

> 'A quantity of light tipi poles were collected from the Indian camps, and by means of these, old pieces of canvas, and blankets, a number were made, and by night all the wounded were carried down the steep slope of the bluffs, across the creek, and down to our camp, the men working in relays.'

Private William Taylor renders a rather contradictory account of these hazardous manoeuvres:

> 'The wounded were moved as soon as possible…………
>
> This work was rather difficult in the case of those who were seriously injured and helpless, for they had to be carried in blankets down a steep bluff and then through the river that was nearly waist deep. The men exercised all the care and consideration that they could, but it must have been a great relief to the wounded when safely deposited in their new 'field hospital', a grassy bed, protected from the sun by a piece of shelter-tent.'

It is obvious that the transferral of the wounded was of the utmost priority and it is therefore likely that the account presented by Private Taylor is the most probable. Taylor was in a much better position than Gibbon to observe the movement as Gibbon would have had other duties to occupy him. These litters were only a 'make-do' and would probably not stand up to the rigours of the return march. Thus, troops from Gibbon's column were set to work making litters for the wounded to be carried back to the supply steamer and it is conceivable that Gibbon may have been confused by the reasons for their actions at this time.

With the evacuation of the wounded well under way, the remainder of Reno's forces spent the rest of the day collecting their personal effects and destroying all the surplus articles that could not be moved. There was still the possibility that the Indians could return and nothing was to be left that they could find of use. The remaining rations were taken down to Gibbon's camp, save for what would be needed that evening. Their final act was to end the misery of a number of badly wounded horses and mules. Gibbon states that

Reno's troops remained on the bluff during the night of the 27th, which appears to be substantiated by Private Taylor:

> 'Soon after five o'clock on the morning of the 28th, the remount of our Regiment swung into the saddle again and bade farewell to that memorable spot and the scattered graves of our late comrades. It had been our enforced abiding place for two and one half days, and for the greater part of the time, it looked as if we had reached the end of our earthly journey. We left it, carrying with us the memory graven deep in our minds of those thrilling scenes when for hours we looked death in the face.'

As the troops of the Seventh busied themselves on the bluff, Captain Benteen rode over the rolling hills to see Custer's battlefield for himself. He was accompanied by Lieutenant De Rudio and Lieutenant Bradley. Also in the party was Lieutenant Nowlan, RQM of the Seventh on detached duty with Terry's column. As they rode to the knoll where Custer lay, they passed the bodies of troopers and horses that increased in number as they cantered forward. De Rudio described the scene:

> '……… and there we found a dead body; that was the first, lying in the bottom of a little coulee. It was so disfigured as to be unrecognisable, but from the marks on his pants we knew it was a trumpeter. Soon we found more bodies, scattered all over, wherever there was a chance to make a stand in the coulee.
>
> At last we got to the top of the knoll where Gen. Custer was, and several others, and the horses appeared to have been killed to form barricades. There were higher points all around, so they could not defend both front and rear, and they appeared to have been overcome by overwhelming numbers.'

Upon their return from the Custer battlefield, Benteen remarked to Lieutenant Maguire, an engineer on Terry's staff:

> 'By the Lord Harry, old man, 'twas a ghastly sight: but what a big winner the U.S. Government would have been if only Custer and his gang could have been taken.'

It may have been a casual comment or Benteen may have been referring to something else. His cousin, Lawrence Cobright, was not only the head of Associated Press but was also very well acquainted with many politicians and military personnel in

Washington. Had Cobright warned Benteen before the last phase of the campaign? If he had, it would explain why Benteen did not go to Custer's aid when he received the messages for help. Years later, Benteen hinted to researchers that there was much more to the battle than he was prepared to disclose.

It was during this cursory inspection of the battlefield that 'Comanche' was discovered. Many have laid claim to the discovery, but most authorities accept that Comanche was found by Lieutenant Nowlan in a ravine. The horse, officially described as a bay of 15 hands in height, was purchased by Captain Myles Keogh, the officer commanding Company I of the Seventh Cavalry. It is believed that Comanche was born in 1862 and it was during a skirmish with the Comanche Indians that he got his name. An arrow had struck his right hind quarters and at that moment of impact he had screamed like a Comanche. From that moment on, Keogh and Comanche had been inseparable. Now he was standing amidst the debris of battle, his rider dead and himself with no less than seven wounds. Contrary to popular belief, Comanche was not the sole survivor of the battle at this point, although that would be his destiny. There were a few other horses on the field struggling to remain alive, although suffering from terrible injuries and it was obvious that they were beyond any help.

Sergeant Stanislaus Roy was detailed with others, to shoot all the wounded horses to put an end to their suffering the following day. However, Comanche was well known to everyone in the Seventh and the fact that he was Keogh's horse may well have saved him. After all, in the wake of such an awful disaster the public, not to mention the army, needed a hero and Comanche was perfect for the part. In any event it was Reno who issued the order that Comanche was to be saved and given the attention he so desperately needed. Gustave Korn, one of the Seventh's blacksmiths, was instructed to give the utmost care and attention to Comanche, which he dutifully did. Comanche faithfully served the army right up to his death on 7th November 1891, when he was believed to have been 29 years old.

Having gathered all the available evidence, it appears that Terry then retired to write the first of his reports to Philip Sheridan. He had faithfully completed his duty in compliance of the General's orders and, having seen the result, may have harboured grave concerns about his superior officer's hidden agenda. The report, written on the 27th June, gives full details of Custer's movements and the ensuing fight, although he made no mention of his own orders to Custer, orders which were to become extremely controversial in later years. The following day, he wrote another report, much shorter this time, giving Sheridan the direction the hostile Indians were believed to have taken:

> 'A reconnaissance was made today by Captain Ball, of the Second Cavalry, along the trail made by the Indians when they left the

> valley. He reports that they divided into two parties, one of which kept the valley of Long Fork, making, he thinks, for the Big Horn Mountains; the other turned more to the eastward.'

Terry had no intention of pursuing the Indians at all, however as he was the commanding officer he knew he should at least make some effort to ascertain the hostiles whereabouts. He was also aware that even if a trail was found it was still no positive indication that was the direction they had actually taken. On the frontier nothing was certain. Thus, Captain Edward Ball set out with a company of cavalry and after riding due south for around 19 kilometres, he reached the point where the trail divided. He turned eastwards and picked up an old Indian trail that led back towards the abandoned encampment. Ball now knew that this was a separate trail to the one previously discovered by Custer and if there were others, as indeed there must be, then the Indians that had congregated on the Little Big Horn must have been of a very formidable number. As Ball and his soldiers followed the Indian's trail they found grass blackened and the air smoky; the departing Indians were setting fire to the terrain after they had passed through.

On the 28th June, Gibbon wrote to the commanding officer at Fort Ellis, Captain D.W. Benham. His letter not only informed Benham of the disaster that had befallen Custer, but also requested him to telegraph the commanding officers at Fort Shaw and Camp Baker to inform them that he and his command were all well. Of course, it was a foregone conclusion that Benham would also telegraph the news of the defeat as well, not only to those he had been requested to but everyone else as well. News such as this was bound to spread fast. Gibbon's letter and the two reports from Terry were carried to Fort Ellis in Montana, by a civilian scout by the name of 'Muggins' Taylor. Terry had instructed the scout to ensure that his reports were telegraphed to General Sheridan as quickly as possible upon his arrival. Thus, Taylor left the camp on the Little Big Horn and reached Fort Ellis during the evening of the 3rd July. Considering the distance he covered, it was a remarkable feat, although it is not known whether he returned to the Yellowstone to follow it westwards or if he cut across country and took the risk of running into the scattered Sioux and Cheyenne.

At five o'clock, on the morning of Wednesday 28th June, Reno and the survivors of the Seventh Cavalry crossed the Little Big Horn and rode on to the battlefield to bury their dead. These men had endured two days of the most ferocious fighting they were ever to experience for the rest of their lives and many of them were still suffering the trauma. If that was not enough, the grisly sight that met their eyes was to be forever imprinted in the minds of those whose duty it was to bury their comrades. Deaths caused by violence are never a pretty sight and given that the Custer battalion had been lying on the open ground for over 60 hours, in a daytime temperature of thirty two degrees Celsius (89.6 F), it is not surprising that many could not be identified and credit should be given to those who attempted to do so. Most of the dead had been stripped naked, save for a few who still wore their underwear, and from a distance they looked white. Captain Godfrey of Company K, described the scene:

> 'The marble white bodies, the sombre brown of the dead horses and dead ponies scattered all over the field, but thickest near 'Custer Hill', and the scattering tufts of reddish-brown grass and almost ashy-white soil depicts a scene of loneliness and desolation, that bows down the heart in sorrow. I can never forget the sight; the early morning was bright, as we ascended to the top of the highest point where the whole field came into view, with the sun at our backs.
>
> "What are those?" exclaimed several as they looked at what appeared to be white boulders. Nervously I took the field glasses and glanced at the objects; then, almost dropped them and larconically (sic) said: "The dead!"
>
> Captain Weir who was sitting near on his horse exclaimed: "Oh how white they look!"

In actual fact, decomposition was already in an advance state, with the blackened and bloated bodies swarming with flies. Captain Walter Clifford, of Company E, 7th Infantry, recorded:

> '........... the bodies swollen and blistered in the sun and each hideous gaping wound with a host of buzzing, quarrelling blue flies.'

Apart from the wounds received during the fight, many of which were horrendous in themselves, mutilation was also prevalent. The degree of mutilation appears to be a moot point with many authorities, however, accounts from the burial party do agree that it was observed. The most common was the crushing of heads, presumably with stone clubs, and the slashing of the limbs, although evisceration and decapitation was also found. Private Slaper wrote:

> 'Some of these disfigurations were too horrible to mention. After being scalped, the skulls were crushed in with stone hammers, and the bodies cut and slashed in all the fleshy portions. Much of this was doubtless done to wounded men. Many arrows also had

> been shot into some of the bodies – the eyes, neck, stomach and other members.'

Private Taylor substantiated this statement when writing his own version of the events, as did many others. Private George Glenn of Company H, gave a graphic account of the discovery of the body of Private Thomas Tweed of Company L:

> 'His crotch had been split up with an axe and one of his legs thrown up over his shoulder. He was shot with arrows in both eyes.'

This was clearly a very emotional experience for the burial parties, with many throats being choked with grief and a large number of eyes swelled by tears. Private Glenn knew Private Tweed quite well. The deceased was a fellow Bunkie and the shock that Glenn felt at seeing his bodily remains so desiccated, must be incalculable. The sickening stench that arose from the putrefying corpses was another unpalatable factor the burial parties had to contend with, which hampered the internment considerably. Private Slaper wrote:

> '……., but the stench was so strong from the disfigured, decaying bodies, which had been exposed to an extremely hot sun for two days, that it was impossible to make as decent job of interring them as we would otherwise have done.'

Sergeant Ryan, of Company M, also noted:

> '………….. that the stench of the bodies was terrible, and several of the men who buried the Deep Ravine dead recalled the smell as so overwhelming as to cause vomiting amongst the burial detail.'

Captain Thomas French found his way across to Reno and asked him if he had any whiskey. Reno was well known throughout the Regiment for his partiality to the liquor, indeed Custer had even warned him about it. Reno replied that he had, to which French retorted,

"Then give me a drink for I am sick at the stomach!"

On reaching the field Reno ordered his officers to split the area between them and advance across it in a skirmish line. Lieutenant Varnum and his scouts were detailed out on to the flanks as a precaution against any hostiles returning to the scene. There were very few implements within the command that the burial parties could work with. Gibbon wrote that shovels and spades had been discovered in the deserted Indian camps, which was of great help with the burials. However, this does not appear to be the general consensus. It is more probable that the burials were carried out with the use of tin cups and knives as best as possible, although in many cases the bodies were covered with just a few centimetres of earth scraped over them and a few stones. When this was not practical, either due to the putrefaction of the bodies or the hardness of the ground, sage bush was simply laid over the top in a vain effort to discourage natural scavengers. It was a respectful gesture, if nothing else. The Custer brothers were afforded a little extra care, but even their graves did not exceed 30 to 35 centimetres in depth. Identification and the re-burial of the dead would be a major problem over the years to come.

Since the event there have been three serious attempts to re-bury the remains. In 1877 Captain Michael Sheridan, acting on the orders of his brother, General Phil Sheridan, returned to the battlefield ostensibly to exhume the remains of the identified officers, place them in pine boxes and return them to their families for re-burial. The only exception being the remains of Lieutenant John Crittenden, who was re-buried on the field where he had been killed at the request of his father. Captain Sheridan's men found the bones of the fallen, once again exposed to the elements and identification could only be presumed from the markers that were found nearest the remains. Bones that could not positively be identified were, once again, covered with earth, stones and sage brush. Four years later, Lieutenant Charles Roe, of the 2nd Cavalry, was detailed to exhume the bones and re-bury them collectively in a mass grave. Roe also erected a granite monument on the top of the hill where Custer had been found. However, it was not until 1890 that the marble markers were placed across the field to commemorate where each soldier fell. These can still be seen by visitors to the battlefield today. (Having buried, re-buried and removed the remains it begs the question how did those later parties of Roe know where to place the markers as there is no records to show exactly where they fell on the fields save for Custer himself ?)

On the top of a ridge, furthest from the river lay the remains of Lieutenant-Colonel George Custer and those who had fallen with him. Interpreter Fred Girard was the first to locate the body. Captain Edward Godfrey described the scene as told to him by Girard:

> 'He found the naked bodies of two soldiers, one across the other and Custer's naked body in a sitting posture between and leaning against them, his upper right arm along and on the topmost body, his right forearm and hand supporting his head in an inclining posture like resting or asleep.'

Accounts vary, although most seem to agree that apart from a wry smile on his lips, his expression was relatively calm. Custer had a bullet wound in his left chest and another in his left temple, but other than these wounds he had not been mutilated or scalped. Here again, accounts concerning the wound in Custer's temple are conflicting, leading to confusion and the mistaken assumption that he had committed suicide. Godfrey has repeatedly stated that there were no powder burns surrounding the wound, a profound statement considering he was only repeating what Girard had told him. Sergeant Ryan, whose detail actually buried Custer's body was more descriptive:

> 'He had been shot in two places, one bullet had entered his body on the right side and passed nearly, but not quite through. The second bullet, and undoubtedly the fatal one, passed through his head entering close to the right ear and coming out of the left ear.'

How Sergeant Ryan managed to note the wounds to such an extent has never been clarified. Such a description would put some modern pathologists to shame! However, as he does not mention the presence of powder burns, it is safe to assume that either he did not think them worthy of note or there were none to note. A twist in the tale comes from Rain-In-The-Face, a Hunkpapa Sioux who was a prominent participant of the battle and one of the few Indians that would have been able to recognise both George and Tom Custer, the latter of which he had an intense dislike. On his deathbed in 1905 at the Standing Rock Agency, Dakota, Rain-In-The-Face made a confession to a missionary by the name of Mary Collins:

> 'Yes, I killed him. I was so close that the powder burns from my gun blackened his face.'

In view of the fact that Rain-In-The-Face could have identified both George and Tom Custer, the possibility of being able to do so in the heat of battle is highly unlikely. It is also difficult to discern whether his confession refers to George or Tom. It was a known fact that he hated Tom Custer with a vengeance and many of the bodies had been shot in the head by the Indians after they had been killed. In any event, whichever account is true, it does appear that there is no justification to the popularised theory that George Armstrong Custer took his own life.

The body of Captain Thomas Custer was found lying face down on the ground, a little distance to the left of his brother. Like many others on the field, he was bereft of his clothing with numerous arrows bristling from his body and the back of his head. All of his scalp had been removed, leaving just a few small tufts of hair on the nape of his neck and his skull had been completely smashed in. To make a positive identification, the body was turned over only to reveal the horrific mutilation that had been inflicted. He had been split down the centre of his body leaving his entrails protruding out; his throat had been cut; and the muscles of his arms and thighs sliced through. It was not possible to identify the body as being that of Tom Custer at first. Prolonged contact with the hard soil had completely flattened what was left of his face and decomposition had made any facial features non-existent. One of his arms had been shattered by a bullet and closer inspection of the arm, despite the mutilation and the blackening from decay, revealed a tattoo of the 'Goddess of Liberty and a flag' together with the letters 'T.W.C.'

Nearby lay the remains of Custer's Adjutant, Lieutenant William Cooke. A Canadian by birth, he was well known throughout regiment for his magnificent side-burns, long lengthy whiskers that converged with his moustache before falling in two distinct points on to his chest. The hostiles had obviously been very interested in Cook's prolific whiskers, for they had scalped one side clean off. Again, he had been stripped naked and horribly mutilated.

Other bodies that were identified on Custer's 'Last Stand Hill' were those of 25-year old Boston Custer and his cousin, 18-year old Harry Reed. They were discovered at the foot of the hill approximately 45 metres from where Private Tweed lay and not a great distance from the remains of Captain George Yates, of Company F. A little way to the right of Custer's position, another hill rose from the ravine and it was here that the bodies of Lieutenant James Calhoun (Custer's brother-in-law), Lieutenant John Crittenden and the men of Company L were found. A high ridge ran between Custer's and Calhoun's positions which was littered with bodies of fallen troopers. Amongst them lay the corpse of Captain Myles Keogh. He had been stripped of his clothing, except for his socks, and although he had not been scalped or otherwise mutilated, his body bore multiple stab wounds in addition to the bullet holes. Across Keogh lay the body of his trumpeter, John Patton.

Sergeant James Butler was discovered where he fell, in Medicine Tail Coulee. From his position it appears that he was one of the first to fall, valiantly trying to cover the retreat of his troopers.

Newspaper correspondent, Mark Kellogg was found on the flat ground below Custer's final position. Stripped and mutilated, Kellogg could only be identified by the distinctive straps on his boots. True to his word, Kellogg was with Custer at the death! Ironically, even though Kellogg failed in his mission, his employer the 'Bismarck Tribune' was the first newspaper to reveal the extent of Custer's defeat.

Yet again, there is another controversy over the burials. According to Lieutenant Nowlan, he says that he had marked the graves of the officers by driving a stake into the ground. Driven into the stakes were cartridge shells that contained folded slips of paper with the officer's names on them. He also prepared a sketch of the battlefield to show the location of the officer's burial sites. It has not been verified that Nowlan did, in fact, create such markers. Sergeant Ryan, whose detailed accounts of the bodies he buried is amazing, does not verify this action and neither do the other members of the burial parties. However, in view of the fact that Nowlan accompanied Captain Sheridan in removing the officers from the field the following year, it is possible that he made a rough sketch of the area to show the burial sites and this is what he used to recover the bodies. (The sketch, if it ever existed has never been authenticated.)

The bodies of Lieutenant's James Porter, Henry Harrington and James Sturgis, plus Doctor George Lord, were never found or at least, never identified. It is presumed they were all killed as they were never seen alive again and bloodstained clothing had been found in the abandoned village.

The overall death toll for the army was horrendous:

16 Officers, including two Surgeons.
21 Sergeants.
24 Corporals.
180 Privates.
10 Civilians, scouts and interpreters.

In addition there were 52 wounded, of whom some died of their wounds at a later date. Casualties experienced by the hostile Indians remain unknown. As was the custom, their dead and wounded were carried from the battlefield. Estimates have varied over the years, however, according to the Indians themselves their fatalities range from as little as 30 to around 140. With so little information available it is impossible to determine. In the abandoned camp circles, the few tipis that were still standing contained the bodies of fallen warriors, roughly 22 in number. Of course it must be noted that although some may have been killed in this epic struggle, others may have died as a result of wounds sustained at the Battle of the Rosebud. One thing is certain, though, markers have been placed on the battlefield to indicate where the soldiers fell (or were found). There are no such markers to indicate where any Indians fell, save for one wooden plaque that tells an interested visitor that a Cheyenne leader, Lame-Wolf-Man fell nearby. Admittedly it would be difficult to place markers as no record was kept, but it should be remembered that these warriors gave their lives as well.

The Battle of the Little Big Horn was also a financial disaster for the army, in addition to the cost in lives. Of the soldiers who fell no equipment, weapons, ammunition or clothing were to be found. The Indians had picked the field clean, including harnesses and saddles. Anything they deemed useful was taken, including cavalry horses that had not been wounded, although this booty did not serve them as well as they thought. Army horses were used to being fed corn, whereas Indian ponies could exist on grass or shoots, thus many army mounts did not last long in Indian hands.

It is doubtful that Sheridan had given any thought to the terrible loss of life, the trauma experienced by other soldiers who had to view the carnage or the huge financial cost of such a field campaign when he first envisaged his plan to deal with Custer. It is also doubtful that neither Crook nor Terry had any idea concerning the manner in which they were being used, for Sheridan was extremely adept in subterfuge. Terry does appear to have given the matter some considerable thought whilst camped by the Little Big Horn. Apart from Sheridan, only he would have known exactly what his orders were and he must have realised that politics is a very dangerous game, for he absolutely refused to comment on the disaster in the subsequent years and, interestingly, accepted all criticism aimed at himself as Custer's commander, not allowing anything to tarnish Custer's reputation. Terry was in a very precarious position. If he did suspect foul play he could not divulge it or he may be next. Sheridan was a powerful man and he had very influential friends in high places. He could not discuss the events with Crook either, even though he knew Crook had not done his duty. Crook also had political connections in high places. His best friend appears to be none other than William McKinley, who at present was adjutant to Rutherford B. Hayes, both of whom would become future Presidents. Thus, Terry kept quiet and just did his duty.

Private William Taylor of Company A, later visited the field of battle and wrote:

> '…………, and on every hero's cenotaph I seem to see carved the word 'Duty'.

If they achieved nothing else, Custer and his men who rode to their deaths with him, did their duty.

Chapter 6

A Very Precious Cargo

The remains of Custer and his battalion having been interred to the best of their ability, the burial party returned to the camp with many of the soldiers extremely traumatised, if not in a complete state of shock. Now the formidable task of moving the wounded back had to be organised. Official records for Wednesday 28th June 1876 are grossly deficient of information regarding the wounded, although it does appear that First Lieutenant Gustavus C. Doane, of Company C, 2nd Cavalry, volunteered to construct horse litters from what materials he could find in the abandoned Indian village. Foraging for canvas and poles to assemble hand litters was already under way, but overall the process proved to be slow and many of the wounded were sorely in need of the comforts of a post hospital. By late afternoon four of the proposed five horse litters had been assembled and all of the hand litters had been completed. Thus, with the added fear that the hostiles could return at any given moment, it was decided to strike camp and begin the march back to the confluence of the Little Big Horn with the Big Horn, where the wounded could be transferred to the 'Far West'.

As the sun slowly disappeared behind the hills to the west, the wounded were carefully transferred to the prepared litters. Mules from Custer's pack-train had been chosen to bear the burden of the few horse litters in the belief that their sheer exhaustion of the campaign would make them more manageable. However, they actually proved to be somewhat recalcitrant at first and grave doubts were expressed as to whether it would be safe to move the wounded this way. Two men were assigned to each of the mule litters in order to steady the mules, which did prove exceedingly helpful although later the men were doubled as the heat and the weight of their burdens proved the task a little difficult for the animals.

Movement along the trail in the darkness was also a huge problem and many litter bearers stumbled on the uneven ground or tripped over weeds and sage brush, sending their wounded comrade tumbling to the ground. The repeated halts and constant change of carriers made their progress slow and laborious and, as the night wore on, fatigue also became a major problem. Musician George Berry of Company E, 7th Infantry, and his partner had been detailed to carry a wounded trooper who weighed far heavier than they did and he later recalled his experience:

> '…………. he was badly wounded, too …………shot in the small of the back, and didn't want to be put on the ground any oftener than could be avoided; but we had to set him down pretty often in order to rest, as there was no road…………..'

Private Edward Stumpf, also of the 7th Infantry, commented:

> 'It was one of the most trying jobs I ever experienced, dark, no road, hill up, hill down, the wounded moaning, groaning and us tired to death.'

Stumpf had not suffered the horrific ordeal that the Seventh Cavalry had and yet he was already exhausted!

John Gibbon also recorded the scene when he wrote in an article for 'The American Catholic Quarterly Review' in 1877:

> '…………we moved through the darkness, the silence of the night broken only by the tramp of men and horses and the groans of the wounded……………
>
> Long, tedious and slow, the hours of that sad night wore on, and it was past midnight before we reached camp at a distance of only four and a half miles [approximately 7 kilometres]'………… I have seen in the course of my military life many wounded men, but I never saw any who endured suffering, privations, and the fatigue of travel, more patiently and cheerfully than those brave fellows of the Seventh Cavalry.'

It was obvious to all that the march could not continue in this manner. The hand litters were too awkward and cumbersome to use and the bearers, despite frequent changes were already becoming physically exhausted. Accidents were happening at an alarming rate. Saddler Mike Madden of Company K, whose leg had been amputated below the knee by Surgeon Porter, was dropped to the ground twice during that first night's march and others had experienced similar mishaps. Captain Williams, the Senior Surgeon, duly advised Gibbon that the wounded would not be able to travel much further under the present circumstances. Gibbon ordered a halt and instructed Lieutenant Doane to construct additional mule litters and horse travois, such as the Indians used. Gibbon describes the latter as being:

> '............. a couple of lodge poles, having one end fastened to the saddle of a pack horse, and the other trailing on the ground, the two being fastened together just behind the tail of the horse by a wicker-work platform, on which the patient reclines. The light flexible poles act as springs, and, except over very rough ground, the movement is far from disagreeable or rough.'

The halt was not to be enjoyed by everyone. The remaining mules of Custer's pack-train were now thoroughly scrutinized and the most gentle or the best broken were turned over to Doane for the transportation of the wounded. A number of Companies were sent back to the abandoned village to collect the materials that Doane could make use of and to destroy any other property not needed. What items that could not be burnt were broken up. The soldiers still in the column ahead, could look back and see large columns of smoke rising from the valley. By afternoon, Doane had supervised the construction of the additional litters and was giving the handlers instructions on how they should be used in order to give the minimum discomfort to the wounded. Lieutenant Doane worked constantly and tirelessly to ensure the safe transportation of the wounded, a fact that has never received the recognition it deserved. By the early evening 19 mule litters and 10 travois were occupied by wounded troops and ready to resume the march, with the less seriously wounded men travelling on horseback.

At six o'clock on the evening of the 29th June, the column resumed the march. They had only travelled a few kilometres when two mounted figures were observed on the bluffs to their left. As they approached the column it became apparent they were the two couriers that had been sent to the 'Far West', to inform Captain Marsh to expect large numbers of wounded men. The couriers, Private Goodwin of the 7th Infantry and a guide named Bostwick from Fort Shaw, had left the camp prior to the commencement of the return march and had caused concerns for their safety as they had not been seen since. Terry ordered a brief halt while the couriers made their report and, after ascertaining that the steamer was but a short march away, pushed the column forward keeping close to the bluffs, as Bostwick had also informed them that they would have to scale them to reach the mouth of the Little Big Horn where the steamer was moored.

Darkness closed in and for a while the weary soldiers were able to find their way by the light of the moon. It was not to last. On reaching the plateau at the top of the bluffs, the sky became overcast, obscuring the moonlight and rain began to fall. Bostwick now had the sole responsibility of guiding the column across the terrain in complete darkness. Periodically the moon managed to break through the clouds and officers could assure themselves that the column had not separated. Slowly and relentlessly the column pushed on. However, in their eagerness to discover the trail that led down from the plateau to the river, the advance guard found itself separated from the main column and they had to follow the sound of bugle calls to re-join the command. The darkness and rain was proving to be a problem and before long even Bostwick could not find the ravine that led to the river. Not all was lost though, for through the shroud of the sombre night a Crow scout appeared leading a travois on which a wounded Crow lay. Half-Yellow-Face could not understand English and as the column did not have an interpreter it took a little while for the Indian to understand what was wanted of him. Finally, Half-Yellow-Face perceived their plight and took the lead, but even he ran into difficulties with the rain and the darkness. Following the Crow as closely as they could, the column weaved across countless ravines before finding themselves hemmed in on each side by gulches, the height of which was incalculable in the dark. They had no option but to retrace their steps, a manoeuvre that was easier said than done. In the confusion that followed, one of the mules bearing a litter stumbled in a hole and Mike Madden found himself hurled to the ground yet again!

Uncertain that they were even moving in the right direction, the column pushed on. The enveloping night, dense with falling rain, added to their difficulties of traversing uneven terrain immensely. Now and again, advance riders caught a glimpse of a light, but it soon disappeared and their hopes faded with it. What had been considered to be but a short march had turned out to be a gruelling nightmare. They knew they were in close proximity to the river and the waiting steam boat, but they could not find the trail. The prospect of having to bivouac on such a bleak plateau with little respite for the wounded and in the heavy rain, was not even worth considering.

The column was halted and, accompanied by a staff officer, Gibbon rode ahead in an effort to discover the trail. Finally, the two officers succeeded in making their way down towards the river, where they saw a light flickering ahead of them. As they advanced they were challenged and as luck would have it, they had found Captain Stephen Baker of the 6th Infantry, who was in command of the guard assigned to the 'Far West'. Baker wasted no time in mounting Gibbon's horse and was already heading back up the trail to locate the column, as Gibbon turned and approached the steamer. In Gibbon's account he states that he ordered men to build fires alone the route he had taken, to hasten the arrival of the wounded. Other accounts claim it was Captain Marsh, who would have had time to prepare them beforehand. Whoever issued the order has been lost over the years, but the fires served their purpose because the hillside was ablaze with light, through which the wounded were safely brought down. However, Gibbon was amazed at the efficiency of Marsh and his crew, for he later wrote:

> 'They were all up and expecting us, on the boat; and the lower deck, enclosed (sic) with canvas, was prepared with beds to make our wounded as comfortable as possible.'

Private William Taylor of Company A, Seventh Cavalry, also recorded their arrival at the 'Far West':

> 'About one o'clock in the morning the head of the column, looming weirdly through the darkness in the flickering firelight, approached the boat. Captain Marsh had caused a portion of the deck to be thickly covered with grass, and over it spread a lot of tent flies, making the whole like an immense mattress and in a short time, the fifty-two stricken men well placed on board and with them Keogh's horse, Comanche. The men were laid in rows on the grass covered deck and Dr. Williams and H.R. Porter set about examining and dressing their wounds.'

Saddler Mike Madden could relax now. There was nowhere to fall!

Comanche, although still in a serious condition, was still alive and Farrier Gustav Korn intended to keep him that way. Having dressed his terrible wounds, Korn had gently led the horse across the trail alongside the wounded men and as the men were laid on the deck of the steamer, Comanche was also made as comfortable as possible. Marsh ordered a grass-padded stall built and found a veterinary surgeon to care for the horse. It is believed that the veterinary surgeon was found amongst Gibbon's forces and if that is so, why had he not helped Korn to care for Comanche before now? It was well into the early hours of Friday 3oth June and already, with the rain having stopped, the dawn sun was spreading a myriad of colour across the sky, heralding a new day. For the survivors of the Seventh Cavalry their ordeal was all but over.

Captain Grant Marsh had already received news of the disaster that had befallen Custer and his men. In fact during the last few days that his steamer had been moored at the mouth of the Little Big Horn, he had actually received the news no less than three times! It is generally assumed that Marsh reached the Little Big Horn before or on the 26th June and that either the following day or the next (accounts vary) a Crow scout brought the first news of the defeat. This was the famous Curley, a Crow scout who was known to have been with the scouts of Custer's battalion, and there are numerous variations of his story. Marsh, his engineer, his pilot and Captain Baker were idly fishing when Curley burst through the brush and brought his pony to a halt on the riverbank. Some accounts say he was naked, others describe him as having a cloth around his head, wearing a black shirt, a breech-clout and moccasins. In any event, he was recognised and the crew waved him aboard the steamer. Once on board, Curley dropped to his knees and began rocking from side to side. With no interpreter available, it took some time before they could understand what the distraught Indian was trying to tell them. Nevertheless, through the use of sign language the news became clear: Custer was dead and Reno was in grave danger.

At the time of the battle, Curley was just 17 years old and freely demonstrated his excitable nature, which does not help when trying to unravel the irregularities of his evidence. He first stated that he had wrapped himself in a Sioux blanket and crawled away from the battlefield for about three kilometres (1.8 miles). However, this does not appear feasible. The weather was extremely hot, even when it rained, and as the Sioux and Cheyenne had been stripped almost naked for the fight, any blankets to be found would probably have been in the hostile camp circles. If Curley had gone there, his distinctive Crow scalp lock would have signed his death warrant. In later years, he said that he concealed himself in the carcass of a disembowelled horse and waited for the Sioux to leave before making good his escape. Many historians discount any Curley story, saying that he probably ran away before the fight began. That does not make sense either, for during subsequent interrogations Curley knew many facts concerning Custer's last moments, that have since been verified only by archaeological investigations. Curley was young and very scared. Custer's last fight was the first major battle with the Sioux that he had witnessed. As the battle raged, he was probably scared that he would be discovered and killed by the Sioux. The ground seemed alive with hostile Sioux and Cheyenne no matter where he looked. The true facts concerning his miraculous escape are unlikely to ever be known. He may have witnessed the dreadful battle from a distance before running for his life, for how else would he have known that Custer was already dead and Reno was in danger? His fears did not abate on reaching the steamer, for he was now scared that the army, who had engaged him as a scout, would punish him for not discharging his duty. It is unfortunate that Curley changes his story every time he is questioned about it, which does not help historians to find the truth. He may have any number of excuses concerning his actions or the relating of his traumatic experience. What confuses the issue is that all those who noted his story, wrote different accounts of the same event, until eventually Curley became a myth in his own right.

Marsh gave the young Crow food and water and then directed him to ride north to the Yellowstone, where a base camp had been established. There is no doubting that the Captain and his crew were stunned by the news and they spent a very uneasy night with Baker's sentries becoming 'trigger happy' and jumpy at every sound. When 'Muggins' Taylor arrived at the steamer just before dawn, he was greeted by a fusillade of shots fired at him by the sentries. Fortunately none of them found their mark! En route to Fort Ellis and carrying Terry's dispatches,

Taylor confirmed that Custer had been killed and that Reno had a large number of wounded. He also stated that he had been chased by Sioux horsemen through the night, which can now be revealed as fanciful embellishment as the Sioux had moved away from the approaching column and then divided, each group going their separate ways. In any event, Marsh had been forewarned to expect the arrival of many wounded and before Terry's couriers, Goodwin and Bostwick, arrived with fresh orders, the resolute Captain had begun preparing his craft to receive them. Grass was cut and spread across the deck; tarpaulin stretched across to shield the wounded from the sun; and medicine chests were hauled up from the hold and opened. Marsh knew he would be carrying a very precious cargo and he would be ready to do so when the time came.

Little has been recorded of Terry's actions during the evacuation of the wounded. From available records it appears that Gibbon was more instrumental in making the decisions, even though Terry was the senior officer. On his arrival at the 'Far West' Terry and his staff officers went on board, leaving Gibbon in command of the column. From various accounts it does appear that Terry had been deeply shocked at the carnage on the battlefield. It was the first time he had seen the aftermath of a fight with hostile Indians. He had conferred with Indians when making treaties, but he had never fought them in combat. Shocked as he was, Terry still retained his composure in front of his forces, particularly Gibbon and Reno. Of course it is also possible that Terry may have realised that he had been politically used and he was now considering his own position. Terry definitely had problems at this point, whether it was some sort of trauma from the scenes of battle or concern for his own future is not clear and we will probably never know, but Terry did not let his problems show to his men. He was too much of an officer and a gentleman for that. Terry found Captain Marsh in his cabin and instructed him to use all his skill to navigate the treacherous rivers safely, adding that every wounded man now aboard the steamer,

"...... was the victim of a blunder – a sad, terrible blunder."

Just after dawn, Marsh gave the order to cast off and the 'Far West' slowly edged its way through the confluence of the Little Big Horn and Big Horn rivers. It was just over 85 kilometres (almost 53 miles) to the mouth of the Big Horn, where its water converged with the Yellowstone, and Marsh had to use all his skill to keep the steamer in the deeper channel, avoid the small islands and ride the fast flowing rapids. He had instructed his engineer to keep up a full head of steam within the limits of safety of course, and the steamer responded wonderfully. By late afternoon the 'Far West' had covered the distance without any incidents and after entering the Yellowstone, was safely moored by the bank where Gibbon's supply camp was situated. Here, Marsh was instructed to wait the arrival of Gibbon and his forces, a strange order considering the urgency of getting the wounded away. However, Gibbon's troops would have to cross the Yellowstone in order to reach the camp and without the steamer it would have been very difficult to accomplish.

Around five o'clock Gibbon crossed the Little Big Horn to the northern side and ordered his column to bivouac for the night. It had been a strenuous march and his troops were totally exhausted. In the early hours of the morning of the following day, the column resumed the march and after making about 32 kilometres (just under 20 miles), another halt was made beside the Big Horn. It must be remembered that the majority of Gibbon's forces were infantry, making progress slow and tiresome. On 2nd July, Gibbon pushed forward once again and the column arrived at the Yellowstone, where all the soldiers were ferried across to the supply camp by the 'Far West'.

Terry had re-established his headquarters at the camp by the time Gibbon had arrived. Here, on 2nd July, he wrote a telegram to Phil Sheridan outlining the evacuations of the wounded by steamer to Fort Lincoln and he informed the General that he would be sending one of his aides, Captain E. Smith, to answer any questions he way wish to ask .The telegram also informed Sheridan that he had only just received Colonel Sheridan's dispatch containing information that the hostiles were gathering in numbers along the Rosebud. This dispatch ominously appears after the event and it does look suspiciously like it was a deliberate ploy to withhold valuable information. Terry concludes the telegram by stating that he has still received no word from Crook and once again, voices concerns at the lack of cavalry horses:

> 'At least a hundred horses are needed to mount the cavalrymen now here.'

There is no doubt that Terry was concerned about the events surrounding Custer's defeat, for on the same day he wrote another telegram to Sheridan detailing the plans of operation, as he saw it. He opens the telegram:

> 'I think I owe it to myself to put you more fully in possession of the facts of the late operation.'

Terry then gives a fully detailed account of the plans and subsequent discussions he had had with Gibbon and Custer, before the departure of the Seventh Cavalry. He repeatedly states that Custer knew Gibbon would not be able to reach the Little Big Horn until 26th June and that had Custer waited, the operation would have been successful as far as he was concerned. He conveniently omits to tell Sheridan that Gibbon's forces did not reach their destination until the 27th June, a full 24 hours late! Terry is clearly trying to absolve himself of any blame, however, his conclusions are primarily based on information he has been given by Captain Benteen, an officer who is known to have intensely disliked Custer and, it must be remembered, an officer who obstinately refused two requests from Custer to bring aid to his forces. Terry, of course, still has no knowledge of the huge numbers of hostile Indians that had gathered to fight and yet, he asserts that no blame should be placed on Custer. He also informs Sheridan that he will send him a copy of his written orders to Custer in another dispatch, adding:

> '……….. these were supplemented by the distinct understanding that Gibbon would get to the Little Big Horn before the evening of the 26th.'

If this telegram is compared to Custer's written orders, no such understanding can be found. It appears that Terry has realised just how ambiguous those orders were and he is now trying to justify his actions. If, as he states, Gibbon had been instructed to reach the Little Big Horn before the evening of the 26th June, why was the column a full 24 hours late, a column that also included Terry and his forces? This anomaly has never been explained and apart from his official reports, Terry refused to discuss or comment on the death of Custer for the rest of his life. He would not allow anything derogatory said or written about Custer either. The only conclusion that can be reached is that Terry is not only covering his own tracks but those of others as well, for he writes:

> 'I should very much like instructions from you, or if not instructions, your views of the situation based as they might be on what has taken place elsewhere as well as here.'

Based on the assumption that Terry has no knowledge of Crook's engagement on the Rosebud, his withdrawal or Crook's whereabouts for that matter, his request is extremely interesting. He may not be aware of the instructions that Sheridan relayed to Crook, but he was certainly aware of those he had received from the General and by now, he must have fully comprehended the implications those instructions had. Thus, he requests further instructions not wishing to jeopardise the agenda by using his own initiative, as an area commander should.

Both of these telegrams were carried to Fort Abraham Lincoln by Terry's adjutant, Captain E. Smith, who travelled with the wounded on board the 'Far West', arriving at Bismarck on 5th July. Smith duly telegraphed the dispatches to Sheridan on the morning of the 6th July, before proceeding to report to the

General in person. Sheridan should have already received the reports carried by 'Muggins' Taylor, sent by telegram from Fort Ellis. However, due to a break in the line at Bozeman, Sheridan did not receive those reports until after he had received those from Smith. This 'break in the line' was not a mechanical fault but a human one, as a letter to Sheridan, dated 5th July, from Captain D. Benham of Fort Ellis clearly illustrates:

> '……….. on the afternoon of July 3rd …………
>
> Taylor arrived at this post from Genl. Terry's command with important dispatches ………………..
>
> I immediately in person took the dispatches to the telegraph office in Bozeman and was there informed that the line was in working order to Pleasant Valley.
>
> On the 4th of July I went to see if the telegrams left at the office on the 3rd had been sent and found the telegraph office closed.
>
> This afternoon on visiting Bozeman, I enquired if the telegrams left at the office on the 3rd had been sent and was informed that they had been forwarded by mail this morning. I deem this neglect of duty and criminal negligence on the part of the telegraph operator and report it accordingly.
>
> If the telegraph rates are charged on the dispatches above referred to between Bozeman and Helena, the bill should be repudiated and proceedings instituted against the company for neglect of duty……….'

Clearly Benham is annoyed and rightly so. Having no telegraph system of its own, the army had to rely on civilian telegraph offices to send urgent dispatches. As Benham points out later in the letter, he should have been informed that the dispatches had not been sent and he would have sent them to Sheridan by courier, which would have arrived 24 hours earlier!

At the supply camp on the Yellowstone, 14 of the wounded men had recovered sufficiently to be carried ashore. They were placed in the care of Lieutenant Paulding and, according to him, a 'general hospital' was established by Field Orders on 4th July, although he gave no details of its size or construction. With the hot weather, typhoid and scurvy were making an appearance amongst the men, including the wounded. Paulding was having to care for an average of 35 to 40 cases at any one time. Medical supplies took weeks to be delivered and Paulding had to make do with those he had. Major Sloane, Medical Director of the Department of the Dakota, had requested a three month supply of medicines, enough for 300 men, to be sent from Fort Lincoln. However, apart from the length of time they would take to reach the Fort an additional time delay would have to be taken into account before any fresh supplies would actually reach Paulding. Henry Porter had accompanied John Williams on the 'Far West' to continue their care of the severely wounded, thus Paulding had to cope on his own with the few medical orderlies he had been assigned.

Around 5 o'clock on Monday 3rd July, the 'Far West' slipped her moorings and began her journey to Fort Abraham Lincoln and Bismarck. Due to the numerous snags, sand bars and the ever changing current, steamboats did not generally travel the Yellowstone at night. But these were extraordinary circumstances and Marsh pushed the vessel forward at full-steam, reaching an average of 32 kilometres (just under 20 miles an hour)! Occasionally the steam gauge touched the danger point, but onward the steamer soared. Marsh knew he was taking chances, but he also knew the lives of his precious cargo were at stake; the wounded needed medication desperately now. In actual fact, the extreme rate of speed that Marsh pushed his craft has never been rivalled by a steamer on the Yellowstone since. The speed with which he travelled up the Big Horn had been an astonishing feat in itself, but the dash down the Yellowstone was wild and unimaginable.

During the trip the surgeons worked under increasing pressure to care for the wounded and their supplies were rapidly dwindling. These men worked continuously without rest and as a consequence only one of the wounded died before they reached Bismarck.

The 'Far West' sped along the Yellowstone all night and in the early hours of the following day stopped briefly at the mouth of the Powder River, where an army camp had been established. Marsh collected the personal equipment of the officers of the Seventh Cavalry that had been left there prior to the campaign. The camp had heard rumours of the defeat from Indian scouts as they passed through, but they had dismissed them as being outrageous. Marsh confirmed the rumours and then departed before he could be pressed for any further information. In the engine room, blackened firemen pushed wood into the fireboxes to give Marsh his speed. Occasionally the steamer's whistle would echo along the cliffs, sending herds of deer stampeding through the trees and brush. Onward the 'Far West' rushed as if the Devil was following her stern, sometimes just brushing the banks and other times skimming the reeds and sand banks.

At Fort Buford a brief stop was made to put a wounded Indian scout ashore, but Marsh soon had his craft well under way again before awkward questions could be asked. Bad news always travels fast! Now they had reached the wide Missouri, with its treacherous undercurrents, although Marsh did not even give them a second thought. On reaching Fort Stevenson another brief stop was made. Terry had given Marsh explicit instructions on military protocol and it was here that the intrepid Captain draped the derrick and jack-staff of the steamer in black, to honour the dead and wounded. If the occupants of the fort had any questions, this action would have silenced them. Marsh did not hang around to find out. As the 'Far West' gathered steam, the last leg of the journey raced by and as dusk turned to night the tired crew looked forward to reaching their destination and a well-earned rest.

It was 11 o'clock that night when the 'Far West' finally slowed down and tied up at the wharf that served Bismarck. Across the river lay Fort Abraham Lincoln, the wounded men of the Seventh Cavalry had reached the safety of their home. It was Wednesday 5th July and Marsh had covered an incredible distance of 1142.6 kilometres 9 well over 700 miles) in just 54 hours! Bismarck lay in darkness, with the silence broken only by the odd bark of a dog. All that was about to change. No sooner had the steamer fastened her mooring lines, many crew members began racing through the streets shouting the news of Custer's defeat and rousing the residents from their slumber. Lights appeared in the windows as the populace turned out, many of whom were still wearing their night-shirts. Everyone in Bismarck had family, friends or acquaintances serving in the Seventh and as the news broke they were stunned. Marsh, together with Dr. Porter and Captain Smith, located Clement Loundsberry of the 'Bismarck Tribune'. Loundsberry was not only the editor of the 'Tribune' but he also served as a stinger for the more impressive 'New York Herald' and as an ex-army officer he knew he had the scoop of the century. Loundsberry then accompanied the men to the home of J.M. Carnaham, the only telegrapher of this frontier town, where they roused him and told him the news.

At the telegraph office, Loundsberry listened intently as the officers relayed their story and after making a few additional notes and asking even more questions, for he must have viewed their tale with disbelief at first, he scribbled a short message and handed it to Carnahan to transmit to New York:

> 'Bismarck, D.T., July 6 1876:
> General Custer attacked the Indians June 25, and he with every officer and man in five companies were killed. Reno with seven companies fought in entrenched positions three days. The Bismarck Tribune special correspondent was with the expedition and was killed.'

However shocked Loundsberry must have been, he did not allow his emotions to override his professionalism. For over an hour he listened to Marsh, Porter and Smith as they retold their dramatic stories, while Carnahan transmitted Kellogg's notes across the wire. The telegrapher then sent a long account of the fight that had been written by one of Gibbon's officers. Loundsberry continued his interview and carried on writing, then Carnahan finally transmitted

Loundsberry's handwritten account. Loundsberry and Carnahan stayed in the telegraph office for over 24 hours, during which time the telegrapher sent over 15,000 words which ultimately cost the 'New York Herald' a staggering $3000! Loundsberry was handsomely rewarded with a bonus of $2,500 from the eastern newspaper, although it is not known whether Carnahan received anything extra for his hard work. Marsh, Porter and Smith left the office a little after midnight and took the long suffering wounded across the river to Fort Lincoln. Unfortunately, it would not be until morning, on 6th July, before they would all be settled in the post hospital. Obviously it had been more important to relay news of the battle before transferring the wounded ashore and it does pose the question, did Captain Marsh make his mad dash through the Yellowstone and Missouri rivers to deliver the wounded as quickly as possible or to be one of the first to break the news of Custer's defeat? It is a question, like so many others, that will never be truthfully answered. Nonetheless, the fact remains that Marsh did deliver his precious cargo safely and in record time.

Comanche, Captain Keogh's stalwart war-horse, also survived the trip, although by the time the steamer had reached Fort Lincoln he was unable to walk. Gustav Korn had not left the horse once during the entire journey and he accompanied the animal as he was carried to the stables in a wagon, where his body was supported by a sling. Under the watchful eye of the regimental veterinary surgeon, Carl A. Stein, and the tender care of Korn, Comanche made a full recovery over the next 12 months. By then his status as the sole survivor of the battle had been established and he was revered as a national hero. Over the subsequent years, myths and legends swirled around the horse like a host of flies, none of which have any proven credibility, thus contrary to popular belief, the officers' ladies never rode him nor did the commanding officer's daughter. Comanche was never ridden by anyone, although a strong bond did develop between the horse and Korn, who was assigned to be his attendant permanently. On 10th April 1878, Colonel Sturgis of the Seventh Cavalry issued General Orders No. 7:

1) The horse known as 'Comanche', being the only living representative of the bloody tragedy of the Little Big Horn, June 25th 1876, his kind treatment and comfort shall be a matter of special pride and solicitude on the part of every member of the Seventh Cavalry, to the end that his life shall be preserved to the utmost limit. Wounded and scarred as he is, his very existence speaks terms more eloquent than words, of the desperate struggle against overwhelming numbers of the hopeless conflict, and the heroic manner in which all went down that fateful day.

2) The commanding officer of Company I will see that a special and comfortable stall is fitted up for him, and he will not again be ridden by any person whatsoever, under any circumstances, nor will he be ever put to any kind of work.
3) Hereafter, upon all occasions of ceremony of mounted regimental formation, Comanche, saddled, bridled and draped in mourning, and led by a mounted trooper of Company I, will be paraded by the regiment.

Although it is clear that Sturgis is showing concern for the welfare of the horse, he contradicts his own orders. In paragraph 2, he states 'nor will he ever be put to any kind of work' and he follows this up with paragraph 3, by stating that he 'will be paraded by the regiment'. In any event, on all ceremonial parades, Comanche led his late officer's Company, draped in black mourning and with a pair of cavalry boots reversed in the stirrups.

When the Seventh Cavalry was moved back to Fort Riley, Kansas, the same frontier post where the regiment was formed on 21st September 1866, Comanche moved with them. Still attended by Korn, Comanche remained in excellent health until Korn was killed at Wounded Knee on 29th December 1890. Farrier Samuel J. Winchester was detailed to replace Korn, but no matter what he did, Comanche deeply felt the loss of his friend and showed it. He grew increasingly morose until he died the following year on 7th November at 29 years of age. Winchester was with the old war-horse and recorded the sad event:

> '............ in memory of the old veteran horse who died at 1:30 o'clock with colic in his stall while I had my hand on his pulse and looking him in the eye...................... This night long to be remembered.'

Comanche's death was sorely mourned by all the troops in the Seventh Cavalry and the officers were determined to preserve his remains. They telegraphed a renowned taxidermist, Lewis Lyndsay Dyche, at the University of Kansas to see if he was able to do the job. Dyche agreed to preserve the remains for a fee of $400, although he apparently later waived the fee if the army would agree to allow the university to permanently keep Comanche. Unfortunately, no official records of the deal are available, although the military authorities must have agreed to the proposal, for Comanche still stands proudly within the confines of Dyche Hall at the Kansas University of Natural History, a poignant reminder to all of courage in the face of adversity.

Acknowledgements

When I first embarked, over 30-years ago, on the research concerning Lt. Col. Custer's death at the Little Big Horn, I had no idea of the number of people it would involve and looking back I am astounded by their genuine encouragement and their precious time they gave to my project. Their enthusiasm and generosity forms the foundation of this book and it's companion, which details the aftermath. Although there are far too many to name individually, I will give specific credit to a few, however I thank you all.

First of all I would like to express my heartfelt gratitude to Tara, Commissioning Editor, and Harriet, Production Editor, at Pen & Sword Military for all their hard work in producing this book and for believing in my ability to change history. My appreciation knows no bounds.

From early on the United States Army was a willing contributor and I thank Elaine Everly, Col. Robert Waggoner and Richard Sommers Ph.D for their valuable help; not to mention Renée Klish, Marlana Cook and Michel Diaz of the United States Military Academy at West Point.

Many other American authorities gave up so much valuable information and I thank Neil Mangum, Custer Battlefield National Monument; James Davis, State Historical Society of North Dakota; Allan Clark, Eastern Montana College; Linda Weirather, Parmly Billings Library; and Kellen Cutsforth of the Denver Public Library. I am grateful for all your help. Others include William Meuse, the Springfield Armoury; L. K. Goodstal, the Remington Arms Company Inc.; and G. M. Wilson, the Armouries H.H. Tower of London, for information on weapons. Individually, I sincerely thank Col. Charles Custer, a descendant; Lawrence Frost, author; Sam Cahoon, photographer; and Shannon Gering of the University of Oklahoma Press. Sadly, many people who gave so much to my research have passed on, however they will always be remembered and my gratitude will always be with them.

Finally I would like to thank my husband Brian and my daughter Hayley for their patience, understanding and belief in my search for the truth, even though at times there seemed to be no end in sight. In particular I thank Hayley for all the technical help she has given, which proved to be so invaluable.

In conclusion, I thank you all most sincerely.

Bibliography

ABRAMS, MARC H., *Sioux War Dispatches*, Westholme Publishing: U.S.A.: 2012

AGONITO, ROSEMARY, *Buffalo Calf Road Woman,* Twodot: Montana: 2006

ALLISON, E.H., *Surrender of Sitting Bull,* South Dakota Historical Collection Vol.6: 1912

AMBROSE, STEPHEN, *Crazy Horse and Custer*, Simon & Schuster U.U. Ltd: London: 2003

ANDREWS, RALPH, *Curtis' Western Indians*, Bonanza Books: New York: 1962

ANDRIST, RALPH K., *The Long death,* Macmillan Publishing Co.: New York: 1964

ANGLO, MICHAEL, *Custer and the Myth*, Jupiter Books: 1977

ARMSTRONG, VIRGINIA I., *I Have Spoken*, Sage Books: Chicago: 1971

BAILLY, EDWARD, *Echoes from Custer's Last Fight*, 'Military Affairs': Winter: 1958

BARRETT, S.M., *Geronimo*, Sphere Books: London: 1970

BENTEEN, FREDERICK, *An Account of the Little Big Horn Campaign*, Ghent Paper: Washington

Letters to Edward W. Field 8 – 2 – 1886, Military Research Collection: Carlisle Barracks

Letters to Theodore W. Goldin 1891 – 1896, Military Research Collection: Carlisle Barracks

The Custer Fight, Hollywood: 1933

BLISH, H.H., *A Pictographic History of the Ogalalla Sioux*, Lincoln: Nebraska: 1967

BRADY, CYRUS T., *Indian Fights and Fighter,* University of Nebraska Press: Nebraska: 1971

BRANDON, WILLIAM, *The Rise and Fall of the North American Indians*, Tempus Publishing: Stroud: 2007

BRININSTOOL, E.A., *A Trooper with Custer*, Cooper Square: New York: 1975

Fighting Indian Warriors, Indian Head Books: New York: 1995

Troopers with Custer, Stackpole Books: Mechanicsburg: 1994

BRITT, ALBERT, *Great Indian Chiefs*, New York: 1938

BRITTON, JACK, *United States Military Medals & Decorations*, MCN Press: Oklahoma: 1979

BROOME, JEFF, *Dog Soldier Justice*, University of Nebraska Press: Nebraska: 2009

BROWN, DEE, *Bury My Heart at Wounded Knee*, Barrie & Jenkins: London: 1970

The Fetterman Massacre, Barrie & Jenkins: London: 1972

Brown, JOSEPH E., *The Sacred Pipe*, Penguin Books: Baltimore: 1971

BROWN, MARK H., *The Plainsmen of the Yellowstone*, Putnam: New York: 1961

BRUST, JAMES S., *Where Custer Fell*, University of Oklahoma Press: Oklahoma: 2005

BURT, MARY E., *The Boy General*, Charles Scribner & Sons: New York: 1941

CAPPS, BENJAMIN, *The Great Chiefs*, Time – Life Books: New York: 1974

The Indians, Time – Life books: New York: 1976

CARROLL, JOHN M., *The Benteen – Goldin Letters*, University of Nebraska Press: Nebraska: 1991

They Rode With Custer, J.M. Carroll & Co. : New York: 1993

CATLIN, GEORGE, *North American Indians*, Penguin Books: London: 1989

CHAMBERS, LEE, *Fort Abraham Lincoln, Dakota Territory*, Schiffer Books: Atglen: 2008

CHUN, CLAYTON S., *U.S. Army in the Plains Indian Wars*, Osprey Publishing: Oxford: 2004

CLARK, W.P. (Captain), *Indian Sign Language*, Hamersly & Co.: Philadelphia: 1885

CODY, IRON EYES, *Indian Talk*, New English Library: London: 1972

COHAN – SCHERER, J., *Indians,* Octopus Books: London: 1974

COLLIER, JOHN, I*ndians of the Americas,* New American Library: New York: 1964

COLLINS, J.S., *Across the Plains in '64*, Nebraska: 1904

CONNELL, EVEN S., *Son of the Morning Star*, Book Club Association: London: 1985

COX, KURT H., *Custer and His Commands*, Greenhill Books: London: 1999

COZZENS, PETER, *The Earth Is Weeping*, Atlantic Books: London: 2016

CROOK, GEORGE (General), *Autobiography*, University of Oklahoma Press: Oklahoma: 1946

CURTIS, EDWARD S., *Native Americans*, Taschen: London

CURTIS, NATALIE, *The Indian Book*, Harper & Bros: New York: 1907

CUSTER, ELIZABETH, *Boots and Saddles*, University of Oklahoma Press: Oklahoma: 1968

Following the Guidon, University of Nebraska Press: Nebraska: 1994

Tenting On The Plains, University of Oklahoma Press: Oklahoma: 1982

CUSTER, GEORGE A. (Lieutenant – Colonel), *My Life on the Plains,* W.H. Allen & Co. Ltd: London: 1982

The Custer Story (Letters of G.A. & Elizabeth), Devin – Adair: New York: 1950

DARLING, ROGER, *General Custer's Final Hours*, Potomac – Western Press: Virginia: 1992

DE BARTKE, JOE, *Life and Adventures of Frank Grouard,* The Buffalo Bulletin

DE LAND, CHARLES, *The Sioux wars,* South Dakota historical Collection: Vol.15: 1930

DELORIA Jnr, VINE, *Behind the Trail of Broken Treaties*, University of Texas: Texas: 1985

Custer Died for your Sins, Macmillan Publishing: New York: 1969

DILLON, RICHARD H., *North American Indian Wars*, Magna Books: Wigston : 1983

DIPPIE, BRIAN W., *Custer's Last Stand*, University of Montana Publications: Montana: 1976

DODGE, RICHARD (Colonel), *The Hunting Grounds of the Great West*, 1877

DONOVAN, JAMES, *A Terrible Glory*, Little, Brown & Co.: London: 2008

Custer and the Little Big Horn, Crestline: New York: 2001

DU BOIS, CHARLES G., *Kick the dead Lion*, The Reporter printing & Supply Co.: Billings: 1961

DUNN, J.P., *Massacres of the Mountains*, New York: 1886

DUSTIN, FRED, *The Custer Tragedy*, 1939

EASTERWOOD, T.J., *Memories of Seventy – Six*, New York Herald: 1876

EDGERLY, WINFIELD S., *Narrative of the March of Gen. G.A. Custer,* Ghent Papers: Washington

FARB, PETER, *Man's Rise to Civilisation*, Granada Publishing Ltd: London: 1971

FEHRENBACH, T.R., *Comanches*, Pimlico: London: 1974

FELTON, MARK, *Today Is A Good Day To Fight,* The History Press: Stroud: 2009

FIELD, RON, *Forts of the American Frontier 1820 – 91*, Osprey Publishing: Oxford: 2005

U.S. Army Frontier Scouts, Osprey Publishing: Oxford: 2003

FOUGERE, KATHERINE, *With Custer's cavalry,* The Caxton Printers: Idaho: 1940

FOX, RED (Chief), *The Memories of Chief Red Fox*, W.H. Allen: London: 1971

FROST, LAWRENCE A., *Custer Victorious,* University of Nebraska Press: Nebraska: 1990

The Court Martial of Gen. G.A. Custer, University of Oklahoma Press: Oklahoma: 1987

GARLAND, HAMLIN, *General Custer's Last Fight as Seen by Two Moon*, McClure's Magazine Vol 11: 1898

GARST, SHANNON, *Crazy Horse, A Great Warrior of the Sioux*, 1950

GHENT, WILLIAM J., *Accounts of the Custer Fight given to General Hugh Scott by two Crow Scouts, 'White – Man – Runs – Him' and 'Curley'*, August 24th 1919

Ghent Papers: Library of Congress: Washington

Criticism of Godfrey's Custer Article

U.S. Army Military History Institute

Carlisle Barracks: Pennsylvania

GIBBON, GUY, *The Sioux*, Blackwell Publishing: Malden: 1970

GIBBON, JOHN (Colonel), *Gibbon On The Sioux Campaign of 1876*, The Old Army Press: Nebraska: 1970

GIDLEY, M., *With One Sky Above Us*, Webb & Bower Books: Leicester: 1979

GOBLE, PAUL, *Red Hawk's Account of Custer's Last Battle*, Brigham: Utah: 1976

GODFREY, EDWARD S., *Address at the Custer Battlefield on the 40th Anniversary of the Battl*e, Parmly Billings Library: Billings

Custer's Last Battle, Century Magazine: January 1892

Diary of captain E.S. Godfrey: Battle if the Little Big Horn 1876, Ghent: Papers: Washington

Letter to Major C.H. Asbury 18 – 1 – 1929, Eastern Montana College: Billings

The death of General Custer, The Cavalry Journal Vol. XXXVI: July 1927

Voluminous Material Covering all of his Military Life, Military Research Collection, Carlisle Barracks: Pennsylvania

GOLDIN, THEODORE, *Battle of the Little Big Horn: Securing water*, U.S. Military History Institute: Carlisle barracks: Pennsylvania

GOODRICH, THOMAS, *Scalp Dance*, Stackpole Books: Mechanicsburg: 1995

GRAHAM, W.A., *The Custer Myth*, Stackpole Books: Mechanicsburg: 1995

The Lost Is Found: Custer's Last Message Comes To Light, The cavalry Journal Vol. LI: 1942

The Reno Court of Inquiry, Stackpole Books: Mechanicsburg: 1995
The Story of the Little Big Horn, Stackpole Books: Mechanicsburg: 1994
GRAY, JOHM S., *Centennial Campaign of the Sioux war 1876,* University of Oklahoma Press: Oklahoma: 1988
Custer's Last Campaign, University of Nebraska Press: Lincoln: 1991
GREENE, JEROME A., *Evidence of the Custer Enigma*, Outbooks: Reno: 1979
Indian War Veterans, Savas Beattie LLC: New York: 2007
Slim Buttes 1876, University of Oklahoma Press: Oklahoma: 1891
GRINNEL, GEORGE B., *The Cheyenne Indians*, Yale University Press: New haven: 1923
The Fighting Cheyennes, University of Oklahoma Press: Oklahoma: 1956
GURNEY, GENE, *The Pictorial history of the U.S. Army*, New York: 1966
GWYNNE, S.C., *Empire of the Summer Moon*, Constable & Robinson: London: 2011
HAGEMANN, E.R., *Fighting Rebels and Redskins*, University of Oklahoma Press: Oklahoma: 1969
HAMMER, KENNETH, *Custer in '76, Walter Camp's Notes on the Custer Fight,* Brigham: Utah: 1976
Men With Custer, The Old Army Press: 1972
HARDORFF, RICHARD G., *Cheyenne Memories of the Custer Fight*, University of Nebraska Press: Lincoln: 1998
Lakota Recollections of the Custer Fight, University of Nebraska Press: Lincoln: 1997
HATCH, TOM, *The Custer Companion*, Stackpole Books: Mechanicsburg: 2002
HEDREN, PAUL L., *We Trailed the Sioux*, Stackpole Books: Mechanicsburg: 2003
HENRY, WILL, *Custer's last stand*, G & D: 1968
HOEBEL, E. ADAMSON, *The Cheyennes*, Holt, Rinehart & Winston Inc: New York: 1960
HOIG, STAN, *The Sand Creek Massacre*, University of Oklahoma Press: Oklahoma: 1961
HOOK, JASON, *American Plains Indians*, Osprey Publishing: Oxford: 1985
The Apaches, Osprey Publishing: Oxford: 1987
HOOK, RICHARD, *Warriors at the Little Big Horn 1876*, Osprey Publishing: Oxford: 2004
HOWARD, O.O., *My Life and Experiences Among the Hostile Indians,* Hartford: 1907
HUGHES, HOWARD, *The American Indian Wars*, Pocket Essentials: Herts: 2001

HUMFREVILLE, J. LEE, *Twenty Years Among Our Hostile Indians*, Hunter & Co.: New York: 1903

HUMPHRIES – MILLER, D., *Custer's Fall*, Transworld Publishers: London: 1965

HUNT, BRIAN V., *Reno Court of Inquiry,* Big Byte Books: 2015

HUNT, FRAZIER, *Custer, Last of the cavaliers*, Cosmopolitan Book Corp.: New York: 1928

HUTCHINS, JAMES, *7th U.S. Cavalry 1876,* Military Collector & Historian: Vol.X No.4: Winter 1958

HYDE, GEORGE E., *A Sioux Chronicle*, University of Oklahoma Press: Oklahoma: 1980

Indians of the High Plains, 1959

Red Cloud's Folk, University of Oklahoma Press; Oklahoma: 1961

Spotted Tail's Folk, University of Oklahoma Press: Oklahoma: 1961

JACKSON, DONALD, *Custer's Gold: U.S. Cavalry Expedition of 1874*, Yale University Press: Yale: 1967

JOHNSON, ERIC S., *No Greater Calling*, Schiffer Publishing: Atglen: 2012

JOHNSON, MICHAEL, *The Native Tribes of North America*, Compendium Publishing: London: 1999

Tribes of the Sioux nation, Osprey Publishing: Oxford: 2000

JOHNSON, SWAFFORD, *History of the U.S. Cavalry*, Hamlyn: London: 1985

JONES, DOUGLAS C., *The Court Martial of George A. Custer*, Scribner: New Jersey: 1964

JOSEPHY Jnr, ALVIN M., *500 Nations*, Alfred A Knope: New York: 1994

KATCHER, PHILIP, *The American Indian Wars 1860 – 1890*, Osprey Publishing: Oxford: 1995

U.S. Cavalry on the Plains 1850 – 90, Osprey Publishing: Oxford: 1995

KERRIGAN, EVANS E., *American War Medals & Decorations*, Viking Press: New York: 1964

KERSHAW, ROBERT J., *Red Sabbath*, Ian Allan Publishing: Hersham: 2006

KIDD, J.H., *Personal Recollections of a Cavalrymen*, Sentinel Printing Co.

KING, CHARLES, *Campaigning with Crook*, New York: 1890

KLOKNER, JAMES B., The *Officer Corps of Custer's Seventh Cavalry*, Schiffer Military History: Atglen: 2007

KOSTER, JOHN, *Custer Survivor*, Chronology Books: New York: 2010

KUHLMAN, CHARLES, *Legend into History*, Stackpole Books: Mechanicsburg: 1952

LA FORGE, OLIVER, *A Pictorial History of the American Indian*, Spring Books: London: 1966

LANGELLIER, JOHN P., *Bluecoats*, Greenhill Books: London: 1995

Longknives, Greenhill Books: London: 1996

LAVENDER, DAVID, *The Penguin Book of the American West*, Longman's: London

LECKIE, WILLIAM H., *Military Conquest of the Southern Plains*, University of Oklahoma Press: Oklahoma: 1963

LIBBY, ORIN G., *The Arikara Narrative of Custer's Campaign & the battle of the Little Big Horn*, University of Oklahoma Press: Oklahoma: 1998

LONGSTREET, STEPHEN, *War Cries On Horseback*, W.H. Allen: London: 1970

LUCE, EDWARD, *Custer Battlefield National Monument*, National Park Service Historical Handbook Series 1, Washington Government Printing Office:1949

McCHRISTIAN, DOUGLAS C., *The U.S. Army in the west 1870 -1880*, University of Oklahoma Press: Oklahoma: 1995

McCLERNAND, EDWARD, *The Indian and the Buffalo in Montana*, The Cavalry Journal: January 1927

McCRACKEN, HAROLD, *George catlin and the Old Frontier*, Bonanza Books: New York

McGINNIS, ANTHONY R., *Counting Coup and Cutting Horses*, University of Nebraska Press: Nebraska: 2010

McLUHAN, T.C., *Touch The earth*, Sphere Books: London: 1972

MACLEAN, FRENCH L. (Colonel), *Custer's Best*, Schiffer Military History: Atglen: 2011

MAGNUSSEN, DANIEL, *Thompson's Narrative of the Little Big Horn 1876*, A.H. Clark: California: 1974

MALLERY, GARRICK (Colonel), *Gesture Signs and Signals of the North American Indian*, Bureau of American Ethnology: Smithsonian Institute: Washington: 1881

MANCHIP – WHITE, JON, *Everyday Life of the North American Indian*, Batsford: London: 1979

MARQUIS, THOMAS, *Custer and the Little Big Horn*, 1969

Keep the Last Bullet for Yourself, Two Centuries Publishing: New York: 1976

Wooden Leg: A Warrior Who Fought Custer, University of Nebraska Press: Nebraska: 1957

MARSHALL III, JOSEPH M., *The Day The World Ended*, Penguin Books: London: 2008

MEED, DOUGLAS V., *Comanche 1800 – 74*, Osprey Publishing: Oxford: 2003

MERRINGTON, MARQUERITE, *The Life of General George Armstrong Custer*, University of Nebraska Press: Nebraska: 1971

MEYER, ROY W., *History of the Santee Sioux*, University of Nebraska Press: Nebraska: 1967

MICHINO, GREGORY F., *Forgotten Fights*, Mountain Press Publishers Co.: Montana: 2008

Lakota Noon, Mountain Press Publisher Co.: Montana: 2007

The Mystery of E Troop, Mountain Press Publisher Co.: Montana: 2005

MILES, NELSON A. (General), *Personal Recollections*, 1897

MILLS, ANSON, *My Story*, Washington: 1918

MILLS, CHARLES K., *Harvest of Barren Regrets*, University of Nebraska Press: Nebraska: 2011

MONNETT, JOHN H., *Where a Hundred Soldiers were Killed*, University of New Mexico Press: Albuquerque: 2010

MOONEY, JAMES, *The Ghost Dance*, J.G. Press: U.S.A.

MOORE, JOHN H., *The Cheyenne*, Blackwell Publishers: Oxford: 1996

MOORE, MARIJO, *Eating Fire, Tasting Blood*, Running Press Book Publishers: Philadelphia: 2006

MOQUIN, WAYNE, *Great Documents in American Indian History*, Da Capo Press: New York: 1973

MORRIS, JAMES M., *History of the U.S. Army*, Bison Books: London: 1986

NEIHARDT, JOHN G., *Black Elk Speaks*, Sphere Books: London: 1974

NEVIN, DAVID, *The Soldiers*, Time – Life Books: New York: 1974

NICHOLS, RONALD H., In *Custer's Shadow*, University of Oklahoma Press: Oklahoma: 2000

Men With Custer, Custer Battlefield Hist. & Museum Assoc. Inc: Montana: 2000

OGDEN, H.A., *Uniforms of the United States Army 1774 – 1889*, Dover Publications: New York: 1998

OLSON, JAMES C., *Red Cloud and the Sioux Problem*, University of Nebraska Press: Nebraska: 1965

OVERFIELD II, LOYD J., *The Little Big Horn 1876*, University of Nebraska Press: Nebraska: 1990

PANZERI, PETER, *Little Big Horn 1876,* Osprey Publishing: Oxford: 1995

PARKS, JACK, *Custer*, Nordon Publications: New York: 1975

PARSONS, JOHN E., *Firearms In The Custer Battle*, Stackpole: Harrisburg: 1953

PEGLER, MARTIN, *U.S. Cavalryman 1865 – 1890*, Osprey Publications: Oxford: 1993

PHILBRICK, NATHANIEL, *The Last Stand*, The Bodley Head: London: 2010

RED FOX, *The Memoires of Chief Red Fox*, W.H. Allen: London: 1971

REEDSTROM, E. LISLE, *Custer's 7th Cavalry*, Sterling Publishing Co.Inc.: New York: 1992

REYNOLDS, QUENTIN, *Custer's Last Stand*, Random House: New York: 1952

RICKER, ELI S., *Voices of the American West Vol 1: The Indian Interviews*, University of Nebraska Press: Nebraska: 2005

Voices of the American West Vol 2: The settler & Soldier Interviews, University of Nebraska Press : Nebraska: 2005

ROBERTS, DAVID, *Once They Moved Like the wind*, Pimlico: London: 1998

ROBINSON III, CHARLES M., *The Plains Wars,* Osprey Publishing: Oxford: 2003

ROBINSON, DOANE, *Crazy Horse's Story of the Custer Battle*, South Dakota Historical Collection Vol 6: 1912

ROSENBURG, BRUCE, *Custer and the Epic Defeat*, Penn. State University Press: 1974

ROWLAND, WILLIS, *The Story of White Elk as Told to Willis Rowland at Lame Deer, Montana May,* 25th 1927: Billings Library: Montana

RUSSELL, DON, *Custer's Last Stand*, Abram's: New York: 1971

RUTLEDGE, LEE A., *Field Uniforms of the Indian Wars Army 1866 – 1871*, North Cape Publications: California: 1998

Field Uniforms of the Indian Wars army 1872 – 1886, North Cape Publications: California: 1997

SANDOZ, MARI, *Cheyenne Autumn*, Eye & Spottiswood: London: 1966

Crazy Horse, the Strange Man of the Ogalallas, Knopf: New York: 1945

Hostiles and Friendlies, University of Nebraska Press; Nebraska: 1959

The Battle of the Little Big Horn, J.B. Lippincott Co.: New York: 1966

SCHERA, JOANNA COHAN, *Indians*, Octopus Books: London: 1974

SCHMECKBIER, LAWRENCE E., *The Office of Indian Arrairs*, John Hopkins Press: Baltimore: 1927

SCHMITT, MARTIN F., *General George Crook*, University of Oklahoma Press: Oklahoma: 1986

Fighting Indians of the West, Bonanza Books: New York

SCOTT, DOUGLAS, *They Died With Custer*, University of Oklahoma Press: Oklahoma: 1998

SCRUDDER, RALPH, *Custer Country*, Binford: Oregan: 1963

SELBY, JOHN, *U.S. Cavalry*, Osprey Publications: Oxford: 1972

SETON, EARNEST T., *Sign Talk*, Doubleday: New York: 1918

SEYMOUR, FLORA W., Indian *Agents of the Old Frontier*, Appleton – Century: New York: 1941

SPENCE, LEWIS, *Myths & Legends of the North American Indians*, Parragon: Bristol: 1998

STEVENSON, JOAN N., *Deliverance from the Little Big Horn*, University of Oklahoma Press: Oklahoma: 2012

STEWART, EDGAR, *Custer's Luck*, University of Oklahoma Press: Oklahoma: 1955

Penny – an – Acre Empire in the West, University of Oklahoma Press: Oklahoma: 1968

STILES, T.J., *Custer Trials*, Vintage Books: 2016

TAYLOR, COLIN, *The Native Americans*, Salamander Books: London: 2000

The Plains Indians, Salamander Books: London: 1994

The warriors of the Plains, Hamlyn publishing: London: 1975

TAYLOR, WILLIAM O., *With Custer on the Little Big Horn*, Penguin Group: London: 1996

TILLET, LESLIE, *Wind on the Buffalo Grass*, Crowell: New York: 1976

TUCKER, PHILLIP, *Why Custer was Never Warned*, Universal Publishers: Irvine: 2017

TURNER, DON, *Custer's First Massacre*, Humbly Gulch Press: Texas: 1968

URWIN, GREGORY J.W., *The United States cavalry*, Blandford Press: London: 1985

The United States Infantry, Blandford Press: London: 1988

UTLEY, ROBERT M, *Bluecoats and Redskins*, Purnell Books: London: 1975

Cavalier In Buckskin, Salamander Books: London: 2001

Custer and the Great Controversy, Westernlore: Los Angeles: 1962

Custer Battlefield National Monument, Dept. of the Interior: Washington: 1969

Frontiersmen in Blue, Macmillan: New York: 1967

Life In Custer's cavalry, University of Nebraska Press: Nebraska: 1987

The Last Days of the Sioux Nation, Yale University Press: 1963

VAN DE WATER, FREDERIC, *Glory Hunter*, Bobbs – Merrill Co.: Indianapolis: 1924

VAUGHAN, J.W., *With Crook at the Rosebud*, Stackpole: Harrisburg: 1956

VESTAL, STANLEY, *Sitting Bull,* University of Oklahoma Press: Oklahoma: 1857

Warpath, Houghton Mifflin: Boston: 1834

VIOLA, HERMAN J., *Is It A Good Day To Die*, University of Nebraska Press: Nebraska: 2001

Trail to Wounded Knee, National Geographic: Washington

WALKER, J.R., *The Sun Dance and Other Ceremonies of the Teton Dakota,* Forgotten Books: U.K.

WELCH, JAMES, *Killing Custer*, W.W. Norton & Co.Inc.: New York: 1994

WELSH, WILLIAM, *Report and Supplement Report of a Visit to Spotted Tail's Tribe of Brule Sioux Indians*, Philadelphia: 1870

WHITE – BULL, JOSEPH, *The warrior Who Killed Custer*, University of Nebraska Press: Nebraska: 1968

WHITTAKER, FREDERICK, *A Complete Life of General George A. Custer*, Sheldon & Co.: New York: 1876

WILLIAMS, ROGER L., *Military Register of Custer's Last Command*, University of Oklahoma Press: Oklahoma: 2012

WINDOLPH, CHARLES, *I Fought With Custer*, University of Nebraska Press; Nebraska: 1974

WINDROW, MARTIN, *Military dress of North America 1665 – 1970*, Ian Allan: London: 1973

WOOD, NORMAN B., *Lives of Famous Indian Chiefs*, American Indian Historical Pub.Vo.: Illinois: 1906

YENNE, BELL, *Indian Wars*, Westholme Publishing: 2006

ZIMMERMAN, LARRY J., *American Indians: the First Nations*, Duncan Baird Pub: London: 2003

U.S. GOVERNMENT PAPERS

Index to Reports of Committees of the House of Representatives for the 1st Session: 44th Congress: 1875 – 1876

Report on the Material Wealth, Climate and Rainfall and Natural Resources of the Black Hills of South Dakota: 1st Session: 44th Congress: Exec. Doc 51

Report of the Commissioner of Indian Affairs in Relation to the Present Situation of Indian Disturbances in the Sioux Reservations: 1st Session: 44th Congress: Sen. Doc. 52

Indian Affairs, Laws and Treaties 1 – 11: 1st Session: 57th Congress; Sen. Exec. Doc. 452 (3)
2nd Session: 62nd Congress: Sen. Exec> Doc 719

Report of the Expedition to the Black Hills under the command of Brevet Major – General G.A. Custer: 2nd Session: 43rd Congress: Sen. Exec>Doc. 32

Report of the secretary of War – Communicated to the Two Houses of Congress at the beginning of the 2nd session: 45th Congress: Vol. II Part II: 1876/1877

United States War Department Report on the Military Expedition Against the Sioux Indians: Report July 14th 1876: 1st Session: 4th Congress: House Exec. Doc. 184

United States War Department Report 1876: 2nd Session: 44th Congress: House Exec. Doc. I Part II
2nd Session 44th Congress: Sen. Exec. Doc 9

Discussions of H.R. 1335 (X192: 44/1 and X197: 44/1): 2nd session: 44th Congress

LIST OF Killed and Wounded in Action with Sioux, Little Big Horn River, Montana: Official Army List of 1876: National Archives; Washington

Medal of Honor Recipients 1863 -1978: Sen. Comm. Print No 3.:
National Archives, Washington

Transcript of the Reno Court of Inquiry 1878/1879
National Archives Micro. Pub. M – 592: Rolls 1 and 2
National Archives: Washington

U.S. GOVERNMENT PUBLICATIONS

Cavalry equipment 1874

Custer Battlefield 1961

Custer Battlefield 1969

Entrenchment Trail: Custer Battlefield

Horse Equipments & Cavalry Accoutrements 1891

Horse Equipments & Cavalry Equipments for Officers and Enlisted men 1905

U.S. Army Uniforms and Equipment 1889

Index